THE SPITTING IMAGE

THE SPITTING IMAGE

MYTH, MEMORY, AND THE LEGACY OF VIETNAM

Jerry Lembcke

Consulting Editor: Harvey J. Kaye

New York University Press
New York and London

NEW YORK UNIVERSITY PRESS
New York and London

Library of Congress Cataloging-in-Publication Data
Lembcke, Jerry, 1943–
The spitting image : myth, memory, and the legacy of Vietnam /
Jerry Lembcke.
p. cm.
Includes bibliographical references (p.) and index.

1. Vietnamese Conflict, 1961–1975—Veterans—United States.
2. Vietnamese Conflict, 1961–1975—Public opinion. 3. Public opinion—
United States. I. Title.
DS559.73.U6 L46 1998
959.704'3373—ddc21 98-9048
CIP

New York University Press books are printed on acid-free paper,
and their binding materials are chosen for strength and durability.

ISBN: 978-0-8147-5147-3

10 9 8 7 6

For Carolyn
and
Molly Del

CONTENTS

All illustrations appear as an insert following p. 92

Preface ix

1 Introduction: The Spitting Image 1

2 Yellow Ribbons and Spat-Upon Veterans: Making Soldiers the Means and Ends of War 11

- Reasoning about the War, 12
- Reason Abandoned: Toward War with Iraq, 16
- Against the Coalition against the War, 18
- Fighting the Vietnam Syndrome, 24

3 Dear Spiro Agnew: About Soldiers, Veterans, and the Anti-war Movement 27

- War Veterans and the Vietnam War, 29
- Veterans for Peace and the Fifth Avenue Peace Parade Committee, 30
- Veterans, Soldiers, and the Peace Movement Reach Out to One Another, 33
- Turning the Guns Around: GIs and Veterans against the War, 37
- The Moratorium Days of 1969, 44

4 The Nixon-Agnew Counteroffensive: "Good Veterans" vs. "Bad Veterans" 49

- Agnew vs. "An Effete Corps of Impudent Snobs," 49
- "Good" Veterans vs. "Bad" Veterans, 53
- Vietnam Veterans Against the War, 57
- Like Fire and Water, 66

5 Spat-Upon Veterans: The Evidence (or Lack Thereof) 71

- Disproving a Myth, 72
- Grist for the Myth, 76

6 From Odysseus to Rambo: Coming-Home Stories 84
- The "Dolchstoss Legend," 85
- Les Centurions, 87
- From the Fantasies of Robert Welch . . . , 91
- . . . to the Fantasies of Richard Nixon, 93
- The Nixon-Agnew Strategy: Smash the Left, Capture the Center, 94

7 From Badness to Madness: The Mental Labeling of Vietnam Veterans 101
- The *New York Times* and PTSD, 102
- The Psychiatrists, 105
- The Dwight Johnson Story, 107
- Charlie Clements: The "Right Stuff" Gone Wrong, 111
- Warrior Dreams, 115

8 Women, Wetness, and Warrior Dreams 127
- Spit as an Icon, 128
- Female Fluids and (Male) Fears, 129
- The "Evil Eye," 133
- Betrayal: The Alibi for a Lost War, 136
- From Times Square to San Francisco: Memories of Homecomings, 139

9 Myth, Spit, and the Flicks: Coming Home to Hollywood 144
- Vietnam War Movies before 1978, 148
- 1978, 161
- The Road to Rambo, 174
- The Return of the "Political" Veteran, 177

10 We Are What We Remember 183

Notes 189
References 199
Filmography 207
Index 211
About the Author 217

PREFACE

In February 1991, I was asked to speak at a teach-in on the Persian Gulf War. My presentation to the teach-in focused on the image then being popularized in the press of Vietnam-era anti-war activists treating Vietnam veterans abusively. I told my audience that the image was inaccurate and that the media and the Bush administration were using it as a propaganda device to dissuade people from opposing the Gulf War. Drawing on my own experience as a Vietnam veteran who came home from the war and joined Vietnam Veterans Against the War (VVAW), I called the image of spat-upon Vietnam veterans a myth.

Following the teach-in, my comments were published as a newspaper opinion piece, and I got encouragement from readers to write more. My initial research interest was simply to find out where and when, during the fall of 1990, the idea of spat-upon veterans was first invoked. At the time, I thought I might be able to say something interesting about how the image functioned and what political interests were exploiting the image. It wasn't until I saw Bruce Franklin's article in the December, 1991, *Atlantic* on the myth of the POW/MIA that I began to think there was more to this than I had imagined. I had never met Franklin before I called him, and he virtually answered the phone saying he had just been thinking about the myth of the spat-upon Vietnam veteran. He was ecstatic about my interest in the subject and his enthusiasm for what I have tried to do has never waned. This book is obviously indebted to him.

My decision to research the role of film in the making of the myth was also a turning point. A conversation with sociologists Jim Russell and Richard Ratcliff planted the idea that I should look into film. I recalled the idea a short time later while listening to a public radio program about war films. I called one of the scholars featured on the program and got the name of Tony Williams who had just published the definitive filmography of Vietnam War films. His six-hundred-entry volume, coauthored with Jean-Jacques Malo was a godsend. With it, I was able to identify and view approximately 120 films portraying relations between Vietnam veterans and the anti-war movement.

Still, I would not have pursued the film study without the help and encouragement of Steve Vineberg at Holy Cross College, who made me believe that I could do it even though I had no formal training in film. He told me about the film holdings at the Library of Congress and encouraged me to go to Los Angeles to use the film archives at UCLA and the Margaret Herrick Library to study the 1978 movie *Coming Home.* At those institutions, Madeline Matz and Roger Walke, Brigette Kueppers and Dale Treleven, and Faye Thompson, respectively, were very helpful. John Baky at LaSalle University was very generous with films from the Connelly Library's special collection on Vietnam-era culture. Michael Gordon facilitated my appearance at the Milwaukee Oral History Conference, where I presented findings from that research.

The film study was the key to recognizing the connection between the general cultural disparagement of Vietnam veterans and the evolution of the psychiatric category, post-traumatic stress disorder (PTSD). Seeing that PTSD appeared on the screen before it appeared in the journals of the mental health professions was a clue that the legitimation of PTSD as a diagnostic category was indebted to more than science. Heather Brown and Christine Greenway led me into the constructionist literature on mental health that eventually framed the chapter on PTSD. Lucy Candib shared some informative journal articles on PTSD with me, and conversations with Amy Wolfson in the final days before this book went to press increased my certainty that my hunches about the origin and function of PTSD have been right all along.

Sharon Moore at Dinand Library at Holy Cross College was very helpful, as were the librarians at the Wisconsin State Historical Society Library, who led me to archival material on anti-war organizations. Margaret Post took care of innumerable research-related details. The students in my 1995 Holy Cross seminar on the book read and commented on draft chapters and helped sharpen my argument on many points. The efforts of several students are acknowledged in notes throughout the book. I appreciate the special interest that Jeff Drew took in the project. He found the only image of a spat-upon veteran I have seen in a GI Joe comic book. Dave Hummon suggested some readings that deepened my understanding of myth. The Holy Cross research and publication committee supported my work with travel grants and summer research awards.

Early conversations with Vietnam veterans Joe Urgo, Barry Romo, and Tom Gottschang made me feel as if this book was worth doing. Bill Howe and Kathy Howe took time to read drafts and offer their comments. Gary and Mary Lou Fisher provided friendship and hospitality during my research stints in Washington, D.C., Sara Cooper did the same in Los Angeles. I thank Richard Schmitt, Bob Craig, Gary DeAngelis, Jim Nickoloff, Martin Hart-Landsberg, and Mary Hobgood for their friendship and intellectual support. My daughter, Molly Del Howe-Lembcke, kept me current on the images of Vietnam veterans in film. Because of her, two important films, *Forrest Gump* and *Independence Day,* are in the book. I thank my agent, Nan deBrandt, for her confidence in the book and Harvey Kaye, my friend for many years, for taking me to Niko Pfund at New York University Press. Despina Gimbel provided superb editing. I can't imagine there is a better editor anywhere.

Carolyn Howe read endless numbers of drafts and endlessly discussed with me the political and conceptual issues in these chapters. Her presence in my life enabled me to juggle teaching, writing, traveling, and parenting so I could write this book. She has been my constant companion since the early 1970s, and I thank her very much for her loving support.

ONE

Introduction

The Spitting Image

> My flight came in at San Francisco airport and I was spat upon three times: by hippies, by a man in a leisure suit, and by a sweet little old lady who informed me I was an "Army Asshole."
>
> —Barry Streeter, Vietnam veteran

> Spat-upon Vietnam veterans? That's an urban myth.
>
> —Sharon Moore, college librarian

Barry Streeter returned from Vietnam in November 1971. His account of an unfriendly homecoming was collected, along with many like it, by newspaper columnist Bob Greene for his 1989 book, *Homecoming*. Like many stories of abused Vietnam veterans, Streeter's account involved hippies spitting on a soldier as he arrived at the San Francisco airport from Vietnam.

Sharon Moore has different memories of San Francisco. She made her comment just as I had begun to tell her that I was writing a book about Vietnam veterans and the anti-war movement. "You remember," I began, trying to find common ground for a conversation, "during the Gulf War there was a lot of talk about how Vietnam veterans had been spat upon . . ." Sharon cut me off. "Spat-upon Vietnam veterans?

. . . That's an urban myth." She went on to tell me that she had been living in San Francisco while actively opposing the war and waiting for her friend, Terry, to return from Vietnam. Terry returned to McCord Air Force Base near Seattle, flew to San Francisco on a commercial airline, then took a bus into the city. He was wearing a military fatigue jacket when Sharon met him at the San Francisco bus terminal. Teasingly, she asked him if anyone had given him a hard time about his short hair. He replied that everyone had been very nice.

. . . . . .

Stories of war veterans being spat upon occur frequently in modern histories. Many of these stories are about veterans who fought on the losing side of wars, their abusers said to be "fifth columnists" or traitors to the national cause. Following Germany's loss in World War I, for example, German fascists exploited such rumors to arouse popular anger toward groups and individuals who had opposed the war. According to some historians, the image of abused veterans was an important element in the Nazi propaganda that fanned the flames of patriotism and led the German masses into World War II.

In the United States, the idea that Vietnam veterans had met with malevolence gained prominence during the fall of 1990, when the Bush administration used it to rally support for the Persian Gulf War. After sending troops to the Gulf in August, the administration argued that opposition to the war was tantamount to disregard for their well-being and that such disregard was reminiscent of the treatment given to Vietnam veterans upon their return home. By invoking the image of anti-war activists spitting on veterans, the administration was able to discredit the opposition and galvanize support for the war. So successful was this endeavor that by the time the bombing of Iraq began in January 1991 President Bush had effectively turned the means of war, the soldiers themselves, into a reason for the war.

An analysis of news stories gleaned from press accounts from the fall of 1990 reveals that the administration put forth one explanation after another for the impending war, to the point that nobody could reason about the rightness or wrongness of it because the objectives to be served by military means kept changing. When reasoning within a means-ends framework became paralyzed, public opinion about the war derived from emotion, symbolism, and myth. In effect, the administration invoked the image of the spat-upon Vietnam veteran to solidify support for the war and opposition to an anti-war movement that was growing rapidly during December of 1990.

But how accurate is the image of the spat-upon Vietnam veteran? In writing and speeches I have maintained that relations between veterans and anti-war activists were generally friendly and that, in fact, many returning veterans became war protesters. Veterans with whom I have spoken generally agree that the spat-upon veteran image is inaccurate. Barry Romo, the current head of Vietnam Veterans against the War and an active collector of literature, historical materials, and oral accounts related to Vietnam veterans and the anti-war movement, says there is no news-source documentation (such as photographs) of any incidence of anti-war activists spitting on veterans. Yet, during the Gulf War when Vietnam veterans appeared on news programs to speak about having been abused by anti-war activists, some testified to having been spat upon. How are we to understand these competing claims? How are we to make sense of an image so compelling that people believe it happened to them, when that image does not appear to be supported by empirical evidence? I suggest that we must understand the creation and consequences of the image of the spat-upon veteran as part of a cultural myth, a story that symbolizes societal values, which during the Gulf War period was employed to serve political interests.

Proving that something is a myth is no easy task. How do you prove that something did *not* happen? For this book I adopted two strategies. The first was to make the assumption that two mutually exclusive sets of circumstances cannot coexist in the same time and space. In the case of Vietnam veterans and the anti-war movement, I assumed that those two parties could not have been simultaneously hostile to one another and mutually supportive; anti-war activists could not have been spitting on veterans while at the same time befriending them in off-base coffeehouses. Using news accounts and archival materials from leading anti-war organizations such as Student Mobilization against the War in Vietnam, Fifth Avenue Peace Parade Committee, and Vietnam Veterans against the War, I show that relations between veterans and the anti-war movement were empathetic and mutually supportive. On the basis of that provable truth, I argue that the image of spat-upon veterans must be false.

One of the little-known dimensions of the anti-war movement is that veterans of previous wars, World War II in particular, were early participants in the opposition to the war in Vietnam and instrumental in initiating the outreach to Vietnam-era soldiers and veterans. By helping in-service GIs during the early stages of the war, the anti-war movement established a credibility with drafted and enlisted men that manifested itself in a tight relationship between anti-war activists and veterans by 1970.

In turn, the solidarity between anti-war Vietnam veterans and the anti-war movement behooved the Nixon-Agnew administration to drive a wedge between the two groups. One edge of the wedge pressed against the anti-war movement: the creation of images of such reprehensible acts as spitting on veterans, it was hoped, would turn the American people and Vietnam veterans against the movement. At that level, the propagation of the spat-upon-veteran image was simply a propaganda ploy to discredit the anti-war movement. The other edge of the wedge pressed against the Vietnam veterans themselves, as the authenticity of their opposition to the war was questioned. Initially employed in an effort to discredit veterans' exposés of atrocities committed by U.S. forces in Vietnam, this edge of the wedge ultimately took the form of character assassination. By broad-brushing Vietnam veterans as crazy, prone to violence, and otherwise disabled by the war, all Vietnam veterans were stigmatized and pushed to the margins of American consciousness. Although largely successful measured in political terms, the administration's strategy, measured in human terms, added to the trauma of the veterans' war and postwar experience and increased their isolation from mainstream America.

The image of the spat-upon Vietnam veteran had a mythic quality to it that hinged on the belief that veterans who were in solidarity with the anti-war movement were not the real thing. "Real" Vietnam veterans would have been rejected, not embraced, by the anti-war movement. They would have been treated with hostility by the movement, even spat upon. The existence of these patriotic, pro-war veterans was "proven" by the "fact" that anti-war activists were spitting on someone. Who, if not pro-war veterans, were they spitting on? The image of the spat-upon Vietnam veteran, then, served a conjuring function. It called to mind the image of the "good" pro-war veteran as a counterbalance to the image of the "bad" anti-war veteran.

My other strategy for proving that the image of the spat-upon Vietnam veteran is mythical was to hypothesize that anti-war people really did spit on Vietnam veterans and to try to find support for that hypothesis. In scanning the news accounts of anti-war rallies, demonstrations, and marches, and in reviewing the secondary sources and historical accounts of the period, I found virtually no reason to think that the alleged acts of spitting ever occurred. I argue here that myth is less about something that did or did not happen than about the *belief* that it did. In the case at hand, it was therefore necessary to show how it is possible for a large number of people to believe that Vietnam veterans were spat upon when there is no evidence that they were. In effect, my strategy was to set aside the question of whether or not such acts occurred and to show why even if they did not occur it is understandable that the image of the spat-upon veteran has become widely accepted. Indeed, given the manipulation of information and images that began with the Nixon administration and continued at the hands of filmmakers and the news media during the 1970s and 1980s, it would be remarkable if a majority of Americans had not come to believe that Vietnam veterans were abused by the anti-war movement.

One also finds grist for the myth in the historical record, in incidents that provided substance for the creation of the myth. There were press reports, for example, of acts of spitting that took place at anti-war rallies. As reported, the spit almost always flew from pro-war right-wingers onto anti-war activists. But taken out of context, these reports could have gotten inverted and turned into stories about the opposite having occurred. There were also actual incidents of Vietnam veterans being treated abusively, but in all the documentable cases it was pro-war people who were the abusers. And there are, finally, the reports by Vietnam veterans themselves of either having been spat upon or having witnessed buddies being spat upon. For obvious reasons, I gave these reports serious consideration, but their validity was hard to establish. Almost all such reports came years after the incidents were alleged to have occurred, while in the actual time frame in which men came home from Vietnam there are no such reports. When one attempts to validate the stories through follow-up research, many such claims dissolve rather quickly, and in others one finds details that betray a lack of authenticity.

Still, given the passion of the times and the wide range of personalities attracted to the anti-war movement, it would be surprising if some activists had not directed their political emotions toward the men who fought the war. One can maintain, as I do, that organizations such as the Fifth Avenue Peace Parade Committee did not condone hostility toward soldiers and veterans and yet allow for the possibility that individual protesters may have broken rank and, acting on their own, committed hostile acts against veterans.

There is also the likelihood that, once the Nixon administration began its campaign to discredit the movement with stories that activists were anti-soldier, agents provocateurs may have incited aggressive behavior toward veterans. The individual veteran being spat on by someone fitting the description of a war protester would have no reason to think that that person was other than he appeared to be. It is significant, though, that with all the research that has been done on the anti-war movement and the government's actions against it, no evidence has surfaced that anyone ever spat on a Vietnam veteran.

The fact that so many Vietnam veterans came forward during the Gulf War with accounts of having been spat upon suggests that their memories of their own coming-home experiences have been altered by the prevalence of the spat-upon image. What appears at first blush to be an expression of "false memory syndrome," however, has to be understood in the context of how post-traumatic stress disorder (PTSD) came to be constructed by the media and mental health professionals and applied to the interpretation of veterans' experiences. I problematize PTSD within a constructionist framework and show how it is as much a media product as anything else, its utility as much political as medical.

The similarity between the structure and function of the spat-upon veteran stories and of other myths adds credence to the claim that these stories really are mythical. The act of spitting has deep and longstanding symbolic significance in Western culture. In the biblical account of Christ's Crucifixion, for example, Luke writes that Christ was spat upon by those who betrayed him and that that act of spitting confirmed the prophesy of Isaiah. The spat-upon Christ, in other words, confirmed for Luke that Christ really was the embodiment of goodness, which the sinful, fallen betrayers were incapable of embracing without redemption. But historically those who spat upon and killed Christ were seen to be deserving of society's contempt.

That it was Jews who spat upon and "killed Christ" is not without significance for understanding the cultural role played by spat-upon veteran stories. In the late nineteenth century French Jews were scapegoated for the loss of France's war with Prussia, and in the wake of Germany's defeat in World War I anti-Semitism ran rampant. As noted earlier, the image of the German veteran being spat upon by Germans who had been opposed to the war played a major role in mustering the patriotic German sentiments that fed Nazism. In like fashion, the French right wing exploited national frustration over the country's loss in Indochina in 1954 by claiming the military had been sold out on the home front. Anti-Semitism and the image of rejected veterans of the Indochina campaign figured in the rightist propaganda that led the country into its next war in Algeria.

The European pattern of ultranationalist political forces exciting national fears of subversion from within was repeated in the United States during the Vietnam era. From the earliest days of the war, the extreme right wing in America began pushing its line that Washington "insiders" were soft on communism. The war was dragging on, the right claimed, because the government was pursuing a no-win strategy in Vietnam. When Richard Nixon became president in 1969, he made a variation on that line a centerpiece of his domestic political strategy. Nixon believed the American intellectual establishment was under communist influence, that the ranks of journalists and academics were infiltrated by reds. These leftists were inciting students to radical opposition to the war. Opposition to the war, in turn, was undermining the morale of the troops in Vietnam and giving aid and comfort to the enemy. Thus, Nixon argued, the anti-war movement was actually prolonging the war. The president was so convinced that the real enemy was internal that he nearly turned "the war" into a war on the anti-war movement. The idea that anti-war people spat on Vietnam veterans has it origins in Nixon's haranguing of war protesters for their disloyalty to the troops.

Myths can play a positive role in society by helping a people create a common sense of who they are. The stories that make up the myths help establish the boundaries between who and what the people in the society are and who and what they are not. Viewed this way, myths arise out of the common experience of a people and serve the interests of the group as a whole. But the creation of myths can also involve the exercise of power, and their utilization can serve the particular needs of dominant interest groups. The origins of a myth like that of the spat-upon Vietnam veteran lies less in the common experience of the people than in the need of one group of people within a particular society to have another group believe that something did or did not happen. The presence in the stories about Vietnam veterans of young women as the spitters suggests that the stories function to displace the anxiety of defeated male warriors onto scapegoats: the warriors were betrayed on the homefront by the soft and disloyal female element in the culture, not by the inferior Asian other. Because Euro-American culture associates female sexuality with fluids and wetness, male anxiety about loss in war gets imaged as acts of betrayal that take the form of women spitting.

If the image of the spat-upon veteran is mythical, how did it come to be so widely accepted? How have veterans come to believe that it happened to them? Film, more than any other medium, promulgated the image of Vietnam veteran rejection. Major motion pictures like the 1978 film *Coming Home* created an American mind-set receptive to suggestions that veterans were actually spat upon. Meanwhile, the story of the mutually supportive relations between Vietnam veterans and the anti-war movement never made it to the screen. Except for a half-dozen films in the late sixties, we seldom see veterans and the movement in the same story lines. And even in those, we see only individual, decontextualized veterans whose reel life does not even suggest their real-life involvement in such organizations as Vietnam Veterans against the War. Once the war is lost, however, the frequency of references to the anti-war movement's animus toward soldiers and veterans increases. By 1977, two years after the war is actually lost, the first films portraying hostility between the anti-war movement and Vietnam veterans appear. *Tracks* (1977) contains the first clear inference that anti-war activists spat on Vietnam veterans.

Just as important, through film, veterans and the stories of their reentry into American society come to displace the story of the war itself. In these stories we see Vietnam veterans pictured in uniformly unhealthy ways. Well into the 1980s, the vast majority of filmic representations show veterans as dysfunctional or disabled. The few exceptions are either portrayals of political veterans, which are flawed in their own way, or romanticized portrayals borrowed from World War II–era films. From the late 1970s on, Hollywood produces more and more films portraying anti-war movement hostility toward soldiers and veterans. It is little wonder that by the beginning of the Gulf War the image of the Vietnam veteran as victim prevailed in America and t many Americans blamed the anti-war movement for that victimization.

The dissemination of such a myth throughout the popular culture suggests that the power of the media can be commanded for such an end, particularly in a society like the United States where the communications industry is largely privately owned and power is in the hands of a small number of people. To say that mythmaking in America is a monopoly industry would miss the point, however. It is in the chemistry between the deep-seated cultural anxieties of the Western world and the maldistribution of power in a society like the United States that myths such as that of the spat-upon Vietnam veteran are produced.

. . . . . .

It has been said that we frame our understanding of a particular war through our memories of the one that preceded it. Those memories are heavily mediated by images created by film, music, television, and literature, as well as oral and written histories. Thus, and tragically, the Americans fought the war in Vietnam through World War II–vintage understandings of war that were "remembered" for them through film. In turn, the Gulf War was mentally framed, for many Americans, by what they remembered the Vietnam War to have been about.

Whether Vietnam, because it was America's first lost war, has been more mythologized than previous wars, is a matter for debate. In any case, it is significant that the "remembered" Vietnam War was not the war itself but the homecoming experience of the Vietnam veterans. Ironically, if the real Vietnam War had been remembered, the Gulf War might not have been fought. We need to take away the power of political and cultural institutions to mythologize our experiences. We need to show how myths are used by political administrations to manipulate the decision-making process. And we need to dispel the power of myths like that of the spat-upon Vietnam veteran by debunking them.

TWO

Yellow Ribbons and Spat-Upon Veterans

Making Soldiers the Means and Ends of War

> If I go back home like the Vietnam vets did and somebody spits on me, I swear to God I'll kill them.
>
> —U.S. soldier in the Persian Gulf

In early January 1991 the U.S. Congress authorized President George Bush to use armed force to expel Iraq from Kuwait. But for thousands of Americans, including the anonymous soldier interviewed by *New York Times* reporter James LeMoyne (1990b), the reasons for the war in the Persian Gulf had more to do with support for the American men and women already stationed there than it did with Iraq or Kuwait. By the time the United States went to war on January 16, the U.S. soldiers in the Gulf had become the primary reason for the war.

An analysis of news stories gleaned from the press accounts of fall 1990 reveals that the administration had put forth one reason after another for U.S. involvement, to the point that nobody could reason about the rightness or wrongness of the war. With the ends always changing, reasoning within a means-ends framework became paralyzed. At that point, public decision-making defaulted to levels of emotion, symbolism, and myth.

Reasoning about the War

On August 1, 1990, Iraq sent troops into Kuwait in a dispute over boundary and oil rights. A week later the United States began airlifting 200,000 troops to the Persian Gulf. By the end of the year double that number would be in the region as momentum built for a military conflict between Iraq and the United States.

As the number of soldiers dispatched for war grew during the fall of 1990, so too did the list of reasons offered by the Bush administration for the build up. In all, the administration put forth six reasons for U.S. involvement in the war: the defense of Saudi Arabia; putting military teeth in the economic blockade of Iraq; freeing the hostages; the liberation of Kuwait; the removal of Saddam Hussein; and jobs. The six appeared more or less sequentially between August and December of 1990, although they sometimes overlapped with one another thematically and were often conjoined in administrative press statements in packages of two or three.

At the time, the United States alleged that Iraq's movement of troops into Kuwait was a prelude to an attack on Saudi Arabia. On August 6, U.S. Defense Secretary Dick Cheney arrived in Riyadh, the capital of Saudi Arabia, to persuade the cautious Saudis to open their naval bases and airport installations to the Americans. This framing of the initial U.S. troop deployment had a formative effect on how people in the United States would interpret the events that were to unfold over the next months, and it virtually insured that debate over increased military involvement would take place within a discourse of "defense."

The framing of the initial U.S. troop deployments as a defensive measure kept opposition to administration actions frozen during the first week of August. But no sooner was the defense of Saudi Arabia established in the public's mind as the reason for the troops having been sent to the Gulf than the reason changed. On August 9, the United States dispatched an armada of fifty major ships to the Persian Gulf with the stated intention of enforcing the economic sanctions the United Nations had imposed on Iraq three days earlier. The naval blockade created a nonmilitary rationale—the enforcement of economic and diplomatic tactics—for U.S. military forces in the Gulf. It also began weaving the fig leaf of "internationalism" behind which the Bush administration would walk throughout the course of the war and reframed the issue so that it was less a question about the use of military means than about nonmilitary objectives, a maneuver that stymied opposition for most of the month (Kifner 1990).

The third reason for the military buildup, and the keystone of the Bush administration's strategy to muster domestic support for the Gulf War, involved the creation of a hostage issue. On the lead end of the crisis, the hostage issue connected with the defense motif about U.S. intentions in the Gulf: the Iraqis were the aggressors and the United States was the defender of innocent lives. On the other end, as Washington's intentions became more openly offensive, the hostage issue was an important element of the U.S. effort to demonize Iraq's leader, Saddam Hussein.

The hostage issue was also a transitional issue that allowed the Bush administration to begin recasting the crisis from "this is about them"—the defense of Saudi Arabia and the liberation of Kuwait—to "this is about us." In that sense, it was a prelude to fuller discussions of what U.S. "vital interests" were at stake in the region. Moreover, by writing the role of hostage into the script, any Americans who were in the Gulf, including military personnel, could be cast in the role and used as a justification for U.S. military intervention. The hostage issue, in other words, paved the way for means and ends to be conflated and, ultimately, for the troops in the Gulf to be both the reasons for the war and the means of war.

Headlining of the hostage issue began on August 18, coincident with Bush's decision to call up military reservists. Iraq viewed the administration's call-up as further evidence that the United States was moving toward war. Iraq's response was to declare, on August 18, that foreigners in Iraq would endure the same hardships of the economic blockade and war as the Iraqi people. Foreigners, including Americans, would be accommodated in facilities operated by the ministries of Oil and Military Industrialization and the armed forces.

Headlines declaring that Saddam Hussein was taking hostages dominated the news of the war for the next several days. The hostage stories were combined with stories about troops in the Gulf in ways that, at times, conveyed the impression that it was U.S. troops who were the hostages. George Bush abetted the comingling of images by choosing the Veterans of Foreign Wars (VFW) convention on August 21 as the occasion on which to declare the beginning of the "hostage crisis." Other than making the declaration and saying that he would hold the Iraqis responsible for the safety of Americans in Iraq, Bush was noncommittal with regard to the so-called hostages. His speech, which was excerpted in the *New York Times,* moved seamlessly from hostages to troops, to whom he also pledged his support. Then, in a manner that echoed the news media's profiling of civilian individuals and families trapped in Iraq, Bush read family profiles of U.S. soldiers already in the Gulf. This was very personal and moving, but was this supposed to be a speech about civilian hostages or military troops?

On the surface, of course, it was a speech about hostages but the president had said nothing of substance, leaving the symbolism of the occasion to speak volumes. The message was in the medium and the medium was the venue: by declaring the hostage crisis at the VFW convention and conflating the national anxieties about hostages and soldiers, the association between soldiers, veterans, and hostages was forged. The American people could now be asked to go to war to free civilian hostages or to free the troops in harm's way.

The ultimate comingling of hostage and troop-support symbolism was in the use of yellow ribbons—the quintessential hostage/prisoner symbol—for a support-the-troops symbol. Still, it was not a given that Americans would transfer their emotional support for individuals to support for policy. Someone would have to *say* that the two were linked—or that they were *not* linked. Either would do as a means to create a storm of controversy over support for troops versus support for the war. The Democratic National Committee took the latter tack.[1]

On September 16, the DNC expressed support for the American troops in the Persian Gulf while criticizing the Republican administration that put them there (Toner 1990). This support-the-troops-but-not-the-policy statement signaled to the public that there was a debatable issue while evading the important question of how one could oppose the policy without opposing the troops. Therein was the rub. On the surface, the statement legitimized opposition to the U.S. military role. But it did so in the context of hysteria over hostages and troops-as-hostages that was several weeks in the making and already had a grip on the emotions of the American people. Could opponents of the policy voice their opposition without appearing to be attacking the troops? Not likely. Nor was it likely that the yellow-ribbon campaigners would translate their support for the troops into opposition to the war and demand that the troops be brought home. In reality, the DNC had constructed a one-sided discourse that mobilized the pro-war sentiments of the American people.

In mid September the administration began weaving Kuwait into its hostage narrative. Many of the news stories—including the widely reported story about Iraqi soldiers dumping 312 Kuwaiti babies out of hospital incubators—we now know were concocted by a Washington public relations firm, Hill and Knowlton, headed by Craig Fuller, a former chief of staff for then Vice President Bush. For five straight days, from September 25 to September 30, the liberation of Kuwait was the headline story of the Gulf crisis, and then it faded, like the others, to be periodically returned to prominence as events and administrative needs dictated (MacArthur 1992; Kellner 1992).

Reason five was Saddam Hussein himself. The demonization of Saddam Hussein was a logical extension of the hostage issue. If there were hostages to be liberated, they would have to be liberated from someone. The press began the vilification of Hussein by running personal profiles contrasting the Iraqi leader and the emir of Kuwait.

Hussein was called a socialist, an assassin, and the head of a ruling clique, while the emir was characterized as the head of a family and a benevolent patriarch. Expediting the propaganda campaign, the press constructed the one comparison that no one would mistake: Hussein was a modern Hitler (Safire 1990). President Bush added the Hitler-Hussein analogy to his narrative in October and wove the phony incubator story into it. At a Dallas fund-raising event, he spoke of "newborn babies thrown out of incubators" and, in his signature clipped syntax, added:

> Every day now, new word filters out about the ghastly atrocities perpetrated by Saddam's forces. Eyewitness accounts of the cruel and senseless suffering endured by the people of Kuwait; of a systematic assault on the soul of a nation. Summary executions, routine torture. Hitler revisited. ("Bush Talks of Atrocities," 1990)

Reason six was jobs. Presumably, the Bush administration thought that the working people who would not fight for Texaco might fight to protect the oil on which their jobs depended. Although many Americans then and now believed the war was about oil, Secretary of State James Baker's November 14 attempt to equate oil with jobs and thereby sell a war for the oil companies as something that was in workers' interest did not work. The oil crisis that some expected to result from the Iraq-Kuwait dispute never materialized. On January 10, the eve of the first U.S. bombing of Iraq, the *New York Times* editorially shot down the oil-as-a-vital-interest reason for war (see also Friedman 1990).

Reason Abandoned: Toward War with Iraq

On the surface, the administration's resort to "jobs" as a reason for military intervention appeared to be an act of desperation. The administration had, after all, frantically constructed one reason after another for its military buildup in the Gulf. Yet, none of those reasons had convinced the American people that war was necessary. The administration had failed.

Or had it? In the end, the proffering of one reason after another functioned to paralyze rational discourse. No one could make sense of what this looming conflict was all about. And that was the point. The administration had succeeded in making it impossible to reason about the rightness and wrongness of this war. With reason having been neutralized, opinion about the war drew upon emotion, symbolism, and myth. It was the myth of the spat-upon Vietnam veteran that galvanized the sentiments of the American people sufficiently to discredit peace activists and give George Bush his war.

During the previous August and September there had been only scattered reports of active opposition to military intervention, but by early October mainstream religious groups were voicing their disagreement with the administration's policy. Church opposition was based on the principle of the just war. Just-war theorists involved the public in a carefully reasoned debate about whether war was justified in this case. The problem for the administration was that its policy did not pass the test. While some church leaders found "just cause" in the need to expel Iraq from Kuwait, few were satisfied that war was the last remaining resort (Steinfels 1990).[2]

After the November 8 announcement of increased troop deployment, opposition grew. By early December, reports of organizing by students and anti-war groups began to mount. The most troublesome voices from the administration's point of view, however, were coming from within the military. Within a week after the announcement, reports began to trickle out about soldiers resisting service in the Gulf. During the next few weeks, a large number of active-duty soldiers and National Guardsmen sought conscientious objector status. And not all of the in-service dissent was stateside. When Secretary of State James Baker and Chairman of the Joint Chiefs of Staff Gen. Colin Powell visited the troops in the Gulf in November, they faced discontent bordering on hostility. Later, when President Bush made his Thanksgiving tour of the troops, special security measures were taken, and soldiers "were carefully selected and briefed on how to conduct themselves with him." The appearance that the commander in chief had to be protected from his own troops was very embarrassing for the administration.[3]

Then, on December 6, Saddam Hussein delivered what could have been a lethal blow to George Bush's domestic propaganda campaign. Announcing that all Westerners were free to leave Iraq and Kuwait, Hussein took away the most emotionally potent reason for U.S. military intervention: the hostages. The announcement came just at the time, three weeks before Christmas, when the administration could have used real hostages to exploit the separation anxieties of the nation. Moreover, with no American civilians in either Kuwait or Iraq (except those who were clearly there by their own choice) to use as an excuse for military intervention, Bush was on a shorter leash. The hostages issue, finally, had been a large blind hiding the offensive posture of the administration and that, symbolically, had provided a sure means for rallying pro-war public opinion when necessary. With its position uncovered, the administration now had either to abandon its aggressive stance or to confront, more candidly, the growing opposition.

Against the Coalition against the War

As we know, George Bush stayed the course to war and successfully transferred much of the sentiment that had been mobilized around hostages to soldiers. In effect, soldiers became the new hostages that needed to be rescued—by other soldiers, of course. Soldiers thus became the ends and the means of George Bush's war. The fledgling movement against the war, dubbed the "Coalition Against the U.S." in the *National Review* (Horowitz 1991), would have to be engaged.[4]

As the Senate Armed Services and Foreign Relations committees opened hearings on the policy in September, Bush began to complain that critics threatened the success of what was then still called Operation Desert Shield. Bush's strategy was to turn the tables on his opponents by using their anti-war position against them. Implicit in this strategy, previously employed by the Nixon administration in the closing years of the Vietnam War, was the assumption that peace could best be achieved through strength: those who were against the war in Vietnam were undermining the strength of America and thus prolonging the war. Applied to the Gulf War, the reasoning went that those who were opposed to the administration's policies were, objectively speaking, pro-war and by extension would have to be held accountable for the deaths of American soldiers in the Gulf (Lewis 1990).

A conservative group calling itself the Coalition for America at Risk, began running a series of paid television commercials and newspaper advertisements that made the soldiers themselves the reason for the war. The full-page ads in such major papers as the *New York Times* and *Wall Street Journal* featured a large photograph of barren ground with a curvy line running across it. Beneath the picture, in mid-sized type justified to the left margin, was the caption: "It's not just a 'line in the sand' . . . it's . . ." Then, in large block type beneath the caption and centered on the page, was the single word: PEOPLE. The bottom half of the page addressed itself to "all the men and women participating in Operation Desert Shield" with the words, "We are behind you and support you 100%!" Reading down, the ad passed along a "special hello from home" to sixty-three nicknamed soldiers—Slick, Max, Rooster, Elvis, Bilbo, Badfinger, Fuzzy, the Dakota Kid, etc.—in a unit identified as HMLA-367 (Tolchin 1990).[5]

In no sense, however, was this a greetings message to the troops in the Gulf. The audience for this ad was not the troops but the American people. The construction of the ad asked us to make a distinction between the material and the human reasons for the war. It gave us, the readers, permission to choose, but not simply what the war was about. It instructed us about *how* to make choices about support or nonsupport for the war. To choose the "line in the sand" as a reason for what "it" was about was to choose a materialist framework within which logical propositions about the ends and means related to the defense of national boundaries could be debated and adjudicated. It was in effect a choice to make one's decision within the mode of discourse chosen, up to that point, by both the Bush administration and the anti-war theologians. To choose "people," on the other hand, was to choose to make decisions about the war on different, largely emotional, grounds. But which people was this war about? Who were the people in this ad? Not Kuwaitis. Not Saudis. This war was about Fuzzy and Bilbo, the boys from down the block. The war was about the American soldiers who had been sent to fight it.

In other words, the ad conflated the objectives of war with those who had been sent to fight the war. By thus dissolving the distinction between ends and means, the framework within which people could reason about the war was destroyed. In place of a discourse of reason, the ad gave us a discourse of emotion and identity: we were not to *think* about what this war was about, we were to *feel* what it was about. Henceforth, the campaign for the war was framed by symbols, emotion, and myth.

What we were to feel was mediated by the symbols mobilized for the occasion. Most visible, of course, was the yellow ribbon. During December, the yellow ribbon became a symbol of opposition to the anti-war movement. The yellow ribbon campaign dovetailed neatly with two issues from the Vietnam era about which the American people felt great emotion: the prisoner of war/missing in action (POW/MIA) issue and the issue of spat-upon Vietnam veterans. The POW/MIA issue was a natural, but it was the image of the spat-upon Vietnam veteran that figured most prominently in the rhetoric of those supporting the Gulf War. In that image, soldiers were the scapegoats against whom those who had opposed the war directed their hostility. Allegedly, members of the anti-war movement spat on soldiers just returned from Vietnam; the acts of spitting were said to have been accompanied by cries of "Baby Killer!" and "Murderer!"

That image had been cultivated mostly by the makers of such movies as the Rambo series during the 1980s. Those movies were very popular, so the issue of how Vietnam veterans had been treated was undoubtedly a concern shared by many Americans in 1990. But the link between that Vietnam-era issue and support for the Gulf War did not come about spontaneously. In fact, the link was first suggested by members of Congress, themselves Vietnam veterans, who were interviewed for a story that appeared in the *New York Times* on September 16. The story was accompanied by linked photographs: Sen. John Kerry sitting in his office, paired with a photo of the boat he commanded in Vietnam; Sen. John McCain in his office, paired with a photo of himself as a POW hospitalized in North Vietnam.

The story itself framed the linkage between the Vietnam War and the Gulf War in such a way that the treatment of soldiers and veterans became *the* issue. Rep. John Murtha, for example, who had served as a marine in Vietnam, said that on a recent visit to the Gulf "troops repeatedly asked [him] whether 'the folks back home' supported them. 'The aura of Vietnam hangs over these kids,' the Pennsylvania Democrat said. 'Their parents were in it. They've seen all these movies. They worry, they wonder' " (Apple 1990).

The "aura of Vietnam." It was not the loss of the war, not the massive destruction of Vietnam itself, not the death of 58,000 Americans and 1,900,000 Vietnamese, not any of the myriad other things the war was more evidently about that was at issue. The aura of Vietnam as framed in this story—what the war in Vietnam was about—was the level of support that soldiers and veterans had received from the American people. To make sure that nobody missed the point, the *Times* linked the package—Vietnam veterans, the Gulf War, and hostility for the anti-war movement—with reports from the Gulf like the following:

> One soldier asked that his name not be used and also asked that an officer step away to permit the soldier to speak freely to a reporter. . . . "When we deployed here, people cheered and waved flags," he [said], "but if I go back home like the Vietnam vets did and somebody spits on me, I swear to God I'll kill them." (LeMoyne 1990b)

These sentiments, brought to the surface during the middle weeks of the Gulf War buildup, were then played upon by Operation Yellow

Ribbon in December. Operation Yellow Ribbon carried out its campaign through such state and local organizations as "Operation Eagle," headquartered in the Boston suburb of Shrewsbury, Massachusetts.[6]

Claiming the support of the U.S. Army, Navy, and Air Force, the Marine Corps, and Coast Guard Reserve units, Operation Eagle functioned on three levels. One level involved the collection of items that Operation Eagle leaders claimed were needed by soldiers in the Gulf. Using the stationery of the Third Marine Division Association, Operation Eagle solicited donations of reading material, board games, videos, sports equipment, and personal items such as lip balm and sunglasses. The solicitation listed a "hotline" number for further information without revealing that the number belonged to the Defense Logistics Agency in the Department of Defense.[7]

Additionally, Operation Eagle/Yellow Ribbon carried out a propaganda campaign in the public schools. The program sent Operation Eagle leaders and military personnel into schools and got students involved in writing letters to soldiers in the Gulf. Students who wrote letters were given red, white, and blue Operation Eagle hats.

The school campaign gave Operation Eagle enormous visibility and, through the thousands of children directly touched by military personnel who went into the schools, indirect access to the hearts and minds of thousands more adults. Most important, however, the political fallout from Operation Eagle's appearances in the schools created a pretext for attacks on the anti-war movement. When parents and interested citizens objected to Operation Eagle's self-evidently propagandistic project, the press and grassroots conservatives construed their objections as anti-soldier.

Operation Eagle's war against the anti-war movement was the third, and most important, level at which it, operated. When a Worcester, Massachusetts mother objected to the presence of Operation Eagle in her son's school, the local press ridiculed her in an editorial. Two days later, the paper ran a large cartoon showing a soldier with an envelope addressed to "Any Soldier, Desert Shield," the generic address that

Operation Eagle had been telling school children to use. The soldier was tipping the envelope so that a large amount of what looked like tiny scraps of paper were pouring out of it. The cartoon has him saying, "Some grade school kids from Worcester mailed us . . . CONFETTI?!?" A second soldier is shown saying, "Nope . . . those are kids LETTERS . . . edited by some protest group."

Within days, the paper was flooded with letters that parroted the themes of soldiers, hostages, Vietnam, and the anti-war movement that the Bush administration had so ably stirred together during the previous weeks. One writer said war opponents were causing him flashbacks to the 1960s. "I hope and pray," he said, "Gulf war veterans will never return to the unfriendly and unsupportive country my generation returned to." Another letter claimed that anti-war activists had broken the hearts of thousands of Vietnam veterans. Still another asked if the peace activists opposing the Gulf War were "the same people that spit on the GIs when they came home from Vietnam." A supporter of Operation Yellow Ribbon, when asked why she was at a rally to protest the war, told an interviewer:

> The first reason, the first time I came out, the reason was, is, because of what happened to the Vietnam vets. I felt that they were treated so badly and they fought for their country and they were treated so bad that I tried to make up for it in this way. . . .
>
> I heard *they* [motions to peace vigil] were going to be here. And I didn't know anybody else was going to be here but I came down to protest the protesters. That's the only reason I came. Was to protest the protesters. I want the boys over there to know that there *are* people over here who are behind them and they're not gonna have to come home ashamed of their uniform; they're not gonna be having to take their uniform off at the airport so they can sneak into their own country and not be called murderers and everything. (Porter 1991)

Across the country, the role played by Operation Eagle in Massachusetts was played by other affiliates of Operation Yellow Ribbon. One that drew national attention was in the Chicago suburb of Schaumburg where efforts to block an Operation Yellow Ribbon group from entering Dooley Elementary School drew a response from President Bush. That story, carried in the pages of major newspapers across the country, reinforced the feeling that the real line of conflict in the Gulf War was drawn between those who supported and those who opposed the troops (Mills 1991).

But the yellow ribbon was only a symbol. The "real" thing was the image of the Vietnam veteran abused by the anti-war movement. That image was invoked countless times during the Gulf War period, sometimes in news accounts intended to be sympathetic to the war protesters:

> Vietnam-era protests often were directed at the soldiers themselves, revealing an ugly streak of elitism at best; this year's demonstrators see the GIs as victims. "You won't see protesters spitting on soldiers as they come off the plane," predicted Greg Sommers, director of the Fayetteville, NC branch of Quaker House, a pacifist organization. (Adler 1991)

The not infrequent invocation of the spat-upon veteran image by those who had been active opponents of the Vietnam War, and were now opposed to the Gulf War, may have been opportunism on the part of some, as suggested by David Horowitz (1991).[8] More likely, though, the self-incriminating statements of anti-war activists testified to the hegemony that the image of the defiled Vietnam veteran had acquired through the medium of popular culture and the power of the news media to keep the image in the faces of the American people during the period of the Gulf War buildup.

Fighting the Vietnam Syndrome

The dispatching of troops to the Gulf was an exercise in what is sometimes called "armed propaganda," a way of persuading through action. A substantial component of the propaganda campaign was directed at the American people. Armed propaganda substitutes for reason and rational argument through its appeals to the emotions. It communicates through a discourse of military symbolism, not words and logical propositions. Once the Bush administration had paralyzed the ends-means discourse, the armed propaganda technique enabled it to reduce public opinion on the war to the levels of emotion and symbolism.[9] The image of the spat-upon veteran functioned during the Gulf War as a "perfecting myth." Perfecting myths, explains Virginia Carmichael in her book *Framing History*, provide a justification for the world while simultaneously reinforcing the relationship between individuals and the state. They insure, she argues, "individuals' voluntary acquiescence to, support for, and daily investment in a specific history not of their choosing."[10]

By this reading, the Gulf War was a kind of necessary shock therapy to jolt the American people out of their reluctance to go to war, a reluctance that, allegedly, was a hangover from the defeat in Vietnam. The Gulf War was to be a demonstration of military prowess so awesome that positive identification with it would be irresistible. Opposition to the war, by the same token, would look so hopeless that the few pathetic souls who dared would be automatically subjected to devastating scorn and belittlement (Cloud 1991).

. . . . . .

The Gulf War brought scholars to a new level of appreciation for the audacity of governmental power at the turn of the twenty-first century. As economist Andre Gunder Frank (1992) observed in his analysis of Gulf War propaganda, the capacity of today's high-tech news management to brainwash a global population makes fascist mind control of the World War II era look like child's play.

Most of the historical analysis of the Gulf War has focused on the media and the ability of the government to censor the press.[11] The analysis made here is more in keeping with that of Neil Postman, who points out in his book *Amusing Ourselves to Death* that control over *how* we know is more important than control over *what* we know. While it is true that the government controlled the content of news during the Gulf War, it is more important to understand how it was able to influence significantly the way the American people thought about—or did not think about—the war. Its control was more Huxleian than Orwellian, its problematic more epistemological than empirical.

Few analyses, moreover, have had sufficient historical depth to recognize the foreshadowing of the Bush administration's tactics in the way in which the Nixon-Agnew administration prolonged the Vietnam War. From the mobilization of paramilitary patriots for pro-war rallies through the disparagement of anti-war activists and the exploitation of soldiers already in Vietnam as a reason to keep the war going, the Nixon-Agnew administration did it first.

The historical orientation of what follows does not deny the ongoing relevance of the spat-upon veteran imagery. In his study of political apathy on today's college campuses, Paul Loeb (1994) found that the image of the spitting anti-war activist of the 1960s is an icon of 1990s conservative ideology and is used to intimidate would-be activists. Many of today's students prefer to remain inactive out of fear that activism will lead others to associate them with the 1960s' types who spat on the veterans. It is not surprising then, that as U.S. soldiers were dispatched to Bosnia late in the fall of 1995, a leaflet circulated on the campus of Holy Cross College in Worcester, Massachusetts, expressing opposition to the mission but support for the troops and the "hope that no student today will repeat the mistakes of the generation that proceeded us—by spitting on Marines" (Thompson 1995).

To get beyond this syndrome—a "Vietnam syndrome" of America's political culture—the real story of solidarity between the anti-war movement and Vietnam veterans has to be told, and the image of the spat-upon veteran has to be debunked and its mythical dimensions exposed.

THREE

Dear Spiro Agnew

About Soldiers, Veterans, and the Anti-war Movement

I am writing in response to your criticisms of war critics, which was printed in the *Pacific Stars and Stripes* Saturday, April 3, 1971. The *Stars and Stripes* gave the following account of your speech at the 25th anniversary meeting of the Veterans Administration Volunteer Service:

> Vice President Spiro T. Agnew accused Indochina war critics Thursday of demoralizing American soldiers in the front lines and scorning those who return home. . . . They have been told almost daily . . . that they are fighting in a "worthless" and "immoral" cause.
>
> Agnew . . . said American soldiers in no other war "have had to fight the lonely fight of the Vietnam veterans. . . . This encouragement has come to them—not from Hanoi Hannah, but from some of the leading members of the United States Senate, prestigious columnists and news commentators, academic figures, some church organizations as well as assorted radicals, draft card burners and street demonstrators."

I am an Ensign in the U.S. Navy. I have been in Vietnam one month. In reference to the above quote . . . I *do* feel that I am involved with a worthless and immoral cause, and I feel that we should get out of Vietnam now—totally. It does not demoralize

> me to hear United States Senators, prestigious columnists, etc. say this. . . . In fact, it bolsters my faith in the American people to hear this. . . . What does demoralize me is the feeling that I am being manipulated by the present Administration for political gains, and what is called "saving face." And I find your rhetoric frequently the most demoralizing of all.
>
> "An Open Letter to Spiro Agnew"
> Gene Powers
> ICC Republic of Vietnam
> Box 101 Code 31A
> FPO San Francisco 96626
> April 10, 1971

Gene Powers's "Open Letter to Spiro Agnew" was found in the records of the Student Mobilization Committee to End the War in Vietnam (SMC), located in the State Historical Society Library in Madison, Wisconsin. The letter had been sent to the National Peace Action Coalition and forwarded to SMC. *Pacific Stars and Stripes* was a military newspaper that was widely available to soldiers throughout Southeast Asia during the Vietnam War. Thirty months after this letter was written, on October 11, 1973, Spiro Agnew, facing impeachable charges of tax evasion, would resign as vice president of the United States, the first casualty of the Watergate scandal that culminated in President Richard Nixon's resignation on August 8, 1974.

A remarkable historical document, Gene Powers's letter provides clear evidence that soldiers in Vietnam were being made aware of the anti-war movement and of the administration's opposition to the movement. The issue was as much before the troops in Vietnam as it was before the American people as a whole. The letter, moreover, makes it clear that soldiers serving in Vietnam had before them the option to believe the vice president's interpretation of what the anti-war movement meant to them. In this letter, however, we find an unequivocal rejection of the vice president's view that the anti-war movement was explicitly and unambiguously anti-soldier. Indeed, we find in the letter clear evidence that Ensign Powers embraced the perspective of the anti-war movement. His cover letter to the National Peace Action Coalition—in which he wrote, "Please feel free to print or quote the letter in any way you feel would help the cause"—documents his awareness of organized opposition to the war and his willingness to associate himself with that opposition. Most important, though, Powers's letter raises an interesting question: did the image of hostility between the anti-war movement and soldiers/veterans—an image that would be widely accepted during the Gulf War of 1991—arise out of the actual experience between those groups or was it an image created by political leaders?

War Veterans and the Vietnam War

By 1971, the real story of relations between veterans and the anti-war movement was already more complex than the morality play of "good vets" and "bad protesters" sketched by Spiro Agnew. To begin with, veterans of previous wars were an integral part of the anti–Vietnam War movement from its inception. Veterans' groups led some of the earliest protest marches against the war, and tactics such as draft card burning, which became emblematic of the anti-war movement, and the turning-in of service medals as an act of protest, which became the hallmark of anti-war Vietnam veterans in the early 1970s, may have been foreshadowed by similar actions taken in the mid-1960s by veterans of previous wars.[1] Opposite Spiro Agnew's picket-line portrait of Vietnam veterans across the barricades from anti-war activists is the reality that by 1971 large numbers of Vietnam veterans had already joined the anti-war movement. It is true, however, that some veterans of previous wars not only did not embrace Vietnam veterans but were openly hostile to anti-war Vietnam veterans and ambivalent about Vietnam veterans in general for having lost the first war in American history. The behavior of those superpatriotic veterans actually provided grist for the myth that Vietnam veterans were spat on—a story that will be told in a later chapter.

Veterans for Peace and the Fifth Avenue Peace Parade Committee

The United States had been involved in Vietnam since World War II, when it supported the communist forces led by Ho Chi Minh in their struggle against Japanese occupation. After the war, the United States feared communist expansion in the region and backed the recolonization of Indochina by France. When the French were defeated in a decisive battle against Vietnamese independence forces at Dien Bien Phu in 1954, the United States stepped into the breach.

The cease-fire agreement negotiated after Dien Bien Phu allowed the French to withdraw below the 17th parallel while the communist Viet Minh grouped north of the line. General elections were to be held in July 1956 to reunify the country. Those elections were scuttled because the United States feared the communists would win. Subsequently, the 17th parallel hardened into a political border separating North and South Vietnam. In the South, the United States created a corrupt and repressive client state led by Ngo Dinh Diem. Despite the assistance of thousands of military "advisors," the receipt of millions of dollars in aid, and tons of military supplies from the United States, the Diem regime was never able to defeat its pro-Viet Minh opposition in the rural areas of the South.

Seeking a pretext for bombing North Vietnam, the United States provoked an incident in the South China Sea on August 4, 1964, involving the destroyers *Maddox* and *Turner Joy*. Claiming the destroyers had been attacked, President Lyndon Johnson ordered U.S. jets to bomb the North. On August 7 Congress passed the Gulf of Tonkin resolution that authorized the president to use ground forces in Vietnam. By the end of 1965, there were about 175,000 American troops there. The number of draftees soared accordingly and by summer 1965 opposition to the draft and escalation of the war began to mount (Useem 1973).

One of the first large demonstrations against the war in Vietnam took place in New York City on October 15, 1965, a day designated as the International Day of Protest by several pacifist and anti-war organizations. Organized by the Fifth Avenue Peace Parade Committee, the march up the avenue and a rally in Central Park drew about 25,000 people. World War II veterans were among the marchers greeted with the catcalled words "coward" and "traitor." In response, five veterans issued a call to form what became the Ad Hoc Committee of Veterans for Peace in Vietnam. Fifty veterans attended the initial meeting and agreed to sponsor an advertisement in the *New York Times*. The full-page ad, which carried the signatures of five hundred veterans, ran on November 24, 1965. It featured a picture of a small boy under a caption that read:

> YOUR DADDY DIED IN THE IA DRANG VALLEY.[2]
> Where?
> IA DRANG VALLEY.
> Where?
> IA DRANG VALLEY.
> Why?

The Ad Hoc Committee led a peace march in Washington, D.C., on November 27, 1965, and on December 15 met to form Veterans for Peace.[3] Members of Vets for Peace, as it came to be called, led many anti-war activities during 1966 and 1967. Edward Bloch, a former marine and veteran of World War II, and several other members of Veterans for Peace, led a protest on February 2, 1966, that snarled rush-hour traffic in Times Square. On February 5, a group of veterans attempted to return their discharge papers and medals to President Lyndon Johnson, and later in the spring members of the Veterans and Reservists to End the War in Vietnam burned their discharge papers as a protest against the government's war policy.[4]

The second International Day of Protest, March 26, 1966, drew thirty thousand to a demonstration in New York City. Chicago, Boston, San Francisco, and other major cities across the country also saw marches and rallies against the war. The *New York Herald Tribune* reported the presence of "clean-cut veterans with red-bordered blue overseas caps lettered 'Veterans for Peace in Vietnam' " in the parade down Fifth Avenue. The paper also noted that the parade had been led by a contingent of veterans. The *New York Times* ran a striking front-page visual that paired a photograph of marines going ashore in Vietnam with a photo of the anti-war march. The caption, running atop the two photos read: "Marines Land South of Saigon—Marchers Protest Policy on Vietnam." Pictured prominently in the photo of protesters was a large placard reading: "Veterans and Reservists for Peace."

March 26 also saw an escalation of hostility against the anti-war movement. In New York City, the office of one of the sponsoring organizations of the Day of Protest, the Committee for Independent Action, was firebombed, forcing A. J. Muste, described by the *Herald Tribune* as "the 81-year-old dean of American pacifists and the parade's chairman," to ride in a car surrounded by volunteer bodyguards. Another group, the Viet Nam Peace Parade Committee, was reported to have received anonymous telephone calls warning, according to one member, that "if we march we can be assured we will all be dead by 4 P.M." Along the parade route, protesters were met with taunts of "traitor," "Commie cowards," and "kill a Commie for Christ." Eggs were thrown at marchers in New York, Boston, and Oklahoma City. In Chicago and Washington, D.C., marchers were heckled by members of the American Nazi Party. Most interestingly, we find in the news reports of the March 26 demonstrations some of the first instances of spitting; however, in all such instances it was the protesters who were being spat upon by war supporters.[5]

The accounts of early hostility toward the anti-war movement are important because they counterbalance the popular wisdom that protest groups were responsible for the violence (and spitting) associated with the demonstrations. One need only review the newspaper reports from the period to see that acts of physical intimidation and violence against peaceful protesters began early in the period and preceded the notorious acts of physical destruction committed by anti-war protesters, such as the bombing of the Army Math Center at the University of Wisconsin. There is more at stake than the historical record, however, because, as will be argued later, myths involve the assembly of pieces of real events for the construction of stories that, taken as a whole, are not true. The violence and spit surrounding anti-war demonstrations was real, but the demonstrators were usually the victims, not the perpetrators, of those acts.

Although the organized involvement of Vietnam veterans in the anti-war movement was still three years away, they were participating as individuals by the spring of 1966. At a March 3 anti-war meeting chaired by the journalist I. F. Stone at Town Hall in Manhattan, Donald Duncan, who had been a master sergeant in the Green Berets, the elite counter-insurgency force, and was a Vietnam veteran, was the featured speaker. An anti-war article written by Duncan and published in *Ramparts* magazine was duplicated and circulated by Veterans for Peace. Flyers and posters from 1966 and 1967 found in the files of various anti-war organizations show that Duncan was a speaker at many events across the country.

At a May 1966 meeting of Veterans for Peace delegates from several cities, Maury Colow, a veteran from New York, told those attending to "be on the lookout now for veterans returning from Vietnam." Noting that Vietnam veterans would be sought as spokesmen for the pro-war forces, Colow said, "We must do all in our power to get them on the side of peace" (Minutes 1966).

Veterans, Soldiers, and the Peace Movement Reach Out to One Another

The link between the anti-war movement and Vietnam-era veterans, made through Veterans for Peace, was secured through work on behalf of serving soldiers. By helping soldiers who were in service, especially those in Vietnam, the anti-war movement established a record of caring about soldiers' needs. Later, those soldiers, turned veterans, viewed the anti-war movement as a credible ally for veteran-related struggles.

The credibility of the anti-war movement in the eyes of Vietnam-era soldiers and veterans was not something that could be assumed. By the summer of 1966 the movement had been supporting draft resistance for over a year and was now beginning to support, if not encourage, in-service resistance to the war. How would men who had spent a year or more enduring the indignities of military life and the hardships of Vietnam react to criticisms of the war and calls for their involvement on the side of peace? Moreover, was the movement not demanding that very young men take extraordinary legal risks with their futures by asking them to refuse induction or orders to fight in Vietnam—risks that movement activists would not have to take because they were too old for the draft or exempt from service because of their class, race, or gender. Indeed, weren't the veterans of previous wars asking Vietnam-era young men to do something they themselves had never done, namely, resist induction and service in wartime?

As the writer of an internal memorandum for the Fifth Avenue Peace Parade Committee phrased the problem:

> One reason we cannot get 100,000 men to refuse to go to Vietnam is that we cannot offer them sufficient protection. Being put in the brig, placed on a diet of bread and water for 9 days, forced to forfeit $85/mo in case of private [sic], placed in solitary confinement, etc, is not protection. All this for AWOL. . . . If I were a GI and saw a peace movement such as ours which opposes the war in Vietnam and supports those who refuse I would LOOK TO THEM TO PROTECT MY RIGHTS IN REFUSING TO GO. They can say to us that it is easy to say DON'T GO, BUT WE ARE NOT GOING TO JAIL, WE ARE NOT GOING TO BE PLACED IN THE BRIG [emphasis in original]. (Memorandum c. 1966)

In the summer of 1966, the outreach to in-service GIs through legal-aid work began in earnest. Noting that " 'the grass-roots disgust' at American actions in Vietnam had recently spread to many members of the U.S. armed forces," the Vietnam Peace Parade Committee (another name for the Fifth Avenue Peace Parade Committee) said in an August 4 news release that "civil-liberties lawyers in New York have reported a 'great jump' in the number of clients on active duty who refuse to carry out American military policy in Vietnam" (News Release 1966).

The first major case involving support for in-service resistors was the case of the "Fort Hood Three." Ordered to report to the Oakland Army Terminal on July 13, 1966, for shipment to Vietnam, three GIs stationed at Fort Hood, Texas, refused to go. While on leave prior to their July reporting date, they had traveled to New York City to seek support for their action. They were referred to Vets for Peace and the Parade Committee.

At a June 30 press conference attended by Stokely Carmichael, A. J. Muste, David Dellinger, and Staughton Lynd, all prominent members of the anti-war movement at the time, the Fort Hood Three announced their plan to report to Oakland and their intention to refuse shipment to Vietnam. Speaking for the three, Dennis Mora said:

> We represent in our backgrounds a cross section of the Army and of America. James Johnson is a Negro, David Samas is of Lithuanian and Italian parents, Dennis Mora is a Puerto Rican. We speak as American Soldiers.
>
> We have been in the army long enough to know that we are not the only GIs who feel as we do. Large numbers of men in the service either do not understand this war or are against it. . . .
>
> We have made our decision. We will not be part of this unjust, immoral, and illegal war. We want no part of a war of extermination. We oppose the criminal waste of American lives and resources. We refuse to go to Vietnam.[6]

On July 7, while on their way to a public meeting at the Community Church in New York City, the three GIs were abducted by federal agents and taken to the stockade at Fort Dix, New Jersey. They were court-martialed and sentenced to two years in prison. Subsequent demonstrations for their release and improvement in the conditions of their confinement helped to focus the attention of the anti-war movement on the issue of GI rights and advertised the fact that the anti-war movement was there to help soldiers.

As the anti-war movement was reaching out to help soldiers, soldiers extended their voices and credibility to the movement. The archives of anti-war organizations contain hundreds of letters and petitions recording the widespread support of GIs for the anti-war movement. They began coming in long before the peak of campus protest activity in 1968 and 1969, and they took interesting forms. One from 1966, found in the files of the Fifth Avenue Peace Parade Committee, was co-signed by George J. Bojarski and fourteen other members of an infantry platoon in Vietnam and had been sent to Mayor Orville Hubbard of Dearborn, Michigan. Hubbard had placed a question on the ballot for the November 8 elections that read: "Are you in favor of an immediate cease-fire and withdrawal of U.S. forces from Vietnam so the Vietnamese people can settle their own problems?" Forty-one percent of Dearborn voters (14,124) had voted in favor of the resolution. Bojarski had read about the ballot and the election results in the *Detroit News*. The letter he and this cosigners wrote read, in part:

> Myself and my entire squad (3rd squad A3/12) agree with you and would like to thank you for your concern over the matter. After being out in the field for over a month and then reading the article about the vote you can imagine how mad we were.
>
> All in favor of you and the 14,124 citizens of Dearborn who voted for *us*, thank you.
>
> Of course the rest of the platoon feel as we do but I am just a representative of my squad writing our thanks for your effort.[7]

Bojarski's supposition that his views were "representative" of other GIs may or may not have been accurate. Little research documenting the extent of GI resistance in Vietnam was conducted during the war years, in part because the military authorities made such an undertaking almost impossible, and the research findings that are available do not reach back as far as 1966. There is an authenticity about documents like Bojarski's letter, however, that belie revisionist portrayals of GI resistance as marginal, inspired by campus radicalism or, as Spiro Agnew would have had it, a fiction.

In fact, the government's own data draws a picture that looks more like Bojarski's than Agnew's. In his book *Days of Decision* (1989), Gerald Gioglio presents the following summary of the data on GI resistance:

> During the Vietnam era there were approximately 10 million men in uniform. Among those in uniform, 563,000 men received less-than-honorable discharges (including 34,000 who were imprisoned following court-martial). There were 1,500,000 AWOL and 550,000 desertion incidents. . . . The rate of AWOL offenses increased as the war dragged on, ranging from a low of 38.2 per 1,000 men in 1968 to 84.0 in 1971. The desertion rate ranged from 8.4 per 1,000 men in 1966 to 33.9 per 1,000 in 1971. Nonjudicial punishment meted out by officers to enlisted men ranged from 137 per 1,000 men in 1968 to 183 per 1,000 in 1972. Added to this were escalating problems associated with substance abuse, petty and serious acts of sabotage, and assaults on officers and other cadre. (P. 319)

Turning the Guns Around: GIs and Veterans against the War

During the latter half of 1966, conferences were held in Cleveland, Ohio, in an attempt to forge some kind of national organization that would unite the many anti-war organizations working locally and regionally across the country. On November 26, the Spring Mobilization Committee to End the War in Vietnam (Spring Mobe, for short) was established to coordinate efforts to organize a massive, nationwide demonstration on April 15, 1967. A. J. Muste, from the Fifth Avenue Peace Parade Committee was the chair of Spring Mobe, and David Dellinger, Robert Greenblatt, Ed Keating, and Sidney Peck were vice chairmen.

One of the objectives of Spring Mobe was to broaden the base of popular involvement in the movement through outreach to labor, student, professional, religious, civil rights, and other sectors. Cooperation with Students for a Democratic Society (SDS) in the organizing of a student strike to coincide with the April action resulted in the formation of the previously mentioned Student Mobilization Committee at a conference held at the University of Chicago on December 28.

Organizing for April 15 was a mammoth undertaking: the New York Peace Parade Committee itself distributed over a million leaflets. Buses, trains, and car caravans were mustered to bring thousands to New York and San Francisco from across the country. A special organizing project on the Rosebud Indian Reservation in South Dakota brought a bus of Native Americans to New York. On April 15, four hundred thousand marched against the war in New York, and seventy-five thousand marched in San Francisco—record numbers of protesters for both cities (Halstead 1991).

The April 15 mobilization also notched up GI organizing to a new level. For the first time, organizers gained access to the New York City Port Authority bus terminal, enabling them to pass out leaflets and talk to GIs passing through the terminal. This was a major accomplishment because the Port Authority terminal was a central transfer point for GIs moving between the many military installations in the mid-Atlantic region. The success of April 15 was followed by an increased commitment by SMC to work with GIs. Following the pattern begun by the Peace Parade Committee and Veterans for Peace the year before, SMC became a major player in the fight for GI legal rights.

The first case taken up by SMC was that of Howard Petrick, a private from a working-class family who had spoken at the Chicago SMC conference. Petrick, a member of the Young Socialist Alliance (YSA) before he went into the military, was actively engaged in educating and organizing his fellow soldiers against the war. Stationed at Fort Hood, Texas, he kept a stash of anti-war literature in his locker and regularly leafleted his mates. Petrick's literature was eventually confiscated. Threatened with court-martial, he went public with his case and got the support of SMC and some sympathy from the press, which was attentive to the First Amendment implications of his case. Shortly thereafter, he was thrown out of the army although he later won his honorable discharge on appeal. Petrick would go on to become a major figure in the formation of SMC's GI Press Service, which was probably the most important institution in what became known as the GI Movement (Halstead 1991, 302).

The most important outcome of April 15, however, may have been that it brought together in New York City the six Vietnam veterans who formed Vietnam Veterans Against the War (VVAW). For the next two years, the group played an important educational role in the movement by providing speakers for public events, running newspaper ads, and publishing its newspaper, *Vietnam GI*, later renamed *The First Casualty*.

Links between the anti-war movement and Vietnam-era soldiers and veterans continued to build throughout 1967. The march of one hundred thousand people on the Pentagon on October 21, 1967, brought the movement and uniformed soldiers assigned to defend the Pentagon face to face for the first time. What effect that encounter had on GIs as a whole is unclear, but the photographs of veterans wearing Vets for Peace hats handing leaflets to Pentagon guards and of civilian anti-war activists putting flowers in the barrels of the weapons held by the troops stimulated still more interest in organizing the troops.

In 1968, a group of VVAW members supported Eugene McCarthy, the peace candidate, for president. McCarthy lost the Democratic party nomination to Hubert Humphrey at the party convention which began in Chicago on August 26. During the convention, Chicago streets and parks were filled with protesters. Throughout the week activists fought with the Chicago police over access to the streets leading to the convention and over rights to assemble in the parks. The fighting was brutal, leaving more than a thousand people injured and one dead. Over six hundred were arrested. The week following the convention, SMC held a conference at which a panel of active-duty GIs and Vietnam veterans talked about organizing GIs. As a result, the focus in spring 1969 was on organizing the Easter GI-Civilian demonstrations.

The Easter demonstrations were larger than expected. On April 5, 100,000 marched in the rain in New York City. The next day 40,000 marched in San Francisco to demand an end to the war and freedom for soldiers held in the Presidio stockade. In Chicago, where thirty thousand rallied, one of the speakers was Pvt. Joe Miles, an experienced black nationalist organizer stationed at Fort Bragg, North Carolina. Miles, together with other GIs, some of whom were already veterans of Vietnam, formed GIs United Against the War in Vietnam, which later spread to other bases. When eight GIs were arrested and confined on charges stemming from their attendance at a meeting of GIs United at Fort Jackson, South Carolina, they became known as the "Fort Jackson Eight" and were soon a cause célèbre. The "Eight" were defended by radical lawyer Leonard Boudin. Boudin was the attorney for Benjamin Spock, the doctor and baby-book author who was also a prominent figure in the anti-war movement. Despite support from students at the University of South Carolina and war opponents across the country, the eight GIs received dishonorable discharges when the charges against them were finally dropped (Halstead 1991, 450).

The relationship between the anti-war movement and Vietnam-era soldiers and veterans was galvanized during 1969. The two organizational elements in that chemistry were the GI movement and Vietnam Veterans Against the War. The impetus for a GI movement against the war came as a result of the involvement of the Socialist Workers Party (SWP) in the anti-war movement. The SWP, and its youth affiliate, the Young Socialist Alliance, were opposed to the war but viewed draft resistance as futile and class-biased. It was futile because no matter how many individuals refused induction, the number would never be large enough to impair American military capacity in Indochina, and class-biased in that working-class and poor youth did not have the same access to the means of avoiding the draft, such as educational deferments, flight to Canada, and medical excuses from friendly family doctors, that middle-class youth had.

The YSA was very influential in the Student Mobilization Committee. When questions related to the draft came up, the YSA's position was that the draft, as an institution, should be opposed but that draft resistance or evasion by individuals should not be encouraged. Rather, young men who were drafted should be supported in their efforts to expand GI rights within the military. Expanding GI rights meant, in turn, resisting the tyranny of military authority and the illegality of the war in Vietnam, both of which, argued YSA, had more potential for undermining the war-making capacity of the United States than did draft resistance. Essentially, the YSA positions on the draft and GI organizing were an expansion of the traditional Trotskyist notion that a "proletarian army" was a contradiction in terms given the capitalist objectives of the U.S. mission in Vietnam. Eventually, averred the SWP/YSA leaders, that contradiction would be the undoing of America's imperial policy.

The YSA's position produced tension within the anti-war movement between the peace wing of the movement, led by people like David Dellinger who favored acts of individual resistance, and the anti-imperialist wing of the movement, led by members of the political Left, such as Fred Halstead of the SWP, who favored more organized acts of opposition. Mostly that tension seems to have been constructive, and by 1969 the work with GIs really began to pay off as men who had been part of the in-service GI movement began coming out of military service and joining the anti-war movement as veterans.

In 1969, a group of Vietnam-era veterans formed the GI Press Service (GIPS) as an office within Student Mobe (SMC). The files of GIPS are rich with memoranda, correspondence, and records of meetings, conferences, and demonstrations that authenticate the link between the anti-war movement, GIs, and veterans, and testify to the extensiveness of the solidarity between the movement and servicemen, past and present.[8] GIPS saw itself as the "Associated Press of the GI movement." It was designed to perform three functions: (1) to serve as a link between local GI projects and newspapers, disseminating information and providing something of a national overview of the anti-war movement; (2) to serve as a channel of information to those anti-war GIs who did not have access to a local GI paper; (3) to serve as an organizing tool for the GI anti-war movement and to increase GI participation in national anti-war actions.

GI Press Service, the title of the publication put out by GIPS, had a press run of twenty-five to thirty thousand that went out in bundles to over three hundred active-duty GIs on the subscription list. The publication was then handed out to other GIs on and near military bases everywhere, including Vietnam. A typical issue of *GI Press Service* would contain letters from GIs, reports on legal cases being fought by anti-war GIs, announcements of such upcoming anti-war activities as conferences and rallies, information on where to obtain legal counseling, and reports on the latest crackdowns on dissent by military and civilian authorities. In addition, at least thirty-five underground GI newspapers, with names like *About Face* (Camp Pendleton), *Fatigue Press* (Fort Hood), *Last Harass* (Fort Gordon) and *Short Times* (Fort Jackson), sprung up on major military bases across the country.

A sample of the letters printed in GI newspapers is found in *Turning the Guns Around: Notes on the GI Movement*, by Larry Waterhouse and Mariann Wizard (1971). Their sample includes a letter reporting on the "fragging" of an officer by enlisted men ("The Bond," December 16, 1970); a letter telling of a "People's Trial of the Army" held by soldiers at the Shelter Half Coffeehouse at Fort Lewis, Washington ("AFB," March-April, 1970); a letter from Vietnam reporting that 109 men of the First Air Cavalry Division's Third Brigade were being court-martialed for refusal to fight ("AFB," August 1970); a letter from prisoners in the Fort Ord, California, lockup telling of a prisoner riot ("All Ready on the Left," September 1970); a letter from Cecil Field, Florida, reporting that five soldiers had broken into the arsenal and made off with 150 pistols ("The Bond," November 18, 1970).

Military authorities attempted to suppress distribution of dissident publications by confiscating literature and coming down hard on GIs who put out or distributed the underground papers. As a result, the writing and printing of anti-war material was often times pushed off base to the local variant of a nationwide network of coffeehouses that sprung up to support the GI movement. According to Waterhouse and Wizard (1971, 83):

> One of the most important functions of the coffeehouses has been as the office where GI underground newspapers are put together. Production of any newspaper takes a lot of work, and the GI press is certainly no exception. GIs who work all day on the base devote their evenings and weekends to this task. They solicit stories from GIs who visit the cof-

> feehouses or whom they meet on base, write these and other stories that they have covered, reprint stories from other GI and movement papers, and analyze news stories of national importance. Layout must be done properly, and a printer must be found who is willing to print a "dangerous" publication (sympathetic printers have faced much the same harassment as the coffeehouses themselves) for a reasonable price. Money must be raised to pay the printing costs, and safe transportation must be arranged to and from the printers; otherwise the paper may be "lost" or destroyed en route.

In short, the coffeehouses were places where GIs were "able to meet with each other and interested civilians in a relaxed atmosphere, talk freely around their grievances, and put together their own newspapers away from brass censorship" (Waterhouse and Wizard 1971, 75).

By the summer of 1969, news of the GI movement and growing rebellion in the ranks of troops in Vietnam was out. In early May, United Press International ran a lengthy story on the GI movement which was carried in major papers like the *Los Angeles Times* ("Military Antiwar Drive: Rights vs. Regulations," May 9). On May 23, *Life Magazine* featured a story about what it called "a widespread new phenomenon in the ranks of the military: *public dissent*" (emphasis in original). The eight-page story included striking photographs of GI coffeehouse scenes, a collage of headlines, cartoons, and stories from underground GI newspapers, and photos of soldiers and veterans who were speaking out against the military and the war. Unlike the griping about officers and grousing about food that had always characterized military life, the GI movement against the Vietnam War was described by *Life* as "taking forms that pose an acute dilemma . . . for the military establishment" ("Extraordinary Military" 1969). On August 26, the New York *Daily News* reported the temporary refusal of Company A of the Third Battalion, Twenty-First Infantry, to continue fighting in Vietnam. Commenting on that incident, the columnist James Reston wrote in the August 27 issue of the *New York Times* that President Nixon, "has been worried about the revolt of the voters against the war . . . but now he also has to consider the possibility of a revolt of the men if he risks their lives in a war he has decided to bring to a close."[9]

The Moratorium Days of 1969

GI and civilian protests against the war built to a crescendo in the Moratorium Days against the War in October and November 1969. The idea was that beginning in October "business as usual" would be suspended for one day so that the nation could concentrate on matters related to the war. In November, another moratorium would be held, this time for two days. Each month following, one day would be added until there was an American withdrawal from Vietnam or a negotiated settlement.

The idea for a moratorium came out of the liberal wing of the Democratic Party and was presented to the July 4–5 Cleveland conference that revitalized the Mobilization Committee and renamed it the New Mobilization Committee to End the War in Vietnam, or New Mobe. The moratorium idea was adopted both by New Mobe and, subsequently, by the Student Mobilization Committee. In late summer and early fall, campus teach-ins and locally planned demonstrations helped build momentum for the first Moratorium Day, October 15. One demonstration of eight thousand at Richard Nixon's Summer White House in San Clemente, California, drew "a few dozen" anti-war marines from nearby Camp Pendleton. Teach-in activities at the University of Michigan at Ann Arbor on September 19 carried over to the next day when fifteen thousand people who had been leafleted at a Michigan-Vanderbilt football game joined an anti-war rally at which David Dellinger and veteran Andrew Pully spoke. Pully had been involved with Joe Miles in GIs United. On October 12, at an anti-war coffeehouse in Wrightstown, New Jersey, near Fort Dix, several thousand youths gathered for a rally in behalf of anti-war GIs being held in the Fort Dix stockade. They marched onto the base but were eventually driven back by military police using tear gas.

Like the Student Mobilization Committee, the Vietnam Moratorium

Committee (VMC) made a great effort to reach out to GIs and veterans. In a three-page September 29 memorandum to all GI newspapers, the VMC said: "We are eager to have servicemen join our national campaign to maximize public pressure for peace. We are writing for your help in getting GIs to participate in a 'recurring moratorium' on 'business as usual.' " The memo went on to suggest the kinds of activities that GIs might undertake, including:

- Hold an on-base meeting at which the legal rights of servicemen can be discussed. Invite the base commander to make a presentation about the constitutional rights of GIs.
- Send telegrams to elected officials.
- Hold a fast on moratorium day.
- Invite a congressman to meet with GIs on your base on moratorium day.

The memorandum also included an offer by VMC to pay for a full page of space for a "GI Referendum on Vietnam" to be run in each GI newspaper as well as an offer of legal help for GIs who needed it. In a five-page letter dated November 22, and addressed to "Dear Friends," the Moratorium Committee suggested that "groups invite soldiers to their homes for Thanksgiving and Christmas dinner, sponsor collections for Veterans Hospitals or a general project for assisting the families of soldiers who must spend this Christmas in Vietnam." Letters and memos such as these are important historical documents because they shatter the image of an anti-war movement hostile to GIs and veterans, and they show the falsity of Spiro Agnew's and, twenty-some years later, George Bush's tales of an anti-war movement at odds with all soldiers and veterans.[10]

In New York and Boston over one hundred thousand people turned out to protest the war on October 15. There were fifty thousand in Washington, D.C., twenty-five thousand in Madison, Wisconsin, and Ann Arbor, Michigan, and comparable numbers in many other major cities across the country. The October 24 issue of *Life* magazine called it "a display without historical parallel, the largest expression of public dissent ever seen in this country." The *New York Times* of October 16 ("Some G.I.s in Vietnam Protest") even reported support for the moratorium among the men in Vietnam:

> In the foothills south of Danang, about 15 members of a platoon of the Americal Division wore black armbands as they marched on patrol.
> "It's my way of protesting, one soldier told a reporter. "We wanted to do something, and this was the only thing we could think of."
> Before the day was out, four of the protesting soldiers had been wounded by Vietcong booby traps.

Flushed with the success of October 15, movement organizers looked toward November. Plans for a large march on Washington, D.C., on November 15, the "March Against Death," had been in the making by the student Mobe/New Mobe people even prior to the moratorium idea, but once the moratorium idea was adopted by New Mobe, the New Mobe and Vietnam Moratorium Committee merged their plans for a November action.

On November 9, GIPS and SMC ran a full-page ad in the Sunday *New York Times* that was signed by 1,365 GIs and included the rank and station of each signer. The advertisement, which appealed to Americans to attend the November demonstrations, read:

> We are opposed to American involvement in the war in Vietnam. We resent the needless wasting of lives to save face for the politicians in Washington. We speak, believing our views are shared by many of our fellow servicemen. Join us!

What is remarkable about the ad is that it came after the October 15 moratorium, when GIs had had enough time to measure its impact and public reaction to it. Letters found in the archives of the Vietnam Moratorium Committee reinforce the conclusion that there were servicemen in Vietnam who supported the moratorium. One letter, written by Sgt. James C. Ruh on November 5 read:

> It has been argued by people, such as Vice President Agnew, that the peace demonstrations are demoralizing and dispiriting to those fighting in Vietnam and therefore should not take place. I returned from Vietnam on October 15 and found nothing to be further from the truth.
> In my own infantry company, which I believe to be fairly represen-

tative, the Moratorium had wide support. It was, in fact, very much a morale builder. The men are intelligent enough to realize that the peace demonstrations are on their behalf. They realize that the greater the pressure kept on President Nixon, the sooner they'll get home. Even more importantly, the fewer will be their friends who do not return.

It has also been advanced by these same people, that unless you've been to Vietnam, you don't know what is really going on there, and have no right to criticize it. While this is an obviously fallacious argument, being there does add a personal perspective to the situation, which makes many of your men fighting in Vietnam the biggest critics of the war. They can see what is going on, not what is screened through the media. While many wore black arm bands for the October 15th Moratorium, they are for the large part prevented from demonstrating their feelings on the war. They can give only moral support to the Peace Moratorium, and hope that it is successful.

Peace and Love,
Sgt. James C. Ruh[11]

Interviews conducted by Hal Wingo, a reporter for *Life* magazine, supported Sgt. Ruh's perception that dissent was widespread among soldiers in Vietnam. Wingo (1969) interviewed one hundred GIs from I Corps in the north to III Corps in the south. His findings, as reported in *Life* on October 24, were that "many soldiers regard the organized antiwar campaign in the U.S. with open and outspoken sympathy," and that, "the protests in the U.S. are not demoralizing troops in the field." Pfc. Chris Yapp, a Fourth Division civil affairs team member in a Montagnard village told Wingo, "I think the protesters may be the only ones who really give a damn about what's happening." Pvt. Jim Beck, a 101st Division medic, who had gone to Vietnam partly to avenge the death of his brother at Khe San a year earlier, said, "The demonstrators are right to speak up because this war is wrong and it must be stopped."

The troops in Vietnam did more than write letters. In *The New Winter Soldiers* (1996), Richard Moser writes about the widespread resistance to the war among field units and recounts the stories of the imaginative approaches that GI activism took. In November 1969, one hundred members of the 71st Evacuation Hospital at Pleiku held a protest Thanksgiving fast in solidarity with the moratorium movement back home. This "John Turkey Movement" soon spread to other units. On several occasions, GIs defied military authorities to stage public demonstrations in Vietnamese cities and in some cases even joined with Vietnamese activists.

Buoyed by the positive response from GIs to the October moratorium, organizers for the November march on Washington, D.C., redoubled their efforts to reach out to GIs. A special contingent for GIs was planned and a center for the distribution of all GI newspapers was set up. The VMC scheduled a news conference for Sunday, November 9, at which a group of GIs read statements about the anti-war activities scheduled to occur at military posts around the country on November 15. The VMC also sent out copies of the Department of Defense directive governing the participation of GIs in anti-war activities with information on how GI's could get legal aid if they were harassed by officers for legal anti-war activity.

The November moratorium concentrated on building the turnouts in Washington, D.C., and San Francisco and, with crowds of a half million and a quarter million, respectively, in those cities, the action, coming only one month after the equally massive October mobilizations, was a sign that opposition to the war had reached the proportions of a popular mass movement. In retrospect, however, the period between the October and November moratoriums may have been as important as an incubator for new, pro-war, right-wing strategies as it was for mobilizing for the March Against Death.

FOUR

The Nixon-Agnew Counteroffensive

"Good Veterans" vs. "Bad Veterans"

The trick here is to try to find a way to drive the black sheep from the white sheep within the group that participated in the Moratorium yesterday. —H. R. Haldeman, aide to Richard Nixon

The keystone of the right wing's strategy was to split the liberal and radical elements within the anti-war movement and to split Vietnam veterans from the movement. At one level, the effort to split the movement involved a propaganda campaign to discredit the anti-war movement by portraying it as an alien, un-American, and violent phenomenon. Waged from the White House with Vice President Agnew acting as the mouthpiece, the propaganda campaign was fortuitously assisted by the North Vietnamese.

Agnew vs. "An Effete Corps of Impudent Snobs"

On October 14, Hanoi Radio broadcast an open letter addressed to "Dear American Friends" that encouraged U.S. citizens to participate in the moratorium events scheduled for the next day. The White House distributed texts of the broadcast to Republicans and organized press conferences for Vice President Agnew at which he denounced Hanoi's support for the moratorium. Led by Rep. Gerald Ford of Michigan, Republican supporters of the Nixon-Agnew administration seized on the broadcast as an opportunity to discredit opponents of the war. On October 15, Ford and Sen. Hugh Scott of Pennsylvania introduced resolutions in Congress deploring the "insolent" attempt of Phan Van Dong, Premier of North Vietnam, "to associate those Americans who demonstrate for peace with the cause of our enemy." Astute Democrats in the House and Senate saw the Republican Party machinations as a clever attempt to do exactly what the Republicans were accusing Hanoi of doing, that is, they were trying to associate the moratorium activities in the public's mind with support for the enemy and impugning the loyalty of congressional leaders supportive of the moratorium. Outside Washington, attacks were being leveled against liberal political figures who were supporters of the moratorium. In New York City, where Mayor John V. Lindsay had declared October 15 "a day of mourning" and ordered all the flags in the city flown at half staff "as a patriotic tribute to the dead in Vietnam," his Republican rival in the city's upcoming mayoral election, state senator John J. Marchi, called the mayor's action "a New York version of Dunkirk [sic]" and accused Lindsay of having "planted a dagger in the back of American servicemen in Vietnam" (Bigart 1969).

On October 19, Vice President Agnew made his signature statement on the anti-war movement calling the moratorium leaders "an effete corps of impudent snobs who characterize themselves as intellectuals." According to an account in the *New York Times,* he criticized them for refusing to "disassociate themselves from the objective enunciated by the enemy in Hanoi" and warned that "hardcore dissidents and professional anarchists" within the peace movement were planning "wilder, more violent" anti-war demonstrations on November 15 (Hunter 1969). Then governor of California and experienced cue-taker Ronald Reagan charged in an October 22 speech that some leaders of the moratorium "lent comfort and aid" to the enemy and that "some American will die tonight because of the activity in our streets" (Sullivan 1969). On October 28, the *New York Times* reported ("Wolff Cautions Protesters," p. 20) that on the previous day Rep. Lester Wolff, Democrat of Long Island and a moratorium supporter, had said he would not support the November moratorium unless "the organizers rid themselves of what he called communists in their ranks."

Within days after the October moratorium, it was clear that debate over the war would never be the same. The conservatives had managed to reframe the debate from this-war-is-about-U.S.-objectives-in-Southeast-Asia (that is, assuring the freedom of the Vietnamese people, the repulsion of communism, etc.) to this-war-is-about-the-men-who-are-fighting-the-war. It was a twist on the McCarthyite theme of loyalty, with support for soldiers standing in for patriotism. The corollary of the support-the-troops rhetoric was that anyone who opposed the war was, in the eyes of Nixon-Agnew followers, also disloyal to the soldiers and, by extension, disloyal to the country. The words chosen by Agnew and other conservatives to castigate the leaders of the antiwar movement were undoubtedly carefully chosen. Agnew's use of "intellectuals" as a pejorative characterization of war opponents was an appeal to right-wing and populist fears that highly educated Jews, or "illuminati," were secretly conspiring to destroy the country. His invocation of the terms "effete" and "snobs" as accompanying descriptors was an appeal to working-class resentment of middle- and upper-class privilege. The intended effect of this rhetorical package was to induce suspicions in the public mind as to the motives of the anti-war leaders and cast a shadow of doubt over their loyalty.[1]

The rhetorical ploy of the administration was of the "if you are not the enemy of my enemy, then you are my enemy" variety. By reconstructing the reality that anti-war leaders had refused to *dis*associate themselves from the radio broadcast from Hanoi, the Nixon-Agnew demagoguery created an *association* between the anti-war movement and "the enemy." The coup de grâce of the rhetorical campaign was the linking of the anti-war movement with "communism." Tagging the movement as "communist" was an attempt to convince the American people that the anti-war movement was an alien, un-American force, that the anti-war movement was "them," not "us." In such a political climate, liberal political leaders, their ties to their constituencies already strained by Hubert Humphrey's loss in the 1968 presidential election, would find it very hard to maintain their principled support for the anti-war movement.

Within a week, rumors were flying about a split in the anti-war movement. Supposedly, the liberal wing, which was made up of business people and Democratic Party activists who had been behind the October moratorium, were getting cold feet about their alliance with the more radical New Mobe organization. There was now a question whether the November moratorium would come off at all, since New Mobe had primary responsibility for the November activities. Highlighting the differences between the two factions, the *New York Times* characterized one side (the Moratorium Committee) as a group of politically "moderate," clean-cut kids and the other side (the New Mobilization Committee) as a group of hard-core middle-aged men who included, the *Times* emphasized, David Dellinger, then on trial for conspiracy to disrupt the 1968 Democratic Party's national convention. The *Times* reported that some local anti-war leaders were disassociating themselves from the upcoming November moratorium because of the fear of violence, even though the national leaders of the Moratorium Committee and New Mobe were publicly pledging cooperation and their mutual commitment to a nonviolent event (Rosenbaum 1969). Although the November moratorium came off successfully, it was the last in what had been projected to be a monthly series of moratoriums.

The administration, in its effort to portray the anti-war movement as anti-soldier and therefore anti-American, faced a substantial obstacle in the Vietnam veterans who were a part of the movement. The credibility of the veterans was, of course, enormous. They had been to Vietnam, they had fought the war, and their denunciation of it could not be easily dismissed. Moreover, within the discourse chosen by the administration to rally support for the war and opposition to the anti-war movement, support for soldiers was said to be what the war was all about. How could one support the soldiers and yet reject their experience of the war? Could one embrace the Vietnam veterans without embracing their denunciation of the war?

What the administration needed was an embraceable Vietnam veteran, a "good" veteran, a veteran faithful to the ideals of American foreign policy and the image of male military prowess. But very few Vietnam veterans fit the bill. Research done by the Veterans' World Project at Southern Illinois University found it "difficult if not impossible to find a 'hawk' among Vietnam veterans." "Very few," the researchers reported, "finish their service in Vietnam believing that what the United States has done there has served to forward our nation's purposes" (Gillingham 1972, II-10). The administration's approach to this dilemma began with its countermobilization of veterans from previous wars for pro-war activities in connection with the Veterans Day observances on November 11.

"Good" Veterans vs. "Bad" Veterans

Having put the anti-war movement on the defensive with the loyalty issue, the administration bolstered its offensive by proclaiming November 9–16 "Honor America Week." Veterans Day, was the pivotal date in the administration's plan and pro-war veterans were the primary constituency to be mobilized. It was a bold and potentially explosive move, in that it would undoubtedly raise conservative passions and possibly put thousands of pro-war militants into the streets on the very days of the anti-war moratorium, which was scheduled for November 13–15.

Although it was a tactic intended to play out at the grass roots, there was nothing of the grass roots about the administration's effort. The *New York Times*, in an article titled "Guardsmen Asked to Fly U.S. Flags," published on November 4, noted that "the chief of the National Guard Bureau is asking the nation's 500,000 guardsmen to stage what amounts to a counter demonstration against war protest activities planned for next week." In his appeal, which was termed "unprecedented in the long history of the citizen-soldier organization" by National Guard officers, Maj. Gen. Winston Wilson asked guardsmen to fly the American flag at their homes and drive with their lights on. Conservative organizations, traditional veterans groups, such as the American Legion and Veterans of Foreign Wars, and reserve organizations picked up on the call for counterdemonstrations and within a week planning for countermoratorium events was underway ("War Veterans Plan" 1969.) Among the demonstrations reportedly being organized was one in Charleston, West Virginia where, according to one source, "an atomic explosion of patriotism" was planned. The Charleston demonstrators were expected to include "armed and uniformed policemen." Charleston police chief Dallas Bias was quoted as saying, "We won't creep around in the dark with candles like these traitors do. . . . We'll march at high noon on Monday and let free people fall right in and march behind us to show how they feel about it" ("Nixon Supporters" 1969).

The effect of the administration's action was to foreground, for the public's eyes as well as for the eyes of Vietnam veterans themselves, the image of the "good" veteran. With such conservative veterans organizations as the Veterans of Foreign Wars and the American Legion as players in the street politics of the Vietnam War, there would now be a veteran's voice speaking from the pro-war side. That it was not a voice in any way representative of the Vietnam generation of veterans was not a detail the public was likely to notice. It would be the voice of veterans carrying the imprimatur of established organizations with high visibility throughout the nation—and that would be enough for most people. Moreover, the few hawkishly inclined Vietnam veterans out there would have an ideological pole to gravitate to should they wish to do so. Finally, who better to attack the credibility of Vietnam veterans than other veterans? And what better place to make those attacks than in the VFW and American Legion halls scattered across small-town America? The ultimate effect of the administration's strategy was to displace the Vietnam veteran in the public's mind's eye with the mythological "good" Vietnam veteran modeled after the conservative veterans from previous wars. The existence of the good Vietnam veteran was "confirmed" by the equally mythological existence of the "bad" anti-war activist. The public could be sure that there really were pro-war Vietnam veterans out there because the anti-war people were spitting on someone—weren't they? The singular image of the spat-upon Vietnam veteran thus became the perfecting myth of the Nixon-Agnew administration's strategy to discredit the anti-war movement.

The Veterans Day countermobilizations provide a good measure of the difference between the offensive approach taken by the Nixon-Agnew administration to the anti-war movement and the defensive approach taken by the Johnson administration. Common sense would lead us to expect that Veterans Day observances were always occasions for mainstream American to protest the protesters during the Vietnam War years. But common sense sometimes misleads. In fact, while the Veterans Days of the two years previous to 1969 were preceded by raucous anti-war events that were as threatening to patriotic Americans as the moratoriums, they were not the occasion for conservative countermobilizations. In 1968, the street battle between the Chicago police and the thousands of protesters who had disrupted the Democratic Party's national convention—which all but closed down the city—was watched, live, on television across the country. In 1967, the march on the Pentagon challenged the prestige of military symbolism and the dignity of uniformed service. Yet, while those events, occurring in late summer and mid-fall, respectively, were close enough to Veterans Day to invite a reaction, there was none. Veterans Day in 1967 and 1968 passed without major recognition and with no utilization of the occasion by the political right. What changed in the year from the fall of 1968 to the fall of 1969 was neither the nature of the anti-movement itself (in the sense that it was neither more nor less threatening) nor the positioning of events on the calendar. What had changed was the presidential administration and its strategical approach to the anti-war movement.[2]

The government also began a kind of dirty tricks campaign against

GI organizing efforts leading up to the November moratorium. On October 30, Rep. Bob Wilson, Republican of California and a member of the House Armed Services Committee, issued a press release saying that the Defense Department had warned military personnel "against associating themselves with the so-called 'March Against Death.'" The press release, quoting Brig. Gen. Leo Benade, Deputy Assistant Secretary of Defense, cited legal technicalities, such as the prohibition against GIs participating in such demonstrations while in uniform, or in events that were likely to be violent or bring discredit upon the armed forces, as the reason for the "ban." In fact the congressman's press release, which was picked up by the Associated Press, was merely a scare tactic. But it was a scare tactic that, combined with the government's forecasting of violence in connection with the Washington event, served to cast real doubt over the legality of GI participation. To reinforce the perception that the government really did take the possibility of violence seriously, military troops in the Washington, D.C., area were put on alert for "possible capital duty should violence erupt at the war protest demonstration."[3]

The record of the government's attempt to disrupt the organizing activities of anti-war GIs is important because it makes all the more significant the acts of public resistance that GIs did undertake. Resisting war while a member of the military was a high-risk business. In the short run, a GI ran the risk of an encounter with the military justice system, which was at best problematic and at worst a farcical prospect to be avoided at all costs. In the long run, there was the threat of a dishonorable discharge from the military that would haunt a GI for the rest of his life, staining his reputation and affecting his employment opportunities. This prospect hung over every decision to act or even speak against the war. For every courageous GI who made his opposition to the war known, there were almost certainly several who kept quiet out of fear.

In retrospect, both the mobilization of paramilitary personnel for propagandistic purposes and the employment of dirty tricks against political opponents in the fall of 1969 were prototypes for the future.

Vietnam Veterans Against the War

Vietnam Veterans Against the War emerged from the moratorium days as a full-fledged organization. Its first activity came in February 1970, when it held hearings on American war crimes in Vietnam. In Annapolis, Maryland, and Springfield, Massachusetts, it assembled Vietnam veterans who testified to the war atrocities they had witnessed or taken part in.

In September 1970, VVAW began putting on public reenactments of Vietnam military operations in which members would demonstrate the techniques used by U.S. military troops against the Vietnamese. Inspired by traditions of the radical guerrilla theater groups that had played an important role in educating and mobilizing peasants for liberation struggles in Third World countries, and employing the techniques of improvisational theater, a typical VVAW "performance" would have members dressed in combat fatigues and carrying dummy weapons "raid" a public event, such as an outdoor college graduation. The raid, simulating a search-and-destroy mission on a Vietnamese village, might begin with the setting off of firecrackers (simulating gunfire) to disrupt the event. Then, VVAW members would rush into the audience from all directions and "force" some people down to their knees, "capture" others, and "kill" anyone who appeared to object or resist. While this action was going on, other VVAW members would be circulating through the audience handing out leaflets that explained that what was being reenacted was a common occurrence in Vietnam and that well-meaning citizens of the United States should oppose the continuance of the war.

The best known of VVAW's guerrilla theater productions was a march by Vietnam veterans from Morristown, New Jersey, to Valley Forge, Pennsylvania, in 1970. Beginning on September 4 and marching ninety miles, veterans staged guerrilla actions on small-town main streets and conducted an educational campaign through speaking and leafleting. The march was videotaped, thus giving us a record of the techniques used by VVAW as well as the public response to its efforts.

Most interestingly, the video tape recorded the menacing hostility of older, pro-war, veterans of previous wars toward the Vietnam veterans. Entering Valley Forge on the fourth day of the march, the Vietnam vets are "greeted" by a group of VFW members. We hear a voice from the background saying, "Why don't you go to Hanoi? They need boys like you." On camera, another VFW member says, "You see, I don't blame those fellows for not being proud, because we won our war, they didn't; and from the looks of them, they couldn't." We hear other off-camera comments about the appearance of the Vietnam veterans and, as a maimed veteran on two crutches moves slowly by, a voice wonders if the wounded "have been shot with marijuana or shot in battle." The tape ends with a mass ceremony at Valley Forge at which the Vietnam veterans break the plastic weapons they have carried in the march.

Five months later, VVAW convened the "Winter Soldier Investigation" in Detroit. The term "winter soldier" was taken from Thomas Paine, who had dubbed those who, in the winter of 1776, would shrink from the crisis facing the country "summer soldiers" and "sunshine patriots." More than a hundred veterans gathered from January 31 through February 2, 1971, to testify about the atrocities committed against Vietnamese civilians by U.S. troops. Emblematic of those atrocities was the hamlet of My Lai, where on March 16, 1968, a unit of the Americal Division killed a hundred or more men, women, and children. The killings were first reported by Ronald Lee Ridenhour, a GI who heard about the killings when he was in Vietnam. Ridenhour told authorities what he knew when he returned to the States. In September 1969, the press began to report some of what had happened at My Lai, but it wasn't until investigative journalist Seymour Hersh's series on the massacre appeared in newspapers that the public really took notice. On March 29, 1971, Lt. William Calley was convicted of the premeditated murder of civilians at My Lai.

In his opening statement to the hearing held in Detroit, Lt. William Crandell said:

We intend to demonstrate that My Lai was no unusual occurrence. . . . We intend to show that the policies of the Americal Division which inevitably resulted in My Lai were the policies of other Army and Marine divisions as well. We intend to show that the war crimes in Vietnam did not start in March 1968 [when My Lai occurred], or in the village of Son My or with one Lieutenant William Calley. We intend to indict those really responsible for My Lai, for Vietnam, for attempted genocide. (Vietnam Veterans Against the War 1972, 2)

Although the connection between the atrocities recounted and military policy was hard to make, the testimony offered by the GIs was shocking:

We were taking some grunts out on a beachhead. And there were some fishermen out on the ocean and a couple of our sergeants thought it would be a good sport to use them as target practice. So they swung their 50-calibers around and they just shot the shit out of them, for no reason, I guess.

SP/4 Gary Keyes, Americal Division (VVAW 1972)[4]

From where I was standing I saw maybe two or three male villagers and the rest were women and children—some of the children walking and some of them young enough to be carried, I would say under a year, maybe. The last thing I heard as a command was the gunnery sergeant told them to open fire to keep them back. Their village was on fire and they were in panic; they didn't stop, so they just cut down the women and children with mortars, machine guns, tanks . . .

Pvt. Jack Fronaugh, First Marine Division

Also, we threw full C-ration cans at kids on the side of the road. Kids would be lined up on the side of the road. They'd be yelling out, "Chop, Chop; Chop, Chop," and they wanted food. They knew we carried C-rations. Well, just for a joke, these guys would take a full can if they were riding shotgun and throw it as hard as they could at a kid's head. I saw several kids' heads split wide open, knocked off the road, knocked into tires of vehicles behind, and knocked under tank traps.

SP/4 Sam Schorr, Eighty-sixth Combat Engineers

I saw one case where a woman was shot by a sniper, one of our snipers. When we got up to her she was asking for water. And the lieutenant said to kill her. So he ripped off her clothes, they stabbed her in both breasts, they spread her eagle and shoved an E-tool up her vagina, an entrenching tool, and she was still asking for water. And then they took that out and they used a tree limb and then she was shot.

Sgt. Scott Camil, First Marine Division

The destruction of crops and killing of domestic animals was common whenever the 11th Armored Cavalry Regiment operated in populated areas. Crops were destroyed in the building of defensive positions and animals were run over when the tracks—armored cars, tanks—ran through the villages. Civilian deaths were quite frequent, Vietnamese civilians were killed accidentally when tracks and tanks running through their villages often at excessive speeds, struck them, ran off the road, ran into their houses, hit their bicycles, etc. . . . On one occasion, a North Vietnamese Army nurse was killed by 11th Armored Cavalry troups, subsequently a grease gun of the type used in automotive work was placed in her vagina and she was packed full of grease. On several occasions, enemy graves were violated, their skulls taken out of the graves and used as candle holders and conversation pieces.

Capt. John Mallory, First Air Cavalry

I was a prisoner of war interrogator. I was in Vietnam from '66 to '67. Being an interrogator the way I was, you definitely don't win hearts and minds. I've heard about these "Bell Telephone Hours," where they would crank people up with field phones. I guess we did them one better because we used a 12-volt jeep

> battery and you step on the gas and you crank up a lot of voltage. It was one of the normal things. . . . The basic place you put it was the genitals. . . . The major that I worked for had a fantastic capability of staking prisoners, utilizing a knife that was extremely sharp, and sort of filleting them like a fish. You know, trying to check out how much bacon he could make of a Vietnamese body to get information.
>
> Lt. Jon Drolshagan, Twenty-fifth Infantry

The picture that the Winter Soldier Investigation painted of "our boys" was not pretty. These were not embraceable "good veterans." And because they weren't, the picture painted by Winter Soldier closed the gap between "us," the good guys, and "them," the evil-incarnate Asian others. Since the early days of the war the Vietnamese had been portrayed as terrorists who sneaked through the night to plant hand-carried explosive packages known as "satchel charges" and then mount massed, suicidal human-wave attacks against U.S. installations. The common explanation for this alleged subhuman behavior was that life was cheap for Asians, and the advertised objective of the U.S. presence in Southeast Asia was to keep this alien culture far from our shores. But was evil really so alien? Was terrorism really the mark of the other?

As if to punctuate the poignancy of the questions, Winter Soldier also gave Americans a troubling glimpse of the enemy other—troubling because that glimpse did not confirm the bad-guy image of the Vietnamese anymore than the veterans' testimony confirmed the good-guy image of U.S. soldiers. How were the Vietnamese treating American POWs? S/Sgt George Smith, Fifth Special Forces, testified to having been captured by National Liberation Front (NLF) forces and held as a prisoner for two years. Held under extremely inhospitable jungle conditions, Smith was nevertheless treated well, even receiving mail and Red Cross packages. Smith's testimony, corroborated by the testimony of Marjorie Nelson, a civilian doctor who had been captured and held by the NLF during the Tet Offensive of 1968, contrasted sharply with the U.S. government's version of how POWs were being treated. Such testimony, in combination with the numerous accounts like Lt. Drolshagan's report of abuse of Vietnamese prisoners by American troops, asked the unspeakable: did the American people have their good guys and bad guys mixed up?

The VVAW's Winter Soldier inquiry was basically ignored by the press. So estranged was America from the war it had sponsored that, as David Thorne and George Butler noted in their preface to *The New Soldier: Vietnam Veterans Against the War* (Kerry 1971, 10), "Numerous people, including those connected with the news media, did not believe that many of these men were Vietnam veterans."[5] The grisliness of their testimony, combined with their willingness to indict their own government for war crimes, produced the ultimate "otherization": these were not veterans, at least not *our* veterans. *Our* veterans were "good" veterans.[6]

In April, VVAW tried again to break into the American consciousness by organizing what it called a "limited incursion into the District of Columbia." Named Operation Dewey Canyon III, after Dewey Canyon II, the code name for the U.S./South Vietnamese invasion of Laos that had just ended, the action combined elements of guerrilla theater with lobbying tactics and a dramatic ceremony on the steps of the Capitol at which seven hundred veterans returned their Vietnam service medals ("Veterans Discard Medals" 1971). For five days, from April 18 to April 23, about one thousand veterans from across the country camped on the Mall and told their stories to congressional leaders. When the Senate Foreign Relations Committee began hearings on April 20 to set a date for ending the war, Vietnam veterans crowded into the hearing room to cheer the doves and hiss the hawks (Finney 1971). By the end of its week in Washington, VVAW had gotten the attention of the press, although the *New York Times*, feeding the myth that the anti-war veterans were not real thing, quoted VFW leader Herbert Rainwater saying that the demonstrators were not typical Vietnam veterans. The *Times* noted that "there was no way to take an accurate count of the authentic veterans" at the medal turn-in ceremony ("Veterans Discard Medals" 1971).

These kinds of journalistic ploys had the effect of discrediting the eyewitness testimony of Vietnam veterans. The importance of that effect is hard to overstate because by the spring of 1971 Vietnam veterans were not only condemning the U.S. military role in Southeast Asia, they were also identifying with the Nixon administration's nemesis, the anti-war movement. If the credibility of Vietnam veterans could be even partially neutralized through the press corps' devaluation of what they said, the life of the administration's Vietnam policies could be extended. More seriously, the public questioning of the authenticity of the anti-war veteran also challenged the very reality of the Vietnam veteran's identity. The identity of many Vietnam veterans *qua* veterans was as veterans opposed to the war.[7] Denied their anti-war persona, these veterans ceased to be veterans in the way they understood themselves. Finally, the effect of the press's dismissal of the flesh and blood Vietnam veterans before it, was to posit the existence of a "typical" pro-war veteran. Unseen and unheard, this typical Vietnam veteran was a blank space to be filled in by popular imagination. Just as with the "bad" spitting anti-war activist, the "good" pro-war Vietnam veteran had a mythical quality about him.

Operation Dewey Canyon III established VVAW as a major voice within the anti-war movement. The spokesman for Dewey Canyon had been John Kerry from Massachusetts who, before resigning from the national leadership of VVAW to begin his political career, made a powerful and moving speech before Congress. He reminded congressmen of a 1970 speech in which Spiro Agnew had characterized protesters as "criminal misfits" while glorifying soldiers in Vietnam as "our best men." Kerry called Agnew's statement a "terrible distortion." Those whom Agnew called misfits, said Kerry, "were standing up for us in a way that nobody else in this country dared to." "This administration," Kerry continued, "has done us the ultimate dishonor. They have attempted to disown us and . . . deny that we are veterans or that we served in Nam. Our own scars and stumps of limbs are witness enough for others and for ourselves" (Kerry 1971, 12–24). Following Dewey Canyon III, VVAW worked for improved services and benefits for veterans, sponsored rehabilitation farms, halfway houses, and psychotherapy programs, tried to improve conditions in Veterans Administration hospitals, and supported legislation of benefit to veterans.

With the credibility of VVAW rising and the political conventions of 1972 approaching, the government stepped up its efforts to counter the effectiveness of the anti-war veteran's voice. In fall 1971, a provocateur and government informer named William Lemmer infiltrated VVAW. Lemmer was a shadowy figure with a background that included service in Vietnam. He had been in Washington during Dewey Canyon III and appeared before a congressional hearing with an antiwar petition. In fall 1971, he enrolled at the University of Arkansas and was soon a VVAW coordinator for the Arkansas-Oklahoma region. According to circumstantial evidence later cited by the *New York Times,* Lemmer began receiving money from the government in October to inform on VVAW activities and, apparently, to encourage VVAW members to commit acts that would discredit the organization. On one occasion, according to a VVAW leader interviewed by the *Times*, Lemmer proposed a plan to shoot up the Republican convention: "His plan was that we get automatic weapons, disassemble them and strap them to our bodies, then get into the convention and rip [shoot] people off" (Kifner 1972a).

Later, Dennis Holder, writing in the *Miami Herald,* would describe the VVAW as "an organization thoroughly infiltrated by police and federal informers before and during the convention." In addition to Lemmer, Pablo Fernandez, a Cuban exile who had worked for Watergate burglar Bernard Barker, was recruited by the Miami police department to infiltrate the VVAW and provoke the organization to violence. Fernandez told VVAW leaders where they could get machine guns if they wanted them to disrupt the upcoming Republican convention in Miami Beach. The head of the Miami police department's special investigations section, Adam Klimkowski, later told the press that "we were hoping for an overt act necessary to produce a charge of conspiracy," but the VVAW did not take the bait. Another freelance spy, Vincent Hannard, said he too had been recruited by Watergate burglars Bernard Barker and Frank Sturgis to help disrupt and discredit the activities of VVAW. "It was clear from what they said that I was supposed to incite trouble or riots," said Hannard (Holder 1973).

On July 13, 1972, a federal grand jury charged six VVAW members with conspiracy to "organize numerous fire teams to attack with automatic weapons fire and incendiary devices police stations, police cars and stores in Miami Beach." The indictment included charges that the veterans had plotted to fire lead weights, fried marbles, ball bearings, cherry bombs, and smoke bombs with slingshots at the conventiongoers. The conspiracy was alleged to have been hatched during meetings in Gainesville, Florida, from May 26 to May 28 (Crowder 1972; Kifner 1972a).

Reports to the nation from the August 21 opening day of the Republican convention evoked images of the raucous Chicago Democratic convention of four years earlier. Under a headline reading "Veterans Face Guardsmen in Protest at Miami Beach" (Kifner 1972b), the *New York Times* told of:

- National Guard troops billeted at the Miami Beach High School awaiting security duty.
- A line of Florida Highway Patrol cars with four troopers in each car stretched for four city blocks.
- Helmeted police lounging in loose formations.
- A rally billed as a memorial for George Jackson, the prisoner and revolutionary writer killed at San Quentin Prison.
- Radicals hearing Jane Fonda describe bombings in Vietnam.
- The number of demonstrators at Flamingo Park: thirty-five hundred by mid-afternoon of the first day, which was larger than the number in Chicago during the early days of the 1968 Democratic convention.

• A contingent of eight hundred Vietnam veterans among the demonstrators.

On the second day, three thousand demonstrators circled the convention hall and met conventiongoers with cries of "murderers" and "delegates kill." A splinter group of demonstrators trashed the downtown Miami Beach area in the afternoon resulting in the arrest of 212 people. Thirteen hundred Vietnam veterans led by three disabled veterans in wheelchairs conducted a silent march to the Republican Party's headquarters at the Fontainebleau Hotel, where Ron Kovic, a leader of the march whose story would later be the basis for the movie *Born on the 4th of July,* addressed himself to the delegates assembled inside: "You have lied to us too long, you have burned too many babies. You may have taken our bodies, but you haven't taken our minds" (Kifner 1972c). VVAW leader Barry Romo, referring to Nixon's policy to turn the war over to the South Vietnamese (or, Vietnamization), said veterans wanted "an end of the Vietnam war, not a changing of the color of the skins of those who are dying." The three days of demonstrations climaxed on the night of August 23 with 1,129 arrests, keeping twenty-five judges in eleven courtrooms busy throughout the night (Kifner 1972c).[8]

Like Fire and Water

In physics, there is something called the Pauli exclusion principle, which says that two objects cannot occupy the same space at the same time. Social events are not mutually exclusive in the same sense, of course. Yet, the nature of some social conditions all but exclude the likelihood of coexistence with their opposite: war and peace, for example. In this same sense it is unlikely that the anti-war movement that embraced Vietnam veterans, as described in this chapter, could have coexisted with its opposite: the anti-war movement described in the stories of spat-upon Vietnam veterans. The proof that anti-war activists and Vietnam veterans were mutually supportive, then, constitutes proof that they were not hostile to one another.

The anti-war movement had veterans involved in it from the very beginning. Veterans for Peace, composed of veterans from World War II, was formed in the context of anti–Vietnam War protests that took place during the fall of 1965, and it was in the forefront of efforts to reach out to in-service soldiers and Vietnam veterans. The initial outreach took the form of providing legal services to Vietnam-era military personnel. While this served an important humanitarian function, it also served the needs of the anti-war movement by building a working relationship with servicemen. The sponsorship of the GI Press Service by the Student Mobilization Committee was an integral link in the chain connecting thousands of GIs in a community of resistance to military authority and the war. Scores of anti-war activists were involved in the operation of coffeehouses adjacent to military bases. The coffeehouses provided GIs with refuge and space to organize. Veterans had enormous credibility, and the anti-war movement avidly sought their involvement. The earliest anti-war veterans, like Donald Duncan, appear to have been virtual folk heros within the movement. As time went on and the number of anti-war veterans increased, they formed their own organization, Vietnam Veterans Against the War.

Not all Vietnam veterans were opposed to the war, of course. Some soldiers came home undecided about the war. Some were "hawks," as Polner (1971) found when he interviewed veterans. What the researcher is struck by, however, is the scant evidence of organized pro-war veteran sentiment. I once saw a reference in a letter to a North Carolina group called "B-52s for Peace" and, in 1972, something called "Vietnam Veterans for Nixon" made a brief appearance. Almost no one remembers the latter and those who do, recall it as a political front with no members set up by Nixon's Committee to Re-elect the President. Except for one letter in the *New York Times* I found no record of its existence (O'Neill 1972).

Undoubtedly, there were instances of incivility between veterans and anti-war activists. With hundreds of thousands war veterans and millions of war opponents, one can hardly imagine it otherwise. Given the temper of the times, there were surely intemperate remarks exchanged by soldiers and radicals. Without a script for the occasion, these two parties, whose roles in the war were so different, did not always know what to say to each other. The chances for misunderstandings and hurt feelings from careless comments were great.

Yet, in a Harris Poll of veterans conducted in 1971, only 1 percent of the respondents described their reception from family and friends as "not at all friendly." Only 3 percent described their reception from their own age group as unfriendly (U.S. Senate 1972, 42). The archival record also shows that GIs and veterans did not perceive the anti-war movement as hostile to them. Collections of personal letters and the signed letters to editors of anti-war and other publications, the signed anti-war ads in major newspapers, and, most important, the record of participation by thousands of GIs and veterans in marches and rallies against the war offer ample evidence that the anti-war movement was generally not perceived to be hostile to the interests and needs of servicemen. The fact that relations between the anti-war movement and Vietnam veterans remained close up to the time when the last U.S. troops returned from Vietnam in 1973 suggests that few soldiers and veterans bought the Nixon line that anti-war activity was a threat to the safety of the troops in Vietnam.[9]

Tragically, the effect of the administration's strategy to discredit the experience of anti-war Vietnam veterans may have been more successful. By first ignoring and then questioning the authenticity of veterans' testimony about atrocities and massacres, the administration, with the complicity of the press, added to whatever communications gap there already was between Vietnam veterans and many Americans. The war that veterans wanted to talk about was not the war that most people wanted to hear about. Indeed, with the press sometimes questioning whether anti-war veterans really were veterans, and Vice President Agnew twisting reality in ways that made accounts of military misdeeds sound like anti-war slanders of "good" soldiers, the administration added to the estrangement of America from its veterans and veterans from their own experience.

The effort to discredit the witness of anti-war veterans dovetailed with the fallout from another dimension of veteran involvement in the anti-war movement during the early 1970s. The image of violent veterans who had brought the war home with them was given a mighty boost by the government's case against the Gainesville Six. As was often the case with conspiracy cases brought against radicals in the late 1960s and early 1970s, most of the damage was collateral. The "Six" were acquitted of the actual charges against them but the image of Vietnam veterans armed with automatic weapons storming the Fountainebleau Hotel in Miami Beach was indelible. And the image was not entirely fanciful. Vietnam veterans, dressed in jungle fatigues and carrying plastic facsimiles of real weapons had conducted mock raids in public places to bring the war home to the American people. It did not require a great stretch of imagination to accept the government's claim that VVAW had planned to do the *real* thing at the Republican national convention.

For those lacking in imagination, journalists and psychologists lent a helping hand. A mere three months after it had ignored the testimony of veterans in the VVAW's Winter Soldier Investigation, the media focused on the story of Dwight Johnson, a veteran decorated for combat heroism in Vietnam. Johnson had been killed while attempting to rob a Detroit liquor store at gunpoint. After Johnson's story made the front page of the *New York Times* on May 26, 1971, psychologists began writing about something called "post-Vietnam syndrome." A year later, with tension surrounding the upcoming Republican national convention on the rise and the government's case against the Gainesville Six about to surface, the *New York Times* ran a major op-ed piece on the concept of PVS. Written by psychiatrist Chaim Shatan, the article began the construction of a mental health discourse that would displace the political discourse that had, up to that point, framed interpretations of Vietnam veterans' experiences. The label of "crazy," coupled with the images of Vietnam veterans as violent and gun-toting, opened a chasm between them and the general public that would only get wider for the next quarter century.

The crazy veteran coin had its flip side: if Vietnam veterans were crazy, something or someone had driven them crazy. With the story of the war already being recast as a "coming home" story, the "trauma" suffered by veterans came to be understood in terms having as much to do with their relationship to America as with the war itself. The image of anti-war activists spitting on Vietnam veterans helped perfect the idea that it was the war at home that was the real source of veterans' problems.

FIVE

Spat-Upon Veterans

The Evidence (or Lack Thereof)

"A lot of us were spit on when we came back to this country," said Capers.

"Bullshit," I said. "A lie. An urban myth. I've heard it a thousand times and I don't believe a word of it. And it always happens in the airport."

"That's where it happened to me," said Capers.

"If it happened as much as Vietnam vets claim it happened, no one during those years could have stood up in the airports of America with all that spittle on the floor. You're lying, Capers, and if it happened you should have rammed the teeth down the asshole's throat that did it. That's what I can't believe. A million vets get spit on and no one loses a tooth. No wonder you lost the fucking war."

—Pat Conroy, *Beach Music*

Upon announcing that one is writing a book on the myth of the spat-upon Vietnam veteran, the researcher is met with either approval—"Good, it's about time that someone did it"—or disbelief—"Myth? It's not a myth. It happened." At a conversational level, the safe approach to take with disbelievers is to acknowledge that it is possible, even likely, that some Vietnam veteran, someplace, at some time, endured this humiliation. But that is not the issue any more than whether or not the central myth of feminist bra burning relates to the throwing of a bra into a trash can as part of political theater at the 1968 Miss America Pageant. The issue is that in the memory a large number of people the anti-war movement came to be connected with the image of activists spitting on veterans. Moreover, what is conversationally safe is not the same as good social science. The fact remains that there is scant evidence that any person opposed to the Vietnam War engaged in this behavior.

Disproving a Myth

Innocence, however, is difficult to prove. How can one prove that something did not happen? Challenged to prove innocence, the best that one can do is show that, under the circumstances at a particular time, it is unlikely that certain alleged acts could have occurred. Regarding the allegation that Vietnam veterans were spat upon by anti-war activists, one can present the kind of evidence as in chapter 2, namely, that the anti-war movement was supportive of Vietnam veterans and that, in turn, many veterans joined the opposition to the war. On the basis of that evidence, then, one can argue that it is highly unlikely that that same movement could have simultaneously been acting in a hostile fashion toward Vietnam veterans.

But why should one have to prove innocence? Why shouldn't the burden of proof lie with the accusers? Why shouldn't they have to produce evidence to support their claims?

Proof that the alleged spitting acts actually occurred might take the form of photographs or film in which we are able to clearly identify who is spitting on whom. This would be the most credible type of evidence. GIs returned from Vietnam heavily armed with Pentax cameras bought at base PXs, so it is likely that such photos would exist—if spitting had occurred with the frequency now believed. It is all the more likely that a photo would have been snapped if some GIs had actually been told by the military that they would be greeted by hostile "hippies" upon their return. Surely, some enterprising GI, his photographic talents honed by a year of picture taking in Vietnam (GI photos were processed free, thus inducing many GIs to shoot thousands of slides and prints in Vietnam) would have been quite keen to snap a shot of war on the home front. Indeed, we would expect that J. Edgar Hoover's FBI agents, if not military intelligence itself, would have collected photodocumentary evidence of the alleged perpetrators, which would have been made available to police authorities and the press. This is to say nothing of the kind of direct evidence we would have expected to find in police or court records had anti-war people been accused of such an act at the time, when they undoubtedly would have been arrested. Certainly today if any political or religious group made it a practice of approaching people in public places and spitting on them the perpetrators would be arrested.

The records in which we might expect to find such reports are available to researchers. For example, the Special Committee on Demonstration Observation was established by the Bar Association of the City of New York in the 1970s. The committee, with the cooperation of the police and anti-war groups, sent members of the bar to demonstrations and marches specifically to observe and report on the behavior of the police and demonstrators. Their reports, filed with police at the time, are available from the library of the Bar Association. These reports contain not a hint of hostility between anti-war activists and military personnel or veterans. Indeed some of the reports note the participation of Vietnam veterans in the demonstrations, supplying still more evidence of solidarity between veterans and the anti-war movement.[1]

Slightly less direct but still compelling evidence might be found in news reports from the late 1960s and early 1970s. But a detailed study of news stories in the *New York Times, Los Angeles Times, San Francisco Chronicle,* and selected other sources conducted by sociologists at the University of California at Santa Barbara found no such reports. In all, the researchers examined 495 instances in which there were references to troops or veterans and anti-war protesters. They counted as an anti-troop stance "any portrayal that implied, even indirectly, a troop-blaming orientation" (Beamish, Molotch, and Flacks 1995).[2]

The researchers used an extremely liberal interpretation of what counted as a report of anti-troop behavior. Many of the reports they counted were actually reports of confrontations between activists and uniformed authorities, such as National Guard reservists or military police, who were policing the demonstrations or peace marches. Even by counting such reports as "anti-troop," the researchers reported finding only thirty-two instances, or 6 percent of all the stories over the six-year period, that could be construed as antagonistic behavior by the anti-war movement against GIs or veterans. Although national political leaders frequently labeled the anti-war movement as hostile to soldiers and veterans, Beamish, Molotch, and Flacks concluded that "stories in which the anti-war movement directly or purposely targeted troops are virtually non-existent" (354). They found no reports of anti-war activists spitting on soldiers or veterans.

The fact that there are no news reports of spitting on veterans raises doubts about whether such incidents ever occurred, much less in a number that would justify the now-popular public perception that the spat-upon Vietnam veterans is representative of the treatment veterans received upon their return home. If spitting on veterans had occurred all that frequently, surely some veteran or soldier would have called it to the attention of the press at the time. It is possible, of course, that an individual reporter sympathetic toward the anti-war movement may have received such a report and simply ignored it. But the press corps as a whole was never known to be supportive of the anti-war movement (Gitlin 1980), which makes it hard to believe that there would be no news-source record of these incidents had they occurred. Indeed, we would imagine that news reporters would have been camping in the lobby of the San Francisco airport, cameras in hand, just waiting for a chance to record the real thing—if, that is, they had had any reason to believe that such incidents might occur.

But they had no reason to believe that any such events might happen. Not only is there no evidence that these acts of hostility veterans ever occurred, there is no evidence that anyone at the time *thought* they were occurring. A search of poll results published by the *New York Times*, the Gallup Organization, and the *American Public Opinion Quarterly* between 1968 and 1974 revealed that relations between the two groups was a not a question on America's mind. Further searches of an on-line collection of polls by the Roper Center for Public Opinion and of some key secondary sources, such as John Mueller's *War, Presidents, and Public Opinion* (1973) revealed that when the last U.S. troops were withdrawn from Vietnam in 1973 the question of the anti-war movement's behavior toward veterans was simply not being asked. Nor was there any evidence at the time that Vietnam veterans perceived the anti-war movement as hostile to them or their interests. To the contrary, a U.S. Senate study, based on data collected in August 1971 by Harris Associates, found that 75 percent of Vietnam-era veterans polled disagreed with the statement, "Those people at home who opposed the Vietnam war often blame veterans for our involvement there." Ninety-nine percent of the veterans polled described their reception by close friends and family as friendly, while 94 percent said their reception by people their own age who had not served in the armed forces was friendly. Only 3 percent of returning veterans described their reception as "not at all friendly" (U.S. Senate 1972, 13, 19).[3]

Retrospectively, a 1979 Harris poll (Veterans Administration 1980, 90) designed to measure the "warmth" of feeling between groups, found that anti-war activists had warmer feelings toward Vietnam veterans than congressional leaders or even those who had demonstrated against the war. The poll is outside the time frame when the alleged acts against soldiers would have been committed, and one can only speculate about how the intervening years may have changed the attitude of activists toward veterans. One could imagine that with the cooling of political passions about the war, its opponents, who may have had bad feelings about GIs during the war years, forgave and forgot once the war was over. On the other hand, by 1979 the portrayal of veterans in films like the popular *Taxi Driver* (1976), in which Robert De Niro plays a deranged and dangerous Vietnam veteran, Travis Bickle, who stalks a twelve-year-old prostitute, undoubtedly raised the same specter in the minds of activists that it raised in others: how many Travis Bickles were out there on the streets? In any case, as Appy (1993, 304) conservatively concluded about the poll's findings, "a total reversal in feeling seems unlikely."

That a question that was not on the minds of Americans in 1973 was sufficiently important for Harris to poll people on it in 1979 suggests that what happened between the end of the war and the end of the decade was more important than the homecoming events themselves in shaping popular perceptions about relations between veterans and the anti-war movement. Who put this question into the minds of people? And how, given that as late as 1979 hard empirical evidence from such sources as the Harris poll refuted the notion that anti-war activists were hostile to Vietnam veterans, did many Americans and some veterans come to believe that it was true?

The absence of evidence that Vietnam veterans were badly treated by the anti-war movement, much less spat upon, makes it all the more interesting that by the time of the Gulf War in 1990, many Americans and some Vietnam veterans believed it to be true. It is important to understand how the nation's collective memory was reconfigured over the course of two decades lest we again find those memories exploited for political purposes as they were during the Gulf War.

Grist for the Myth

Myths are made of something, and in the homecoming experiences of Vietnam veterans we can find plenty of grist for mythmaking. To begin with, soldiers returning from Vietnam were not the most welcomed war veterans in history. The standard tour of duty in Vietnam was twelve months, which meant that most of the three million troops who served there came home before the war was over and the outcome was known. Soldiers arrived home throughout the late 1960s and early

1970s while simultaneously thousands of other GIs were boarding planes bound for Vietnam. Sometime during 1969, the flow of troops home began to outweigh the number of replacements going out, but throughout the war period the emotions of the country remained divided between the sadness and anxiety surrounding departures and the pride and elation that accompanied safe homecomings. Further complicating this emotional response was the outpouring of grief for the loss of the fifty-eight thousand who died and the three hundred thousand who were wounded. In short, the vast majority of Vietnam-era veterans reentered a society of divided attention and fractured emotions, a society insufficiently prepared to give veterans their due. Thus was born the perception that Vietnam veterans were neglected.

Soldiers returning from Vietnam also returned to a country that was seriously divided by the politics of the war. The late 1960s and early 1970s were rife with marches, rallies, demonstrations, street politics, inflammatory rhetoric, and violent behavior by both pro- and anti-war forces. Rocks were thrown, windows smashed, cars overturned, offices occupied, heads cracked, buildings bombed, people arrested, campuses occupied, and students shot and killed by National Guardsmen. These were days of rage. Twenty years later, people understandably remembered that it was a climate of division and anger that greeted returning Vietnam veterans. The memory was accurate. But the details of who was doing what to whom, how and why, fade with time. Depending on who is doing the remembering, and with what desired level of precision, the accuracy of detail might be less important than the overall portrayal of the hostility of the times; who was spitting on whom might be less important than the fact that someone *was* spitting on someone.

The most publicized reference to spitting appeared in the October 24, 1969, special issue of *Life* magazine on the October 15 moratorium day. The feature story told of David Moss, owner of a Dallas, Texas, real estate firm. At an October 12 rally against the war, Moss, surrounded by his family and friends, had read the names of Texas men killed in Vietnam. As reported by *Life,* hecklers yelled: "Spit at those people, spit on 'em." "Hippies." "Dirty Commies." In large bold type under a half-page photograph, Moss is quoted as saying, "I intend to state my case, and even when they spit at me, I mean to stand there." Even the casual reader thumbing through this issue of *Life* would have registered the reference to spitting (the story does not say that anyone actually spat), but would the millions of readers who saw the story remember that it was supporters of the war who would have been the perpetrators?[4]

There were actual acts of hostility toward GIs and veterans and, depending on how we interpret these acts, they help clarify the historical record or they become grist for the myth. The fact that most of the documentable hostility emanated from pro-war groups and individuals is a detail that is often lost. Members of such groups as the Veterans of Foreign Wars and the American Legion shunned Vietnam veterans because of the long hair, love beads, and peace symbols that many wore. When VVAW conducted its march and guerrilla theater from Morristown, New Jersey, to Valley Forge, Pennsylvania, in 1971, marchers were harassed by members of the VFW. When Vietnam veterans asked to march as a group in a Greeley, Colorado Veterans Day parade in 1972, they were denied permission to do so by the local VFW chapter. In the Veterans Administration hospitals, wounded Vietnam veterans were treated as second-class citizens by the World War II veterans who worked in and ran the hospitals. The "class of '46", as the Vietnam-era vets dubbed the old-timers, thought Vietnam had not been a "real war."[5]

Public confrontations between anti-war Vietnam veterans and members of the public were not uncommon in the early 1970s. Sometimes these were staged confrontations, parts of guerrilla theater exercises designed to educate civilians about the war in Vietnam. Others were real. In the fall of 1971, for example, I was part of a group of VVAW members leafleting against the war outside the football stadium at the University of Colorado. A Nebraska football fan stepped off the bus from Lincoln and charged at me, throwing a drink in my face and shouting an anti-communist epithet. An observer unaware of my anti-war activities might have seen this incident as, simply, a Vietnam veteran being attacked. Recalled twenty years later, it is easy to imagine how the incident could be turned into grist for the myth.

By changing or omitting key details, the meaning of a story can be changed. Many Americans might remember that U.S. soldiers were physically and violently attacked by other Americans during the war. They remember correctly. They also remember correctly that some who were opposed to the war did the attacking and that those attacks were acts of betrayal that undermined the mission of U.S. forces in Vietnam. Left at that, as it seems to have been in the popular imagination, the story is wholly consistent with the idea that anti-war activists treated veterans badly after the war. But what if we change a couple of details in the story? What if only officers were attacked and it was their own soldiers, opposed to the war, who did the attacking? What if we recognize this as the story of how anti-war soldiers rebelled by "fragging" their officers? Now the meaning of the hostility against soldiers changes and becomes additional evidence of the solidarity between the anti-war movement and GIs, rather than grist for the myth.

Pressed to remember where they first heard that Vietnam veterans had been spat upon, many people will say they do not recall. Many others will say they read it in something that Bob Greene, a syndicated columnist for the *Chicago Tribune*, wrote. In one of his columns in the mid-1980s he posed the following question to Vietnam veterans: Did anyone spit on you when you returned from Vietnam? He heard from over a thousand veterans, some saying they had been spat upon, others saying they had not been. Some said the idea of spat-upon veterans was a myth or folklore. One called it a "figment of someone's imagination," while another called it "unadulterated balderdash!" Greene published some of the responses in a four-part series of columns and printed many more in his 1989 book *Homecoming*. The book contains sixty-three accounts of personal experience with spitting and sixty-nine accounts of spit-free homecomings.

Greene had been skeptical of the spat-upon veteran tales because the stories were too uniform: a dirty, long-haired hippy spits on a clean-cut GI at the San Francisco airport. Weren't hippies too passive to be spitting on anyone, much less on people they allegedly considered to be trained killers? Greene was also unsure enough of the authenticity of some of the letters that he attempted to verify whether the writers were really Vietnam veterans. He doesn't say how many he threw out as bogus, but he added the caveat that there might be "a ringer or two" in the collection he published.

Greene's skepticism was warranted, but in the end he was too willing to suspend disbelief. In fact, there was much more wrong with his testimonies than he acknowledged to his readers. In the first place, there is Greene's own leading question: "Were you spat upon?" Had he asked a more neutral question such as, "What were your homecoming experiences?" the veterans' responses would be much more valid. Second, there is the curious fact that many of Greene's spat-upon veterans claimed the spitter was a girl or a woman. Told this, students of gender behavior are likely to respond, "It has to be a myth. Girls don't spit." This being the case, Greene's stories prompt a different and more interesting question: why were the coming-home memories of war veterans gendered in this way? Whatever the expected male/female balance of spitting frequency is, the stories collected by Greene contain clues to how the political, psychological, and cultural dimensions of memory are linked.[6] Finally, there is the troublesome fact that these claims surfaced fifteen years after they supposedly happened. And those were not just any fifteen years. From the late 1970s on, there was an unrelenting drumbeat of political and cultural interest in the "forgotten" Vietnam veteran. The award-winning 1978 film, *Coming Home,* broke a period of silence about Vietnam by recasting the war as a story about the homecoming of U.S. soldiers. Four years later, the dedication of the Vietnam War Memorial in Washington, D.C., focused the country's emotional energies on its neglect of Vietnam veterans. The enormously popular "Rambo" films presented the nation with specific images of returned soldiers besieged by their peers. While it would concede too much to the power of political and popular culture to believe that a false memory of abuse was simply induced in the minds of veterans by political speeches, news stories, and films, few social scientists would discount the likelihood that Greene's findings were skewed by those factors.

The outstanding fact is that stories of veterans being abused by anti-war activists only surfaced years after the abuses were alleged to have happened. During the period in which soldiers returned from Vietnam, such stories were virtually nonexistent. One reference to spitting on a veteran can be found in Robert Jay Lifton's book, *Home from the War* (1973, 99). A psychiatrist, Lifton was involved with "rap groups" comprised of Vietnam veterans. He reported that "one man in our group told of being spat upon by an anonymous greeter at the airport when he returned." From what Lifton tells us, we don't know if the spitter was pro- or anti-war (this is an important detail because most of the documentable incidents of abusive behavior toward Vietnam veterans involved pro-war people against anti-war veterans), nor do we know the name of the soldier or the circumstances of the alleged incident. By going on to characterize the report as a "kind of mythic representation of a feeling shared by the American people and the veterans themselves," however, Lifton seems to be warning against a literal interpretation of the report.

Another veteran-reported spitting incident occurs in *A Chaplain Looks at Vietnam* (1968), by John J. O'Connor. O'Connor, a Marine Corps chaplain, had served in Vietnam and was pro-war. In describing the rude treatment he later received while speaking at a college campus, he wrote: "I had often witnessed this kind of intellectual weakness in parlor debate, in political oratory, in the placards of many of the protest marchers, in the demonstrations of unreasoned hatred such as that displayed by those spitting in the faces of soldiers guarding the Pentagon" (xiii).

Although it was the soldiers guarding the Pentagon, not veterans, of whom O'Connor wrote, his words could easily have become grist for the image of the spat-upon Vietnam veteran. But what exactly was he saying? Did he witness the spitting? Was he using the image of spitting as a figure of speech? And when was it that the spitting supposedly occurred? It would be ironic if it was during the 1967 march on the Pentagon because that occasion is best remembered through photographs that show protesters gently placing flowers in the rifle barrels of the soldiers standing guard. I wrote to O'Connor, now Cardinal O'Connor, Archbishop of New York, for a clarification and received an equally oblique response from an aide: "[The Cardinal] can neither affirm nor deny what he personally saw or heard recounted by others."[7]

While this absence of hard data is consistent with my findings from my search through news stories and polls, which revealed no basis for the widespread belief that the alleged spitting incidents actually occurred, there are reports from those years that sustain the belief that not all opponents of the war were friendly to returning GIs. The number of such reports is small, however, and some strain credulity. At the top of the list is Murray Polner's book, *No Victory Parades* (1971), which was based on interviews with two hundred Vietnam veterans. Polner cited nine of his interviews for the book, devoting a chapter to each and putting each into the category of "hawk," "dove," and "haunted." None of the nine reported having been spat upon, but all of the hawks expressed animosity toward the anti-war movement. One who had gone to college related that professors "called us killers and damned us about Vietnam." Another made a very generalized statement about "hippies and radicals telling us we did wrong." One of the three hawks repeated a story that had been told to him:

> At Travis Air Force Base an incident occurred which—true or not—spread like wildfire in Nam, and I think was believed by the guys. It seemed very possible to me, too. A vet, just back, was in the men's room when a hippie came up to him. He asked the vet if he had just returned from Nam and when he said yes, he had, the guy shot him in the arm." (P. 10)

Or consider the comments of another hawk:

> Later [George's cousin] reported to him more disquieting news. Antiwar protesters in California, he claimed, were gunning down returning vets

as they arrived home by plane. One of them, he insisted, had only recently been badly wounded at Travis Air Force Base. George believed it to be so, even now . . ." (P. 35)

It should be noted that while *No Victory Parades* manages to convey to the reader the *impression* that Vietnam veterans and anti-war activists were at each other's throats, its actual content does not sustain the impression. With the sole, and rather mild, exception of the one hawk who said his professors had called veterans killers, there are no first-person, eye-witness accounts of anti-war movement hostility toward Vietnam veterans in the book. It's all hearsay.[8]

. . . . . .

Only a minority of Americans participated in the events related to the war during the late 1960s and early 1970s. For obvious demographic reasons they are an even smaller percentage of all living Americans today. Thus, most of those doing the remembering today were not a party to the events themselves; they only remember what filtered through to them from the news media of the time and popular culture since then. To them, the chant "Hey, Hey, LBJ. How many kids didja kill today?" is hard to distinguish from "Baby killer!"—the epithet that protesters are alleged to have hurled at veterans. The conflation of the country's low-key reception for returning GIs with the political division that marked the time is not unreasonable. It happened before.

In Germany after World War I, and in France after its defeat in Indochina, stories very similar to those of the spat-upon Vietnam veteran surfaced. As an examination of those cases will show, they functioned in a very similar way. There is a set of core events essential to stories of this type, which have a similarly self-perpetuating character. In a sense, the basis for new myths are existing myths. Given the right set of circumstances, the will of a people to believe, and the power of a political regime to fashion the necessary symbols and interpretations, an existing myth will be reconfigured for the times.

SIX

From Odysseus to Rambo

Coming-Home Stories

> Stories of warriors betrayed are as old as Greek myth.
>
> —Arthur Egendorf, *Healing from the War*

The classic tale of military victory through subversion is the story of the Trojan Horse in Homer's *Odyssey*. But when Odysseus, the hero, returns home, he finds his house occupied by a horde of young men eating his food and courting his wife. Has his trickery in war while abroad been matched by the duplicity of his wife at home? He can't be sure, of course, but Odysseus takes it as a sign that all is not as it should be. He disguises himself as a beggar and sneaks out to organize his friends for a revolt that will reestablish order.[1]

In modern times, stories of soldiers returning from lost wars bear a marked similarity to Homer's ancient tale. When Confederate soldiers returned home from the Civil War they perceived themselves to be despised by Southern society. Described by one historian as alienated, poor, and mean, they drifted about aimlessly. In December 1865, a small group of them formed a secret organization, the Ku Klux Klan. Disguised in white sheets and led by former officers of the Confederate Army they set out to overthrow the Reconstruction government and restore their own sense of order. The targets of their terror were the white Southerners who allegedly had betrayed the war effort and the black freedmen who had been liberated by the North's victory (Lester and Wilson [1905] 1971; Severo and Milford 1989).[2]

The "Dolchstoss Legend"

The most dramatic instance in which the treatment of war veterans figured in the politics of a country occurred in Germany after World War I. Throughout the war, the German people had endured enormous suffering. Food shortages and other deprivations, suffered unevenly by rich and poor on the home front, added to the pain of human losses in the war. Though the war had begun to go badly by the spring of 1917, the German leadership continued to assure the people that victory was in sight. A soldiers' mutiny in June 1917 and a string of strikes early in 1918 notwithstanding, the people continued to sacrifice while the government tried to repress dissent. When the end finally came late in 1918, the German people felt, with considerable reason, that they had been misled. Why, they wanted to know, had they been asked to sacrifice so much in a losing cause?[3]

Leaders of Imperial Germany, such as Gen. Erich Ludendorff and Field Marshal Paul von Hindenburg, deflected this anger by blaming opponents of the war and supporters of the Weimar Republic for having betrayed the German cause. The Weimar Republic, which was Germany's first attempt to establish constitutional democracy, replaced imperial rule after World War I and was under attack by German rightists from the start. These anti-Weimar forces converged with other reactionary elements to form the fascist movement leading to the triumph of the National Socialist Party and the rise of Adolf Hitler to power in 1933.

During World War I, Hitler had gained notoriety for his oratory against Jews, Marxists, and other "invisible foes" who he said would deny the German people their victory. While recuperating from a war wound, he found "scoundrels" cursing the war and wishing for its quick end. "Slackers abounded and who were they but Jews" (Shirer 1960, 30–31). To ground the idea that German soldiers had been betrayed on the home front, the German right popularized the image of war veterans being abused when they returned home. Hermann Goering, who would later gain notoriety as founder of the Gestapo, described how "very young boys, degenerate deserters, and prostitutes tore the insignia off our best front line soldiers and spat on their field gray uniforms" (Hamilton 1982, 334).

This legend of the "stab in the back," as William Shirer calls it in *The Rise and Fall of the Third Reich*, became a "fanatical belief . . . which, more than anything else, was to undermine the Weimar Republic and pave the way for Hitler's ultimate triumph" (31). But Goering was mythmaking. A closer look at what he did reveals an intriguing similarity between his twist on the German post–World War I experience and the twist that has been given the post–Vietnam War history of the United States. Recognizing the similarity gives us some insight into the creation and function of the stories of mistreated Vietnam veterans.

Most German soldiers returned rather quietly from the war and made the transition to civilian life without fanfare or fuss.[4] Goering's claim that some had had their insignia ripped from their uniforms is based on the fact that, as the war was ending and it was clear that Germany had lost, thousands of soldiers were in revolt against their officers. In acts of defiance against the authority of the old regime and to express their solidarity with a left-wing revolutionary movement that was growing across the land, soldiers ripped the insignia from the uniforms of their own officers (de Jong 1978, 15). So, *some* German soldiers *were* attacked *and they were attacked by anti-war forces*. But the detail that the attackers were themselves uniformed soldiers was left out of Goering's rendition, and it subsequently became lost in the "*Dolchstoss Legend*," the legend of German soldiers stabbed in the back, their military mission betrayed on the home front.

Similarly, instances of attacks on U.S. officers by their own men are all but forgotten in the popular remembrances of the Vietnam War. Many Americans today "know" that GIs were mistreated upon their return from Vietnam. Their images of Vietnam veterans run from the hapless sad sack to the freaky serial killer; for them, post-traumatic stress disorder is a virtual synonym for the Vietnam veteran. But they have never heard of "fragging," the practice of soldiers killing their own officers. The true story of the widespread rebellion of troops in Vietnam and the affinity of GIs and veterans for the politics of the left has been lost in the myth of the spat-upon Vietnam veteran.[5]

Les Centurions

The German story was repeated in France during the 1950s after the French army was defeated in Indochina. Having previously suffered a loss of prestige when it was defeated by the Germans in the early 1940s, the French army had battled Ho Chi Minh and the Communists in Vietnam with little support from the home front. The opposition of the French political left to colonialism translated into left-wing opposition to the war in Indochina. Moreover, given that the war was being fought thousands of miles from home and largely by professional soldiers meant that the general public regarded the war apathetically.

Soldiers returning home after the army's defeat at Dien Bien Phu on May 7, 1954, felt scorned by the public. They had risked their lives only to be told—not only by French Communists but by members of the larger population as well—that theirs was a "dirty war," a "shameful war," a "war which dares not speak its name." According to one account, "uniforms became increasingly rare in French cities, as most officers preferred to promenade in more respectable civilian attire" (Ambler 1966, 94, 100).

Military leaders blamed their defeat on the politicians of the Fourth Republic. Gen. Henri Navarre, who had commanded French forces at Dien Bien Phu, said of France's political leaders:

> They allowed this army to be stabbed in the back. They tolerated the constant treachery of the Communist party and its auxiliaries of all kinds. They allowed a press sure of its impunity to attack the morale of the combatants, to undermine that of the nation and to divulge military

> secrets. The shilly-shallying, the mistakes, the acts of cowardice accumulated over eight years are too numerous and too continuous to be attributable solely to the men, and even the governments, who have successively held power. They are the fruits of the regime . . . a regime which abolishes the national spirit, which isolates the army from the nation. . . . (Scriven and Wagstaff 1991, 154)

The French army was badly in need of a morale boost when revolt broke out in Algeria, then under French colonial rule, in November 1954. The war in Algeria offered it a chance to redeem itself and regain the respect of the nation. But the Algerians were as determined and resourceful as the Vietnamese. Encouraged by the success of the Viet Minh, the Algerian National Liberation Front proclaimed its commitment to a protracted guerrilla war. Following the election of Guy Mollet as prime minister of France in 1956, negotiations with the rebels broke down. The National Assembly passed a special powers act, granting Mollet and the military carte blanche for an all-out war for the preservation of French Algeria.

The myth of betrayal figured prominently in the political sentiment of those French who supported the war in Algeria. "Just as Hitlerism was a revolt against the 'humiliation' of Germany by the Treaty of Versailles," wrote Werth (1958, xvi–xvii), "so National-Molletism was largely a reaction against the widespread French feeling of national humiliation" wrought by France's defeats in World War II and Indochina. But when the government decided to call up reservists and extend the length of military service beyond the normal eighteen months, spontaneous movements against the draft, *mouvements des appelés et rappelés* (Movements of conscripts and reservists) reminded professional soldiers that they were being called upon to fight a war that did not have widespread support.

Unlike the war in Indochina, the Algerian War won the attention of the French public, largely because draftees were involved. By 1958, the French began to show signs of unease about the cost and the conduct of the war. In May 1958, rumors began to circulate that Prime Minister Pierre Pflimin was ready to negotiate with the Algerian nationalists in order to appease the growing number of opponents to the war. With the government preparing to negotiate with the insurgents, French settlers in Algeria along with right-wing extremists and the military seized control of the government in Algiers on May 13, effectively bringing to an end the Fourth Republic. After weathering a revolt by the army and the settlers in the fall of 1959 and an attempted military coup in April 1961, the successor government of Charles de Gaulle granted Algerian independence on March 18, 1962.

The estrangement of many officers following their defeat in Algeria was captured in the best-selling novel, *Les Centurions*, published in 1962. Written by a former paratrooper, Jean Larteguy, *Les Centurions* told the story of Rasperguy, a character transparently based on the real-life paratrooper, Col. Marcel Bigeard. Rasperguy pulls together a group of Indochina veterans who share a sense of alienation from French society and takes them to fight in Algeria. The story depicts metropolitan France as female-dominated and decadent, and military life in Algeria as a cult of the physique that stressed the moral superiority and virility of Rasperguy and his men.

In each of these coming-home narratives of war veterans, we find themes that are also present in the myth of the spat-upon Vietnam veteran. Most important, all the modern stories are about soldiers returning from wars they lost. The fact that we seldom, if ever, hear stories about soldiers in winning armies returning home to abuse suggests that these tales function specifically as alibis for why a war was lost. In the cases cited here, the armies represented the expansionist interests of nations with ideologies of cultural, ethnic, or racial superiority. Unable to deal with their defeat by "inferior" peoples or societies, the losing colonizers look for the reasons for their defeat at home. The myth of the betrayed, abused veteran is a classic form of scapegoating.

Similarities among the stories across nations, continents, and generations abound. Stories of soldiers hiding their uniforms and donning disguises are intended to suggest the contempt that civilian society is alleged to have had for military personnel. The stories of spat-upon

Vietnam veterans are often accompanied by claims that veterans took off their uniforms in the airport as soon as they returned to this country and stuffed them in the nearest garbage can. Many of them tell of girls, women, or unmanly men who are the abusers. In the movie *Hamburger Hill,* the protagonist describes a scene right out of *The Odyssey:* "I'm home from the 'Nam . . . I get home, the wife is sitting cross-legged on the floor, kids running around barefoot, there is a hairhead taking a leak in the john." This gendering of the betrayal helps the defeated male warrior maintain his sense of prowess; with the female betrayer to blame for defeat, the soldier can always believe he could have won had it not been for her. Psychologically, the stories enable him to project his own weaknesses onto others. By rejecting these others, he reaffirms his own manliness and self-worth.

Often, stories of abused veterans become fodder for right-wing political movements and propaganda campaigns that lead to further conflict and war. Modern cases are again strikingly similar in this regard. During the 1980s, U.S. popular culture became infused with references to Vietnam veterans who had been mistreated upon their return from war. The film character Rambo gained cult status as a Vietnam veteran who, having been spat on when he returned home, vented his anger on civilians before returning to Vietnam to avenge the lost war. Writing about the rise of armed paramilitary groups in his book *Warrior Dreams* (1994), James William Gibson calls Rambo "the emblem of a movement that at the very least wanted to reverse the previous twenty years of American history and take back all the symbolic territory that had been lost."

A hallmark of conservative ideology is its appeal to the cultural intangibles of myth and legend; while the left tends to base its arguments on science and material observation, the right appeals more often to emotion and symbolism.[6] The fear of betrayal from within—a constant in the panoply of political sentiment—is most frequently given voice by the political right. The verbalization of that fear, in the context of the American war in Vietnam, could easily have been prompted by imaginative agitators and a casual familiarity with homegrown political traditions like the Ku Klux Klan. No European imports were necessary. Nevertheless, the transatlantic connection was there.

From the Fantasies of Robert Welch . . .

The leading right-wing organization of 1960s America, particularly in matters of foreign policy, was the John Birch Society. Named after a Baptist missionary who had served behind enemy lines during World War II and was killed by Chinese Communists, the society was formed in 1958 by Robert Welch, a Massachusetts businessman. Welch claimed that John Birch was America's first known casualty of the war against communism. The John Birch Society quickly became this country's preeminent crusader against what it saw as a two-hundred-year-old international conspiracy of intellectuals, Jews, and bankers to control the world, and which it deemed responsible for most of the world's woes since the French Revolution. The Federal Reserve System, the United Nations, and fluoridated water were all plots of intellectual elites who, by knowing things the rest of didn't know, were able to control us. These elites were dubbed "insiders" by Welch. They were the communists.

Welch's twist on America's war in Vietnam was that the country's mission in Vietnam was being compromised by communists in the government who were betraying the national interest. Rather than get the war over quickly through an escalation of military means, communists in the government were keeping the war going in order to further the propaganda efforts of the international communist conspiracy. Welch's rhetoric allowed him to appear simultaneously pro- and anti-war: by wanting the war over quickly he appeared to be anti-war, but by arguing for an escalation of the conflict he appeared pro-war. Nonetheless, he put himself on the side of "the people" in arguing that the war, as it was being conducted, was an exploitation of the American people by Washington insiders.

Welch's advisor on Vietnam was Hilaire du Berrier, an American-born adventurer who had fought in the Spanish Civil War and worked with Chiang Kai-shek in China and the French resistance in Indochina during World War II. Described as a long-time French correspondent for *American Opinion*, du Berrier also worked for the Office of Strategic Services and wrote for *Newsweek* magazine after the War. In 1965 he wrote *Background to Betrayal*, which the Birch Society distributed. Welch claimed it was the most comprehensive book published in English on the matter of the U.S. government/communist plot to create chaos in Vietnam "ever since we put Ho Chi Minh in business with our money and equipment in 1944" (Schomp 1970, 146). According to du Berrier, American GIs in Vietnam were in pursuit of a "no-win strategy" that had been concocted by the Central Intelligence Agency and Michigan State University professors. The government's policy in Vietnam only *appeared* to be anticommunist. The hidden intent was to sell out the cause of American freedom and independence to the international communist conspiracy by creating a chaotic situation in Vietnam that North Vietnam's leader Ho Chi Minh could exploit (Schomp 1970).

Hilaire du Berrier drew his lessons from the French experience. In the July–August 1965 issue of *American Opinion*, he wrote:

> If President Johnson really meant business, the next step . . . would be to order the bombing of the dikes on the Red River, upon which the very existence of North Vietnam depends. The French knew the importance of those dikes; they built them. But again, at the darkest moment in the Indo-China war, the French didn't bomb the dikes either. The reason then was that French Communists, their powerful labor union, and all the various shades of Socialists, anti-colonialist "Liberals," and French labor leaders who in their politics criss-crossed the Communist lines, held a knife between the shoulder blades of the government in Paris. America is in that position now. One wonders who is holding the knife at the back of President Johnson. Meanwhile our boys die. . . ." (P. 42)

The idea that the "real" enemy was internal shaped the politics of America's ultraright toward the war in Vietnam almost from the beginning. For them, support for the war was synonymous with opposing the anti-war movement, and their rhetoric soon found its way into

Howard Gottesman hit by an egg while marching against the Vietnam War in Worcester, Massachusetts, on March 26, 1966. (AP/Wide World Photos)

Air Force Capt. Dale E. Noyd arrives at the Federal Court Building in Denver, Colorado, on May 9, 1967, for a hearing on his request to be declared a conscientious objector to the war in Vietnam. (UPI/Bettmann)

FACING PAGE: TOP: Vietnam Veterans Against the War stage a mock search and destroy mission at Boston City Hall, April 14, 1971. Thirty men dressed in army fatigues and armed with toy M-16 rifles "attacked" a subway exit and took "prisoners" who were also members of the group. (AP/Wide World Photos)

BOTTOM: The "John Turkey Movement," November 27, 1969. Members of the 71st Evacuation Hospital at Pleiku, South Vietnam, 1st Lt. Sharon Stanley, Capt. Donald Van Nimwegen, and Spec. 4 Stephen Streeper, fast on Thanksgiving Day to protest the war. (AP/Wide World Photos)

Vietnam Veterans Against the War demonstrating in front of the Dorchester, Massachusetts, Court on January 21, 1972, to support nine veterans on trial for occupying the armed forces recruiting office in Dorchester. (Boston Public Library)

John Kerry, following his arrest with other veterans for their anti-war activities on the Lexington, Massachusetts, Green on Memorial Day, 1971. (Boston Public Library)

John Kerry speaks to Youth Caucus members at Harvard University Freshmen Union, January 9, 1972. (Boston Public Library)

Women pacifists picket the main gate at Ft. Devens, Massachusetts, November 11, 1965. Their signs express their opposition to the war in Vietnam and their personal support for soldiers. (Boston Public Library)

Opponents of the war in Vietnam block a chartered city bus carrying inductees to the Boston Army Base, May 22, 1970. (Boston Public Library)

the political and journalistic mainstream. On March 28, 1966, the New York *Daily News* editorialized that recent demonstrations against the war "gave aid and comfort to the enemy in time of war and thereby fitted the U.S. Constitutions's definition of treason." In April 1967, Gen. William C. Westmoreland, commander of U.S. forces in Vietnam, returned to the United States to lobby for increased troop levels in Vietnam and while on American soil he blasted the anti-war movement as "unpatriotic" and warned that popular opposition to the war would cost lives and prolong the conflict.[7] By the fall of 1969, betrayal had become a central theme of the Republican Party's political rhetoric. As noted earlier, in running for mayor of New York against John Lindsay, a liberal who had come out against the war, Republican John Marchi accused Lindsay of having "planted a dagger in the back of American servicemen in Vietnam" (Bigart 1969).

. . . to the Fantasies of Richard Nixon

The politics of the ultraright resonated deeply with Richard Nixon. Nixon had cut his political teeth as a young Red-hunting member of the House Un-American Activities Committee in the 1950s. His home district in Orange County, California, was widely known as a Birch Society stronghold. The Los Angeles–area Birch Society claimed the membership of several political and economic elites, including members of the Chandler family, which owned and published the Los Angeles *Times*. According to the writer David Halberstam (1979, 118) the *Times*, which was once described as "the most rabid Labor-baiting, Red-hating paper in the United States," virtually created Richard Nixon.[8]

Nixon's approach to the war was Birchesque. He campaigned for president in 1968 as a peace candidate by pointing out that he had been raised as a Quaker and promising to bring the troops home. His path to peace, however, entailed an escalated war. After his election as president, he unleased a ferocious air assault on the Vietnamese and extended the ground war into Laos and Cambodia. When the anti-war movement criticized these measures, Nixon did what any Bircher would do: he decried the anti-war movement as a communist conspiracy that was prolonging the war and that deserved to be treated as an internal security threat.

The Nixon-Agnew Strategy: Smash the Left, Capture the Center

The origin of the myth of spat-upon Vietnam veterans lies in the propaganda campaign of the Nixon-Agnew administration to counter the credibility of the anti-war movement and prolong the war in Southeast Asia. Nixon had won election as a peace candidate, but he was also committed to not being the first American president to lose a war. It was a contradictory agenda. When the Vietnamese undertook a fresh offensive against Saigon from sanctuaries in Cambodia in February 1969, Nixon began bombing that neutral country. Fearing that the U.S. peace movement would use the bombings to build opposition to the war to new heights, Nixon tried to keep the bombings secret. But in May, with U.S. forces taking heavy losses on "Hamburger Hill" in the A-Shau Valley, news of the bombings leaked out. It was time to change the subject (Karnow 1983, 591, 601).

Deploying a propaganda technique that would be honed to perfection during the Gulf War thirty years later, Nixon began to redefine the war. From the spring of 1969 on, the war was going to be first and foremost about the men who were being sent to fight it (and not, mind you, about the people who sent them there). In the first instance, this meant prisoners of war. The administration's clever campaign to muster public opinion around the POW issue was launched on May 19 at a press conference held by Defense Secretary Melvin Laird. Enthusiastically promoted by the media, the POW issue soon dominated war news to such an extent that the writer Jonathan Schell observed that many people were persuaded that the United States was fighting in Vietnam in order to get its prisoners back.[9]

The POW issue created new visions of the war for Americans. As

H. Bruce Franklin (1992, 54) wrote in *M.I.A., or, Mythmaking in America,* "The actual photographs and TV footage of massacred villagers, napalmed children, Vietnamese prisoners being tortured and murdered, wounded GIs screaming in agony, and body bags being loaded by the dozen for shipment back home were being replaced by simulated images of American POWs in the savage hands of Asian Communists." But with the revelations of the atrocities perpetrated by American soldiers against civilians in the Vietnamese village of My Lai in the fall of 1969, America's vision blurred again. Hundreds of thousands turned out for the Moratorium Days in October and November of 1969, making it clear that, while the POW issue could animate pro-war sentiment to a degree, it was not enough.

The POW issue had a certain humanitarian appeal to it, however, which might be extended to all soldiers in Vietnam. The Nixon administration eagerly made the extension. Our boys in Vietnam, it argued, whether they were in prison or in the field fighting, could not be abandoned. Funding for the war would have to be continued, lest the safety of the troops in the field be undermined; rhetoric against the war would have to be curbed, lest the enemy be encouraged and our boys feel betrayed. The thirty thousand GIs who had already died in Vietnam would have been sacrificed for nothing if we were to quit now. The war had to go on until we could have peace with honor, if not victory. As long as there were U.S. soldiers in Vietnam the war had to be supported; to do otherwise would mean abandonment and betrayal. So it was in the soldiers themselves that Nixon found the perfect reason to continue the war.

The success of the October 15, 1969, moratorium against the war moved the administration into a proactive posture against the anti-war movement, and thus began a campaign of "dirty tricks" that would eventually lead to Watergate. The most immediate effect of that campaign was to increase the tension between liberals and radicals in the anti-war movement because the rhetoric employed implied that opposition to the war was tantamount to treason.

In the speeches Spiro Agnew gave after October 15, he blasted the anti-war movement for siding with an enemy aggressor (October 19), for applauding our enemies, condemning our leaders, and repudiating the four hundred thousand American war dead in this century (October 20), for manufacturing homegrown totalitarianism (October 30), for marching under the flags and portraits of dictators (November 20), and for revering totalitarian heroes (December 3). Although such accusations might be dismissed as vice presidential cant for awhile, Agnew's rancor was bound to have an effect if he continued speaking out long enough. And continue he did. On February 21, 1970, he called anti-war activists "the best publicized clowns in our society" and their statements "seditious drivel." He called on leading anti-war organizations, such as Students for Democratic Society, to "transfer their allegiance from Mao Tse-tung and Castro and the Viet Cong to the United States of America." On August 17, 1970, he warned that if a congressional proposal to cut off funding for the war, the McGovern-Hatfield Amendment, passed, it would be known as "the amendment that lost the war in Vietnam."[10]

The press and academe constituted two of Agnew's favorite targets. He continually bashed the press as unduly critical of President Nixon and overly sympathetic to the anti-war movement. At times, he virtually conflated the press with the movement, as when he implied in a speech he gave on November 13, 1969, that if it were not for television's pandering to the radicals, there would not be any marches and demonstrations. Agnew leavened his attacks on colleges and universities with quotes from the architects of the emerging neoconservative movement, Irving Kristol and Sidney Hook. He harangued professors for allowing a climate of permissiveness to pervade the campuses and accused journalists and educators of being soft on basic American values.

The administration's alignment with neoconservativism reassured middle-class liberals. As Barbara Ehrenreich showed in her book, *Fear of Falling* (1989), the social movements of the 1960s were very threatening to certain occupational groups in the middle class, many of whom were also the social base for liberal politics. The middle class generally feared the loss of privilege it saw coming as a result of the rising tide of entitlement movements, and it especially feared what it perceived to be attacks on the integrity of higher education by the student and anti-war movements. Middle-class power, Ehrenreich argued, rested on access to and control of information and knowledge. The institutional site of that power was the college and university system. The cultural permissiveness of the civil rights, women's, and youth movements of the 1960s, moreover, challenged the virtue of the middle-class capacity for deferred gratification. The strategies of the left, focusing as they did on group rather than individual rights, added to the estrangement of liberals from the Left. By the early 1970s, middle-class liberals were vulnerable to the seductions of the right.

The Nixon strategy to end U.S. involvement in Vietnam by turning the war over to the South Vietnamese government appealed to liberals. The plan promised to end the draft and return peace to the campuses while preserving the U.S. position in the global economy. In Vietnam, of course, the North Vietnamese and the National Liberation Front sought a different end to the war. The American political left, meanwhile, viewed Vietnamization as a mask for continued U.S. military dominance in Southeast Asia. Adding their voices to the radical position were the several thousand Vietnam veterans who were integral to the anti-war movement by the early 1970s.

The significance of the neoconservative pull on liberals, both inside and outside the anti-war movement, was amplified by their presence in the opinion-shaping institutions of the country. It is the business of journalists, artists and college professors, claims Ehrenreich (1989, 6), to provide the "spin," the "verbal wrap" that gives coherence to events or serves to justify social arrangements we might otherwise be inclined to question. The power to shape public opinion and, ultimately, to shape America's collective memory about the war rested largely in the hands of these people. As some intellectuals began to move to the political right, so, too, did the ideological constructs that Americans were given for viewing the closing events of the war and postwar years. As history inched the United States closer to the conclusion of its first lost war, the spin doctors began to construct the phrases and images that the public would use to think about and remember that war.

The myth of the spat-upon veteran gained impetus as media portrayals of veterans shifted between 1969 and 1972. Recalling the legitimation given the GI anti-war movement by the media early on, one is struck by the negative portrayal of anti-war veterans a few years later. As late as the Moratorium Days in the fall of 1969, the press was running attractive photo essays on GI coffeehouses. Journalists sent back sympathetic reports of infantry units in Vietnam honoring the moratorium by wearing black armbands and reported on the deep anti-war sentiment in the ranks. Validating the significance of such reports was the commentary offered by such respected observers as James Reston, who in the columns he was writing in the *New York Times,* raised the specter of troop revolts serious enough to impair the military mission in Vietnam.

But troops that wouldn't fight were a more appealing story than ex-troops who had fought and were ready to go public with what they knew about the conduct of the war. The Winter Soldier testimony collected by Vietnam Veterans Against the War in February 1971 was a shocking indictment of the government's policies in Vietnam and a sickening portrayal of a culture that underwrote atrocities against civilians (Vietnam Veterans Against the War 1972). The implications of the stories that anti-war veterans brought home with them extended far beyond America's understanding of the war that was ending to the country's view of itself and its place in the future. Getting beyond the Vietnam War was going to require dealing with the veterans of that war.

Accompanying the administration's effort to discredit the anti-war movement through claims that it was hostile to GIs and veterans and responsible for prolonging war, was the effort to first silence and then discredit the voice of anti-war veterans. The press all but ignored the Winter Soldier proceedings, and when thousand of veterans converged on Washington, D.C., in April 1971 to return the medals they had won in combat and present testimony to congressional committees about the conduct of the war, the press parroted government claims that some of the protesting veterans were phonies. Worse, they might have been less than real men. Speaking before the Armor and American Ordnance Association at Fort Knox, Kentucky, a few weeks later on May 14, Vice President Agnew said:

> The veterans who showed up in Washington last month to demonstrate against the war didn't resemble the majority of veterans that you and I have known and seen. I don't know how to describe them, but I heard one of them say to the other: "If you're captured by the enemy, give only your name, age, and the telephone number of your hairdresser." (Coyne 1972)

Anti-war veterans were genuine, however, and they were not going to go away. They were a boulder in the road to Vietnamization, and they promised to haunt the country's memory of the war. The administration could not silence them and, while its crude attempts to slander them as unmanly homosexuals gave license to the anti-Vietnam veteran bigotry already amassed in American Legion and VFW halls around the country, it wasn't the key to a long-term solution. And the attempt to criminalize them was no more successful. Indeed, the clumsy concoction of a conspiracy case against VVAW backfired when the trial against the Gainesville Eight (two more members of VVAW had been added to the indictment) revealed that it was the government, not VVAW, that was guilty of conspiracy. As writer Fred Cook (1973, 295) put it, "None of the politically motivated trials brought by the Nixon Administration's Internal Security Division of the Justice Department collapsed of its own weight as abjectly as did this one." Moreover, a month after the Gainesville defendants were acquitted, Spiro Agnew resigned in disgrace, to be followed a year later by the president himself. The Gainesville acquittals aside, anything the administration had done to lay to rest the problem of troublesome veterans was tainted by its own shady reputation. The Nixon-Agnew mailed fist approach to the veteran question was a tactical dead end.

. . . . . .

If the end of the Nixon administration meant the end of the campaign to criminalize the behavior of anti-war veterans, it also marked the beginning of the time when the war began to be spoken of in the past tense. In 1973, the last regular troops were withdrawn from Vietnam, and the South Vietnamese government was left to fight on alone. Soon, the question of how the war would be remembered was to displace the remaining issues of the war itself in the public discourse. Vietnam veterans who had fought the war and then fought against the war now became the focus of the struggle over how the war would be remembered. Blanketed by the discourse of disability, the struggle over the memory of veterans and the country alike would be waged with such obliquity as to surpass even the most veiled operations of Nixon's minions. While Nixon's plumbers were wrenching together the Gainesville case against VVAW in the spring of 1972, mental health and news-media professionals were cobbling together the figure of the mentally incapacitated Vietnam veteran. More than any other, this image is the one that would stick in the minds of the American people. The psychologically damaged veteran raised a question that demanded an answer: what happened to our boys that was so traumatic that they were never the same again? As it came to be told, the story of what happened to them had less to do with the war itself than with the war against the war.

SEVEN

From Badness to Madness

The Mental Labeling of Vietnam Veterans

> You have lied to us too long, you have burned too many babies. You may have taken our bodies, but you haven't taken our minds.
> —Ron Kovic, August 21, 1972

Ron Kovic spoke too soon.[1] A Marine Corps veteran who had lost the use of his legs in Vietnam, Kovic was speaking in Miami Beach, Florida, site of the 1972 Republican Party's national convention. He and thirteen hundred other Vietnam veterans were there with thousands more anti-war activists to protest the Nixon administration's continuation of the Vietnam War and the almost certain renomination of Nixon as the Republican Party's candidate for president in the fall elections. By the time Kovic spoke, his charge that the government had lied about the war and that the U.S. military was responsible for the killing of Vietnamese innocents was well substantiated.[2] The *New York Times* had begun publishing the *Pentagon Papers,* a collection of secret Defense Department documents stolen and leaked to the press by Daniel Ellsberg. On March 29, a military court had found Lt. William Calley guilty of murder in the massacre at My Lai. His own mangled body was testimony to the price paid by individual soldiers who had answered their country's call. But the minds of Vietnam veterans were still contested terrain and the battle for them was just beginning.

The *New York Times* and PTSD

On the very day that Kovic spoke, the *New York Times* featured a major front-page story on the mental problems of Vietnam veterans (Nordheimer 1972). The *Times* story was an extraordinary piece of journalism. Its timing, first of all, was deft. The attention of the country's television-viewing public was riveted on Miami Beach, where events as raucous as any the country had witnessed during the Vietnam War years were erupting. The presence of a large number of Vietnam veterans among the protesters was prominently featured in news stories. On the evening of Nixon's acceptance speech, Kovic was interviewed by NBC's Roger Mudd on the convention floor, after he and a few other veterans had gained access to the building. The case against the Gainesville Eight, charged with conspiracy to disrupt the Republican convention by violence, was also in the news at the time.

The *Times* story was placed on the top half of the front page, separated by one column from the lead story on the start of the G.O.P. convention. Its headline read, "Postwar Shock Besets Ex-GIs" and it was accompanied by a three-column-wide photograph of a single GI dragging his duffel bag down an airport hallway. Behind him on a wall is a large banner reading, "Welcome Home Soldier. USA is proud of YOU." The irony of the forlorn soldier brilliantly juxtaposed against the sentiment of the banner is inescapable. The continuation of the story on the inside pages of the paper was set off with a full-page, eight-column headline reading, "Postwar Shock Is Found to Beset Veterans Returning from the War in Vietnam." The continuation covered an entire page and was accompanied by a photograph showing a lone soldier sitting head-in-hand, slumped over a chair at the Oakland, California, army terminal. The caption described him as "weary" and then continued: "One psychiatrist associated with the V.A. Hospital in Minneapolis says that 50 per cent of the soldiers returning from Vietnam need professional help to readjust." With no explanation of what was meant by "professional help" or what it meant in the context of the times to readjust, the association of psychiatry with Vietnam veterans left the impression that the reader should think about Vietnam veterans within a mental health framework.

The association between mental illness and Vietnam veterans was deepened in the text of the story, which was peppered with such phrases as "serious readjustment problems," "emotional stability," "shattering experience," "psychiatric casualty," "mental health disaster," "social problem," "emotionally disturbed," "men with damaged brains," "emotional disorders," "emotional illness," "mental breakdowns," and "severe depression." Even in its attempt to appear discriminating in its characterizations, the story managed to cast a pall over veterans: "The men who suffer post-Vietnam syndrome are not dramatically ill. They do not go berserk or totally withdraw. Instead they are bewildered, disillusioned, unable to cope."

Readers who managed to get beyond the labels found little support for the story's basic claim that significant numbers of Vietnam veterans were suffering from an ailment called post-Vietnam syndrome (PVS). Indeed, deep into the story, the reader learned that there was little hard research on which to base conclusions about the mental health of Vietnam veterans, a fact, however, that did not stop the writer from referring to "countless troubled veterans" a few sentences later.

The *Times* story was clearly not a "news" story in the usual sense of the word. There was little news in the story and even less of what could be called facts. Certainly, there was nothing in the content of the story that dictated its being run on August 21. The story reported nothing, for example, that had occurred on the days leading up to its publication. It was the kind of story that could have been run on the newspaper's science page the following week or month, or in its Sunday magazine at almost any time as a human interest story. Nothing, except for the fact that anti-war GIs were in the streets to protest the start of the Republican national convention on that day, could explain the timing, placement, and content of this story.

Its purpose was not to convey news at all but rather to provide readers with an interpretive framework for understanding those news stories that the *Times* and other news sources would be running during the week of the convention and to stigmatize the veterans. The real news stories reported on the veterans in the streets; this story told readers how to interpret the fact that veterans were in the street: the behavior of these veterans, the reader should understand, was a mental health problem. What's more, this was a mental health problem that resulted less from the war itself than from the homecoming experience of the veterans. The writer noted that the Vietnam War had produced the lowest psychiatric casualty rate in the history of modern American warfare; according to him, the emotional disorders in men who had served in Vietnam showed up only after their return to the United States.[3]

Post-Vietnam syndrome was attributed, in fine print, to both the trauma of the wartime events themselves as well as the silencing and isolation of veterans upon their homecoming. This elasticity allowed PVS and its sequel, post-traumatic stress disorder (PTSD), to function in two ways in conjuring up the "good veteran" image. To the extent that the reported symptoms could be attributed to the trauma of war, the image of these damaged veterans squared with the conventional understanding that war is hell and that the war they fought was a "real" war. These veterans, as much as those of any other war, had been through hell. They had not been anti-war GIs and they were not peacenik veterans. They were *good* veterans. On the other hand, if the observed maladies were due to the trauma of coming home from the war, didn't that also confirm that these were "good veterans"? The reason why the homecoming experience might have been so traumatic was only hinted at by the *Times* story, but the hint was politically loaded: Vietnam veterans had been made to feel guilty by those who thought the war was immoral and had felt hostility from their peers who had not done military service. The inference that it was their peers who were responsible for the guilt-tripping of veterans was, of course, a thinly veiled accusation aimed at the anti-war movement. Why else would the anti-war movement have been anti-veteran if they were not "good" pro-war veterans?

The Psychiatrists

In September 1969, just after the story of the atrocities at My Lai was broken by the U.S. press, a social worker named Sarah Halay interviewed a Vietnam veteran at the Boston Veterans Administration (VA) Hospital. The veteran told her that his company had killed women and children at a village called My Lai, and he described how he was now unable to sleep, had nightmares, and was easily terrified. He was particularly fearful that some of his buddies might kill him because he had witnessed the killing but not participated in it.

When Haley reported her interview with the patient at a staff meeting, she was surprised to learn that the *Diagnostic and Statistical Manual,* published by the American Psychiatric Association and used by mental health professionals to classify mental conditions, had recently been revised and that the new version, DSM-II, issued in 1968, had dropped "gross stress reaction" as a type of war neurosis. DSM-II contained no diagnostic nomenclature to cover a case like that of the veteran she had seen. As a result, her colleagues dismissed the soldier's story as a delusion and classified him as paranoid schizophrenic. A short time later, Haley would join forces with psychiatrists Chaim Shatan and Robert Lifton, opponents of the war, in a campaign to restore war neurosis as a bona fide diagnostic category. That campaign would end when "post-traumatic stress disorder" was included in DSM-III, issued in 1980.

Robert Lifton also read the news accounts about My Lai, and in December 1969 he wrote about how the effects of war on soldiers could explain why atrocities against civilians could happen. In the spring of 1970, amidst the demonstrations against Nixon's invasion of

Cambodia and the shooting of students at Kent State University by the Ohio National Guard, Lifton was invited by Chaim Shatan to speak at New York University. His talk attracted several members of VVAW. Following the talk, he and Shatan began a working relationship with some New York–area Vietnam veterans. In the fall of 1970, they began a series of "rap groups" with veterans, which Lifton later characterized as a form of "street-corner psychiatry." In February 1971, Shatan wrote an op-ed piece on post-Vietnam syndrome for the *New York Times,* but the paper declined to publish it.

The newspaper's lack of interest in Shatan's piece was consistent with its lack of interest in Vietnam veterans in general and anti-war veterans in particular. At about the same time the *Times* rejected Shatan's piece, it also ignored the testimony of veterans at the Winter Soldier hearings convened by VVAW in Detroit. But the newspaper's approach to veterans was about to change. William Calley's conviction for the premeditated murder of civilians at My Lai on March 29 validated what been said in Detroit. In April, hundreds of Vietnam veterans went to Washington to return their medals for service in Vietnam, tell their stories to congressional committees, and lobby for an end to the war. If Richard Nixon could no longer ignore the veterans, neither could the *Times*.[4]

The veterans' story at that point was a political story, through and through. With the exception of German veterans after World War I, there had never been a generation of veterans who had turned so completely against the regime that had sent it to war. When Strayer and Ellenhorn (1975) interviewed Vietnam veterans, they found that *75 percent of them were opposed to the war*. Even more noteworthy was the affinity of these veterans for anti-imperialist politics and the cultural critique of capitalism.[5] That being the case, these veterans loomed as an on-going problem for those ruling-class interests that desired to reestablish the country's military capacity and the populace's will to war. Framing the veterans' story as a political one, however, would add to its legitimation and exacerbate the long-term problem of getting beyond Vietnam.

The Dwight Johnson Story

The *Times* would frame the veterans' story differently and, as that story took shape, its lines began to converge with those being written by the mental health professionals. On May 26, the *Times* ran a front-page story about a Detroit, Michigan, veteran, Dwight Johnson, who was shot and killed while trying to hold up a liquor store at gunpoint. Johnson had been awarded the Congressional Medal of Honor for heroic action near Dak To in the Central Highlands of Vietnam in February 1967. According to the *Times* story, Johnson had gone on a rampage after his tank unit was attacked by North Vietnamese regulars. He single-handedly wiped out the enemy attackers before being taken to a hospital in a straightjacket.

Once back in Detroit, Johnson was unable to find steady work until he was awarded the Medal of Honor. He then rejoined the army as a recruiter and public relations person. The army sent Johnson for medical treatment when he was unable to carry out his duties reliably. At the Valley Forge VA medical center he was diagnosed as suffering from "depression caused by post-Vietnam adjustment problems." In March 1971, Johnson checked out of the hospital on a three-day pass and never came back. On April 30, he was killed in the holdup attempt (Nordheimer 1971).

What was remarkable about the *Times* coverage of the Johnson story was that the paper had ignored the Winter Soldier hearings held in the same city a few months earlier. Several things could explain the newspaper's greater interest in Johnson's death. VVAW's incursion into the nation's capital in April had happened in the meantime, making the need to pay attention to Vietnam veterans more urgent. Or perhaps the *Times* sensed that white fears of militarily skilled black veterans who had been politicized by the war were growing, which would make the story of a war-crazed black veteran holding up a liquor store good copy. In retrospect, however, it appears the greater attention given to Johnson's story was due to it being an individual case. Whereas the story of radical veterans was a sociological phenomenon with vastly broader political implications, Johnson's story lent itself to a psychological interpretation. Spun as a story of all Vietnam veterans in microcosm, it could provide a new starting point for interpreting the coming-home experiences of Vietnam veterans. Mental health professionals did not miss their cue.

Johnson's story became a prominent anecdote in Robert Jay Lifton's seminal writing on PTSD in *Home from the War* (1973). A recognized figure in psychiatry through his study of survivors of the atomic bombing of Hiroshima, Lifton had also been an air force psychiatrist during the Korean War. The notion of "survivor guilt" was central to his work on war and trauma. Survivors, he wrote, live with "residual inner conflicts" having to do with anxiety from the close experience with death, psychic numbing, suppression of feeling, and an overall inability to "formulate one's war-linked death immersion" (38). Initially, Lifton was interested in explaining the participation of U.S. soldiers in atrocities like the massacre at My Lai. What he hit upon was ingenious because it deflected attention away from military policy (where VVAW was trying to focus attention), while simultaneously recasting GIs from their role as agents of imperialism to that of victims. Lifton argued that GIs, griefstricken over the loss of comrades and guiltridden for having lived when others died, sought to diminish their feelings by "continuing the mission" that their buddies had died for. His attempt to understand GIs as "victims" of a war in which the United States had inflicted a kill ratio of about thirty to one on the Vietnamese was a stretch, but once the GI-as-victim image was established, it was easy to shift the locus of the trauma from the war front to the home front.[6]

Chaim Shatan also read the *Times* story on Johnson and later identified it as the "the first public acknowledgment of a Post-Vietnam Syndrome" (1973, 643). Personally moved by the story, Shatan again approached the *Times*, and the paper agreed that it was an "opportune time" to publish his op-ed piece (Shatan 1972) on post-Vietnam syndrome (Scott 1993, 43).[7]

May 1972 was an opportune moment because the credibility of antiwar veterans was high and the Republican and Democratic national conventions were approaching. These would be the first conventions since the raucous events surrounding the Democratic Party convention in Chicago four years earlier, and large demonstrations were planned for both. The Republican convention was especially targeted. VVAW was planning to put together caravans to bring thousands of veterans to the convention to protest the expected renomination of Richard Nixon. Originally scheduled for San Diego, the convention was now rescheduled for Miami Beach, where it was thought security would be easier to maintain. The announcement of the rescheduling came on the same day (May 6) that Shatan's op-ed piece appeared. The timeliness of Shatan's op-ed piece, in other words, had to do with the political developments of the greatest magnitude.

As Shatan told Scott (1993, 44), "After the Op-Ed article, things started mushrooming." Lifton's book came out in 1973, the National Council of Churches sponsored the First National Conference on the Emotional Needs of Vietnam-Era Veterans, and researchers at Cleveland State University and Purdue University put PVS into play. In 1975, Lifton, Shatan, and others began organizing panels at professional meetings with the intention of building support for revising the *Diagnostic and Statistical Manual* to include a category that would cover PVS. Shatan formed a pressure group within the American Psychiatric Association to lobby for the inclusion of the new category in DSM III and the expansion of Veterans Administration services for Vietnam veterans. Jimmy Carter, elected president in 1976, appointed Max Cleland as the director of the Veterans Administration. Previously, Cleland had supported the efforts of Shatan's group as a member of Sen. Alan Cranston's staff. In 1979, Carter signed a law establishing the Vietnam Veterans' Outreach Program (creating the so-called Vet Centers) and declared the week of May 28 through June 3 Vietnam Veterans Week.

In 1980, in the geopolitical context of the Iranian hostage taking and the triumph of the Nicaraguan Sandinistas, DSM III was released with the inclusion of a category for post-traumatic stress disorder. The struggle for recognition of PTSD by its champions was profoundly political. In *The Politics of Readjustment* (1993), Wilbur Scott concluded that the legitimation of PTSD was an instance of medical scientists and their allies discovering something that was previously unrecognized and advancing a diagnosis based on its description. It is a story, he says, that "adds another sociological case to those that illustrate the politics of diagnosis and disease" (28).[8]

The legitimation of PTSD was an enormously important development because it increased the availability of needed mental health resources for thousands of Vietnam veterans. For those who continued to suffer from the wretchedness of their wartime experience, the recognition of their problems was a godsend. But the processes leading to PTSD's legitimation, involving as they did the imperatives of the Nixon-Agnew administration and the press, reached far beyond the boundaries of the mental health professions. In turn, the "discovery" of PTSD—to use Scott's term—had broad political implications. What had also been discovered was a mode of discourse that enabled authorities to turn the radical political behavior of veterans opposed to the war into a pathology, thereby discrediting them in the public mind. It was the media's discovery as much as the psychiatric profession's. As a case of psychologizing the political, the construction of PTSD is a classic illustration of how "badness" can be reframed as "madness."[9]

Although PTSD came into play as a postwar category, it extended the use of psychiatric diagnosis as a substitute for other approaches to discipline problems by military psychiatrists in Vietnam. Peter Bourne (1970, 183), writing from his experience as a medical doctor on a psychiatric research team in Vietnam, noted that this practice taught GIs "that it is legitimate to communicate through the verbal expression of psychological symptoms." In a sense, GIs learned that it was O.K. to be "mad" but not "bad."[10]

Charlie Clements: The "Right Stuff" Gone Wrong

Charlie Clements, whose personal story became known through his book *Witness to War* (1984), learned that lesson well. Clements graduated second in his class from the Air Force Academy in 1967. In the fall of 1969 he was assigned to duty in Vietnam as a C-130 pilot. In Vietnam, he experienced the deceit and self-delusion that were, as he put it, "the order of the day." Seeing at first hand the bombing of Cambodia while listening to the Nixon administration's denial that the war had been extended to that country was more than Clements could abide. He took a leave and, while in the States, spoke at his first anti-war rally and renewed a relationship with an Air Force Academy classmate who had since declared himself a conscientious objector.

When Clements returned to duty he asked for reassignment to nonflying status. The colonel who denied his request referred him to a psychiatrist. For six weeks, the psychiatrist probed Clements's feelings on a variety of issues but showed particular interest in one incident that Clements felt was only tangentially connected with his decision to stop flying. The incident was the death of a friend. "Though saddened and sickened by the experience," recalled Clements, "I had not been overly traumatized. The psychiatrist suspected otherwise and questioned me very closely about the impact of the incident on my thinking." Six months later, Clements found himself in a psychiatric ward.

Had the concept of post-traumatic stress disorder been in play in 1970, Charlie Clements would undoubtedly have been a candidate for the diagnosis. The inability to express grief over the loss of war buddies was said by psychiatric workers to be a prevalent symptom among those who would eventually be labeled as PTSD sufferers. Yet, Clements was admitted to Wilford Hall Hospital at Lackland Air Force Base with the diagnosis "Depressive: Acute, Severe."[11] His time in the hospital might have been a chapter out of Ken Kesey's *One Flew Over the Cuckoo's Nest*, but it was clear, as Clements wrote, that the Air Force held all the cards:

> If I attempted any legal challenge to my incarceration, they could instantly declare me fit for duty and assign me back to Vietnam. When I refused, as I would, it would be a clear case of disobeying orders. I might fight it all the way to the Supreme Court, but the end, without a doubt, would be a stretch in [the Federal Penitentiary at] Leavenworth. . . . I was, after all, the "right stuff" gone wrong. (P. 117)

Clements got out of the hospital after four months, and in the spring of 1971 he was given a psychiatric discharge. In 1980, he graduated from medical school. During the 1980s Clements became famous for his work providing medical aid in the liberated zones of El Salvador, spending many months on the ground with the men, women, and children who were under siege by that country's U.S.-backed military dictatorship.

As an officer and distinguished graduate of a military academy, Clements was, as he said of himself, a special case of the right stuff gone wrong. But on another level his case is instructive, in that it represents the experience of the entire generation of Vietnam veterans in microcosm. War veterans were, by definition, supposed to be made of the "right stuff." They were supposed to be the country's finest, and when a whole generation of them decline their assigned role they were said to have "gone wrong." Such deviance can be treated as a criminal matter or as a medical and psychological problem. In the early 1970s, the story of their "badness" began to be rewritten, with the discourse of psychological trauma supplied by mental health professionals displacing the more political discourse of pacifism and anti-imperialism that had characterized the anti-war veterans' movement. Quite literally, mental health professionals reinterpreted GI and veteran opposition to the war to fit their own paradigm. Writing in the *American Journal of Orthopsychiatry* in July 1973, Chaim Shatan provided an acute example of this tendency: "By throwing onto the steps of Congress the medals with which they were rewarded for murder in a war they had come to abhor, the veterans symbolically shed some of their guilt. In addition to their dramatic political impact, these demonstrations have profound therapeutic meaning" (649).

In the context of the times, anti-war veterans would surely have been surprised to know that their actions against the war were a form of therapy. For them, it was the country that had gone wrong and needed healing, not they. But they weren't the ones telling the story. The ultimate tragedy may have been that what was their finest hour for many veterans, namely, when they found the courage to speak out against the war they had fought, was turned against them as evidence of further damage done to them by that war. Poignant protest was thus pathologized.

The cases of Dwight Johnson and Charlie Clements provide additional evidence that the interpretation given the experiences of Vietnam veterans is more important for our memory than the experiences themselves. Had Dwight Johnson's story been written differently by the press and interested academics it could have well become a fable about economic deprivation, racism, and the exploitation of a war hero's status by military and civilian leaders. As it was, his story became a mental health case study. Clements, perhaps because he had the advantage of an elite college education, had the capacity to resist the pathologizing of his opposition to the war and the wherewithal to control the telling of his own story. His story of political courage and principled pacifism inspired other acts of resistance to U.S. imperialism in Central America during the 1980s.

The juxtaposition of the two cases also underscores the fact that journalists, academics, and other influential spin doctors of the day were making real choices about how the war in Vietnam would be remembered. There *were* choices, and what is interesting from our turn-of-the-century vantage point is that some interpretive voices got amplified by the academic establishment, news media and cultural institutions, while others were ignored. Few Americans today have ever heard of Charlie Clements and fewer still would recognize his story as an important chapter in the story of what happened to Vietnam veterans. Dwight Johnson's story, on the other hand, would be immediately recognized by many Americans as a common coming-home story of Vietnam veterans. Yet, research conducted by Paul Starr under the auspices of Ralph Nader's Center for the Study of Responsive Law in the early 1970s, revealed, according to Starr, that contrary to the growing number of stories about the erratic and violent behavior of Vietnam veterans "there [was] no significant evidence indicating that violence among veterans [was] especially widespread [and no] significant evidence that violent behavior [was] any more frequent among veterans than among other young men from working-class backgrounds." Starr also disputed the notion, central to the image of Vietnam veterans as "alienated," that their year in Vietnam had isolated them from the radical changes taking place back home, changes that they then had a hard time adjusting to upon their return. "By 1969," he wrote, "acid rock, drugs, and peace emblems were as easy to find in I Corps as they were in California" (Starr 1973a, 23, 36).

Starr's book, *The Discarded Army: Veterans after Vietnam*, was a compassionate examination of the failure of institutions like the Veterans Administration to serve the needs of Vietnam veterans. Rather than putting veterans on the couch, he focused on the legal and political dimensions of veterans' problems and raised explicit challenges to psychiatric practice: "Certainly many veterans are ill at ease about their experiences in the war, but it would be wrong to suggest that guilt is a prevalent emotion among them. It is, however, very prevalent among those who write about Vietnam veterans, and this leads to no end of confusion" (35).

In effect, Starr was pointing out that whatever else could be said about PVS/PTSD, it was a construct of well-meaning professionals that had the potential to impute to veterans psychological characteristics that were not their own. Starr would not be the last to raise questions critical of the PVS/PTSD formulation, but the political climate of the country was changing and the marginalization of Vietnam veterans through the medicalization of their image was tailored for the times.[12] Starr would eventually win acclaim for his writing on the social history of American medicine, but his dissent from the psychiatric modeling of the Vietnam veteran experience was lost, along with the stories like Charlie Clements's, as the country's memory of the war was rewritten.

Warrior Dreams

By the early 1980s, the image of the traumatized, psychologically impaired veteran had almost totally displaced the image of the politically active anti-war veteran in American memory. That displacement was essential in order for the myth of the spat-upon Vietnam veteran to have taken root in the culture and consciousness of America.

It was no less essential that the same displacement take place in the memory of Vietnam veterans. False memories are perhaps no more or less common for Vietnam veterans than for any other segment of the population.[13] Occasionally, we get dramatic reminders of this, such as the suicide of Adm. Jeremy Boorda, the Navy's top commander, on May 16, 1996. Boorda was being investigated for wearing ribbons with the *V* device, indicating he had seen combat in Vietnam when, in fact, he had not (Weiner 1996). In another case, it was revealed that Mark Fuhrman, the Los Angeles police officer accused of manipulating evidence in the O. J. Simpson case, had falsely claimed a record of combat service. *New York Times* reporter Fox Butterfield investigated and wrote (1996) that "[Fuhrman] boasted of violent exploits as a marine in Vietnam, yet the closest he got to the ground war there was aboard a ship in the South China Sea."

Boorda and Fuhrman are not the only men of their generation walking around with fanciful warrior identities. Paul Solotaroff, in his book *The House of Purple Hearts* (1995, 57), about homeless Vietnam veterans says, "Check the discharge papers on all those guys telling war stories and you'll find that a third of them never got within twenty klicks of a firefight and another third did their entire tour in Düsseldorf or Fort Dix." He goes on to say that lying about the war has become so prevalent that some therapists now view it as a distinct pathology.[14] B. G. "Jug" Burkett, a Dallas businessman and Vietnam veteran has followed up on some seventeen hundred news stories about "troubled" Vietnam veterans. Using the Freedom of Information Act to glean information about their backgrounds, he has been able to expose about three-quarters of the subjects of these stories as partial or total frauds. Some of them were Vietnam veterans who falsely claimed to have seen combat; others had come nowhere near Vietnam. Oftentimes, the stories combined exaggerated combat biographies with accounts of the mistreatment of veterans upon their return home (Weiner 1996; Whitley 1994).

One of the stories Burkett investigated was that of "Steve," who had been the subject of a 1988 CBS documentary with Dan Rather called the "The Wall Within." Steve claimed to be a Navy Seal who had carried out some gruesome clandestine operations against civilians. Unbalanced by the trauma of his experiences, Steve was unable to function once back in the United States. A classic PTSD case, he became an alcoholic and drug addict, and attacked his mother as a "VC" (Vietcong) before fleeing to the woods of Washington State with some other veterans. Burkett determined that Steve had never been a Seal and that the stories of the other men in the documentary contained fabrications and gross exaggerations, but when he brought the details of his research to the attention of CBS, the network was not interested (Whitley 1994).

The need felt by some Vietnam veterans to fabricate their combat record is understandable. War is a rite of passage in this society. To paraphrase Nietzsche, war is to men what childbirth is to women. The society demands an account of the men it sends to war. It's always the same question: Did you see combat? And the only right answer is "yes." "No" will end the conversation. No one wants to hear about the war experiences of the veteran who did not see combat. No one wants to hear the stories of the men who spent a year at war as clerk-typists, motor pool specialists, mail clerks, or cooks. Who has met the Vietnam veterans who handed out the surfboards at the in-country R and R sites, checked out books at the airbase libraries, or toured 'Nam in the 101st Airborne Band?

What counts as "combat" is, of course, subjective. One out of every ten soldiers and one out of every seven marines are the commonly accepted figures for those who were in the field with a combat unit (Fleming 1985). But most studies of Vietnam veterans allow the veterans themselves to define whether or not they saw combat, a method that confounds the studies of PTSD. Studying the effects of combat on postwar marital relations, for example, Gimbel and Booth (1994) found that when they looked at subjects with self-reported combat experience, an association between combat and marital instability emerged. However, when they employed objective measures of combat experience, such as documented service in Southeast Asia, no such relationship was evident. Individuals, it seems, will alter accounts of the past to create a coherent picture of the present, enlisting exaggerated military experiences to explain current failures.[15]

The reality is that 85 percent of the men who went to Vietnam did not see combat. What they did see, and often participated in, was day-to-day resistance to military authority and the war. But their stories were not the stories that folks back home were ready to hear. That being the case, it is likely that for every veteran whose reluctance to talk about the war was due to the unspeakable violence of his experience, there were others who quickly learned that no one wanted to hear anti-war stories. As mediated by the talented and engaging Robin Williams, Adrian Cronauer's story as the early-morning voice of Radio Vietnam played better on the screen in *Good Morning, Vietnam* than it ever would have as a first-person story in a VFW hall.

All of which is to say that Vietnam veterans felt the pressure to conform to the conventional images of what a veteran is supposed to be. That meant telling easily digestible war stories. As the 1970s progressed, however, the war itself receded in American memory and in the place of stories about the war arose stories about the coming-home experiences of Vietnam veterans. By the early 1980s, a street-corner conversation about "the war" might quickly lapse into a conversation about what happened to "our boys" when they came home. Veterans whose war records didn't fit the motif of war-as-hell could still claim that coming home from war was hell. A story of having been treated badly, especially by anti-war people, was, in effect, a war story and a story about a wad of spit on the uniform might forestall tough-to-handle questions about the medals that weren't there, or experiences that weren't had.

The image of the spat-upon veteran is, of course, only the grounding image for a larger narrative of betrayal. The story that the spat-upon veteran image is supposed to call to mind is how the unwillingness of the country and its leaders to make the ultimate sacrifices for the war effort robbed our young warriors of their victory and the nation of its honor. It is the story of how those who were disloyal to the nation's interest "sold out" or "stabbed in the back" our military. Acceptance of the image of spat-upon veterans entails an acceptance of that larger story of betrayal, and elements of military culture make GIs and veterans particularly vulnerable to its appeal.

The military lays the groundwork for believing that someone back home might betray the soldier when it introduces him to "Jody." Jody is the legendary character who steals the wife or girlfriend while the soldier is away. The introduction to Jody usually occurs in a frightening and crude manner, as when a drill sergeant is screaming at an underperforming trainee to pay attention to his training and forget about his girlfriend because Jody already has her. The introduction, which is usually accompanied by gendered expletives, is repeated with several trainees during the first weeks of basic training. Soon, "Jody" is part of the vocabulary of the trainees themselves as they begin to tease each other about matters of lover and spousal fidelity. When a trainee receives a letter from home, for example, his buddies might ask him if he has been "Jodied"—the term given to the notification that a relationship is over.

The Jody legend functions for career military people to establish a cultural boundary between civilian and military life. The seriousness of military missions requires a high degree of ésprit de corps and the utmost trust in one's uniformed comrades; the boundary insures against divided loyalties and leaves little alternative to dependence on one's military mates. The legend also contributes to a sealing-off of emotional attachments to people who have no relationship to the mission and, perhaps, helps inoculate young soldiers to the reality that, for some, their love life will not survive their hitch in the military.

During the Vietnam War, the paranoia induced by the Jody tales was probably amplified by the high level of distrust between officers and enlisted men. As resistance to the war grew among GIs, and the use of drugs increased, military authorities began covert surveillance of the troops. By 1969, the men in some units were as reluctant to let down their guard against their own officers as they were to relax against the Vietnamese Communists. Many officers were just as afraid of being "fragged" by their own men. This being the case, it would be surprising if much of the hyperattentiveness symptomatic of PTSD was not as attributable to these internal dynamics of military life as to combat itself. The overall paranoid climate of military experience during the Vietnam War likely dovetailed subconsciously at a later time with the allegations of anti-war movement hostility toward GIs and veterans to produce rather vivid images of betrayal in the minds of some veterans.

While neither the wartime Jody legend nor distrust between officers and troops was specific to the Vietnam experience, they played out differently than in earlier conflicts for one simple reason: America lost the war. The anxiety about lover and spousal loyalty, coupled with the suspicion that permeated the culture of the times, predisposed veterans to believe stories of betrayal. There is thus a structural relationship between the historical dimension of the war's outcome and the cultural dimensions of how the war was fought that helps account for the observed symptoms of PTSD.

The perception held by some veterans that they were treated badly upon their return home has also been sustained through comparisons with veterans with other wars. Unlike World War II veterans, it is commonly said, Vietnam veterans did not get any "victory parades" when they returned home. To be sure, World War II veterans had a more generous GI Bill, a more receptive Veterans Administration, and, largely because the United States had won that war, twenty-five years of an expanding economy ahead of them. But the image of World War II veterans returning to ticker-tape parades and trouble-free reentries into civilian life are also the stuff of myth. Psychologist Robert Fleming (1985) points out that most soldiers returned individually from World

War II on a point system for rotation and discharge, not as units, as is commonly believed, and that there was only one large unit parade held. Nor was the portrayal of World War II veterans in postwar culture consistent with the now-believed idea that they were all welcomed home as conquering heros. In 1945, the sociologist Alfred Schuetz wrote about war veterans as "strangers" suffering the effects of displacement from their communities. The classic coming home film of the World War II era was *The Best Years of Our Lives.* The film portrayed the experiences of three veterans who arrived home as individuals with no fanfare and problems that ran the gamut from unemployment and discrimination to alcoholism and divorce. With a little updating, this 1946 film could be the coming-home story of veterans from any war, including Vietnam.

It isn't clear when the homecoming experiences of World War II veterans began to be romanticized, but one image popularly held by the public as late as 1966 was that of the biker veteran. Hunter Thompson, who rode with the Hell's Angels in the mid-1960s, later wrote that the founders of the gang were World War II vets who weren't ready to settle into civilian life.[16] Nor is it clear at what point Vietnam veterans, in large numbers, began to measure their own experiences by the yardstick of World War II veterans' experiences. What we do know is that from the time the Nixon-Agnew administration began its polemics about the anti-war movement's betrayal of the troops, writers and researchers joined in putting the comparison on the table for public consideration. Murray Polner, in his 1971 book, *No Victory Parades,* was one of the first, and ever since writers like Myra MacPherson, who published *Long Time Passing* in 1984, have been using the same yardstick, apparently without ever checking its accuracy. Given that by the late 1980s the country had developed something of an obsession about its failure to give Vietnam veterans a homecoming parade, it is tragic, but not surprising, that the feelings of neglect expressed by many Vietnam veterans stem from the mistaken idea that they did not receive something that World War II veterans did.

Just as the cultural climate set the context in which Vietnam veterans would remember their experience, institutional forces mediated the content of the memories themselves. In his review of Robert Jay Lifton's book, *Home from the War*, Paul Starr expressed serious reservations about Lifton's methodology. Lifton's conclusion—that feelings of guilt were prevalent among Vietnam veterans—was based, said Starr, on observation of a small and "rather special and self-selected group [of veterans], and their feelings were evoked in a highly partisan therapeutic situation" (1973b, 53). Starr's charge that Lifton had "evoked" the very psychiatric conditions that he then claimed to have "found" in the veterans is a powerful insight into in an element of the "false memory syndrome" of Vietnam veterans, namely, that the very identity of veterans, qua veterans, is a social and political construct enabled, in some cases, by the intervention of mental health professionals.[17]

Lifton's work was easily the single most influential work in the voluminous literature on PVS/PTSD. That the gatekeepers of American's intellectual life were willing to overlook the methodological flaws in Lifton's study suggests, again, how imperative it was that a nonpolitical interpretive framework for the Vietnam veteran experience be formulated. And it helps us understand why we find the same methodological flaws in subsequent studies central to PVS/PTSD. The frequently cited study, "Identity, Ideology and Crisis: The Vietnam Veteran in Transition," based on research conducted at Cleveland State University in the mid-1970s (Wilson 1977), for example, asked participating veterans to sign a release form. The form explained that some of the questions were designed to measure how veterans felt about their treatment upon returning from Vietnam. At the top of the form, in underscored upper-case letters, and again in the last sentence of the permission statement, was the title of the study: The Forgotten Warrior Project. Veterans were also told at the outset of their interview that they were participating in "The Forgotten Warrior Project on Vietnam Veterans." It is thus hardly surprising that interviewers found that many of their subjects felt "forgotten."

Whatever notions of themselves and their experience may have been induced in veterans by researchers, the popularization of the image of "forgotten" veterans by the media and mass culture is far more the point. In the early 1990s, there was still no comprehensive study of the GI and veterans movements against the war. Yet, there were hundreds of studies, books, articles, and movies portraying images of neglected Vietnam veterans.[18] News stories conveying the same message proliferate daily. These representations influence how the society sees Vietnam veterans and how Vietnam veterans see themselves. Identities, be those of war veterans or others, are constructed through an interaction of the individual and the social environment. Veterans, knowing that they are thought of by others as forgotten, if not abused, are not immune to adopting those same images as part of their own identity. Indeed, for them *not* to do so would be to exhibit signs that they are inadequately integrated with their social surroundings, a sign that they are not in good mental health.

. . . . . .

In *America's Longest War: The United States and Vietnam* (1979), George C. Herring wrote, "In the immediate aftermath of the war, the nation experienced a self-conscious, collective amnesia" (264). The middle years of the 1970s were a time to forget the war and get on with life. The anti-war movement dissolved and Vietnam Veterans Against the War all but disbanded. Soon, few people remembered that GIs and veterans had actively opposed the war. By the end of the 1970s, when political events like the Soviet incursion into Afghanistan, the taking of U.S. hostages by Iran, and the revolution in Nicaragua began to pull the country out of its shell, memories of the Vietnam War had faded. When we decided to remember it we did so through the representations made available by journalists, scholars, and those who, like the members of the psychiatric professions, had an occupational commitment to the legacy of the war.[19]

The image of the spat-upon Vietnam veteran and the larger narratives that it represented—societal neglect and anti-war movement hostility for Vietnam veterans—was one of those representations. That image functioned in several ways. To begin with, it asked us not to remember the war itself, but the men who fought the war. In some ways, that shift in memory seemed slight, but its effect was profound. Not only are the names, dates, political logic, and other details of the war lost, but the lessons to be learned from it are lost, too. Few college-aged people today know about My Lai, much less what it taught (or should have taught) the country. The focusing of memory on the men who fought the war, at the expense of remembering the war itself, has had the effect of abstracting the warriors from their war. That having been done, however, the next step of recasting the role that U.S. soldiers played in Vietnam, as agents of a near-genocidal war was made easier.

There is a reluctance to examine the role played by U.S. servicemen in Vietnam for fear that such an examination might lead to blaming the victim. The men who went to Vietnam were victimized by the horrors of a war they did not ask for, the objection goes, and to now adjudicate their actions is unfair. That reluctance is well-intentioned and well-founded, but out of a legitimate concern that Vietnam veterans not be hurt again, public discourse has turned away from a critical examination of the U.S. war effort in Southeast Asia. The problem, in other words, is that the reframing of our understanding of the Vietnam War as a story about the U.S. veterans of that war, has created a false issue: should we understand U.S. veterans of the war as victims or executioners? The right answer is neither. The war itself should be the issue, not the men who fought it.

The tragedy is that the creation of the image of the veteran as victim exploits veterans as a buffer between public discourse about the war and the war itself. It is this exploitation of the veteran's image for ideological purposes that constitutes the real victimization. Mythologizing the relationship of veterans to the war and the anti-war movement takes from them the authentic generational identity they have as soldiers who grew as men and took courageous actions to end the war they had been sent to fight.[20]

The image of spat-upon Vietnam veterans also functioned to discredit the anti-war movement. In the short run, the allegation that anti-war activities were anti-soldier functioned to deflect attention away from the Nixon-Agnew administration's own efforts to prolong the war and increase the tension between liberal and radical factions within the anti-war movement. In the long run, the allegation was used disparagingly toward pacifists and peace activists and to delegitimize political dissent. Studying the reluctance of college students to get involved politically in the 1990s, writer Paul Loeb (1994) found that

> students at school after school volunteered stories of protesters spitting on soldiers as their central image of the Vietnam-era peace movement. At every kind of college, in every corner of the country, the slightest mention of antiwar activism of that time would impel them . . . to describe how the peace marchers spat on soldiers, called them names, and drove to bases and airports with the sole purpose of heaping contempt on the already scarred young men as they returned. (P. 77)

Loeb goes on to say that although those images do not square with his memory of those years, such stereotypes "separate current students from previous campus activism that should serve as political inspiration." Many students, he writes, "still use images from the Vietnam era to tar fellow students who take controversial stands." "You might be right about the need to get involved," one student told him, "but I just can't approve of people going out and spitting on soldiers" (p. 77).

To the extent that the image of the spat-upon veteran called to mind a disloyal element that betrayed the nation's soldiers and their mission, it also called to mind the existence of good soldiers who had faithfully given their best in America's behalf. The spat-upon veteran was the good veteran who was abused upon coming home and then forgotten for ten years. Until the 1980s, the good veteran was largely a conjured figure, existing only in the country's political imagination. But the stirring of the nation's global ambitions in the 1980s made it necessary to come to terms with the last war and its veterans in a more tangible fashion. The dedication of the Vietnam War Memorial on the Capitol

Mall gave materiality to the existence of the fifty-eight thousand unambiguously good soldiers who had given their lives in Vietnam, while the legitimation of PTSD provided the grist for the cultural disparagement of living veterans. By the mid-1990s, nary a trace of the political Vietnam veteran could be found in the popular culture, while portrayals of mentally disturbed and dangerous veterans proliferated.

The construction of a fictive hostility between the anti-war movement and Vietnam veterans originated in the Nixon-Agnew administration's obsession with internal enemies and its need to discredit anti-war veterans as impostors. As the war ended and Nixon and Agnew passed ignominiously into history, a more liberal agenda came to the fore. The press establishment and psychiatric professionals collaborated in the construction of post-traumatic stress disorder, which provided a more humane way of framing how Americans thought about Vietnam veterans and their homecoming experiences. In some sense, PTSD provided a necessary obverse dimension to narrative of the betrayed and abused veteran: just as the image of spitting activists conjured up the image of the good veteran, the image of psychiatrically impaired veterans conjured up the political and cultural forces that caused the hurt. Working in tandem, these forces were the impetus behind the myth of the spat-upon Vietnam veteran.

But whatever importance we assign to these institutional forces, elements in the myth of the spat-upon Vietnam veteran remain unaccounted for. For one thing, if we understand the stories of spitting anti-war activists to be at some more fundamental level stories about betrayal, the question, Why spitting? arises. Why are these stories about spitting and not about hitting or some other form of abusive physical behavior? Why is the projectile a bodily fluid and not a rock? What is there about the image of spitting that lends itself to the portrayal of betrayal? A second set of unanswered questions arises because the time and place of origin of these stories cannot be established. It was not that President Nixon claimed on a certain day that anti-war activists had been spitting on Vietnam veterans and the media picked up on this story and impressed it upon the masses. Nor is it the case that the widely believed acts of spitting have ever been depicted in films or other media. Rather Nixon and Agnew alleged the abuse, the press and mental health professionals constructed the supporting images, popular culture alluded to spitting, and the popular imagination supplied the rest. It seems to be the case, in other words, that not only do a large number of people believe that Vietnam veterans were spat upon when they were not, but that they also believe something that no one ever explicitly said happened. Like the origins of other myths, the origin of this one lies deep within the culture of the people who created it, and who in turn are defined by it. As the following chapter will show, the tale of spat-upon veterans has intriguing historical antecedents and broad psychological and political dimensions spanning individual and collective needs.

EIGHT

Women, Wetness, and Warrior Dreams

> Life on the summit isn't only lofty and sublime; it is also dry. The seas continue to flow down below and become the enemy, that gnaws, as it were, at the peaks.
>
> —Klaus Theweleit, *Male Fantasies*

The perception that Vietnam veterans were treated badly by members of the anti-war movement is wholly incongruent with the historical record. Nevertheless, when we consider that the government, the press, the entertainment industry, and mental health professionals all contributed in one way or another to the construction of that idea, it becomes understandable that a quarter-century later large numbers of people believe that veterans were spat upon.

Myths, however, are more than widely believed stories containing elements of fiction. Particular types of stories that reappear throughout history, myths also share certain structural characteristics. Even though they reappear in disparate times and places, they often seem to function in very similar ways. So it is with the stories of spat-upon veterans.

Spit as an Icon

In the stories about American veterans of Vietnam, German veterans of World War I, and French veterans of Indochina, we find elements characteristic of myths. In each, there is some physical act that functions as an icon to elicit an emotional response. In the German case, there were actually two such icons, with the "stab in the back" and "spat-upon veteran" images both figuring prominently in Nazi propaganda. In the French case, the "stab in the back" image was the most prominent, while in the American the "stab in the back" was invoked most frequently during the war years, and the "spat-upon veteran" gained great popularity during the 1980s.

Icons play a crucial role in mythmaking. In societies imbued with myth, *things* become concepts: in a dry climate, water stands for life in stories about life and death. In the scientific world, on the other hand, things are things and concepts are concepts; water stands for water. Scientific thinking combines reason with empirical evidence to reach conclusions about the world, but it does not conflate the material world that is to be known with the capacity of the knower to know; meaning resides outside the object of study (Wright 1975, 20).

But if scientists think scientifically, most people don't. Modern societies, argues Kenneth Burke (1969), look to both myth and science, meaning that people use things, or icons, as references to provide meaning for events and circumstances in situations where science fails or where the meanings provided by science are unacceptable. The successful invocation of the image of the spat-upon Vietnam veteran by the Bush administration during the Gulf War illustrates this point. Once the administration had befuddled Americans about the war by constantly putting forth different reasons for sending troops to the Gulf during the fall of 1990, people abandoned reason (which is to say they abandoned scientific thinking) out of frustration; mentally, they then latched onto the image of the spat-upon Vietnam veteran put before them by pro-war forces.

Simple answers are seductive. A story about one person spitting on another needs no interpretation, no explanation, because everyone understands its implications. By relaying that anti-war activists spat upon Vietnam veterans, the storyteller is implying something about the activists: they are bad people. They should not be supported and anyone who does support them will be thought of the same way, as someone who spits on our soldiers. In turn, the soldiers who are spat upon are implicitly good. We know that because we know something about spit. We discharge spit. We spit when we want to rid our bodies of something unhealthy or undesirable. We spit on things like the ground that are distinct from ourselves, not on our clothes, furniture, or friends. Those who would spit on other people are not like us. They are not good people. They are bad. The people that bad people spit on must be very unlike themselves, therefore they must be good people. Since the people opposing the Gulf War, the thinking went, were of the same type as those who opposed the Vietnam War and spat on Vietnam veterans, the soldiers being sent to the Gulf must therefore also be good soldiers. We had to support them.

Female Fluids and (Male) Fears

Will Wright (1975) has written that myth depends on simple and recognizable meanings which reinforce rather than challenge social understandings. For this purpose, a structure of oppositions is necessary. The stories of spat-upon Vietnam veterans unambiguously reflect this binary, oppositional structure so characteristic of myth. The stories feature polar opposites of "good" and "bad" on two levels. On one level there are the good soldiers and the bad anti-war activists. The good soldiers are an image of something that we want to believe about ourselves and our society. We want to believe that we are good people who do good things in the world. Just as laziness as an explanation for poverty among African Americans really involves a myth about hard work and white success that displaces racism as a reason for inequality (Steinberg 1974), so too the stories of spat-upon veterans give us the image of the good soldiers, which negates the need to evaluate the real war in Vietnam. Our focus blurs, and not by accident.

At that level, the stories of spat-upon Vietnam veterans are more characteristic of urban legends than myth. Urban legends, such as that of "the Hookman" who terrorizes young lovers in parked cars, are orally transmitted tales that express fear about the complexities of modern society (Best and Horiuchi 1985). Unlike traditional legends, which often contain supernatural themes, most urban legends contain themes about human baseness that reflect anxiety about the anonymity and chaos of urban life. Urban legends appear more often during periods of social instability and frequently revolve around encounters with strangers.

But the element of spit in the coming-home stories of veterans also reveals a second level of binary structure, that between man and nature. The man-nature dichotomy lies at the heart of all understandings of human existence. When and how did mankind separate from nature? The answers are provided by the creation myths elemental to human culture. Creation myths frequently entail stories about the emergence of mankind from the sea. Accordingly, we read in the Old Testament book of Genesis: "And God moved upon the face of the waters . . . . and said, 'Let there be a firmament in the midst of the waters and let it divide the waters.' . . . And God said, 'Let the waters bring forth abundantly the moving creature that hath life. . . .' "

The prominence of water in creation stories correlates with the scientific understanding that human life emerged from aquatic life, but its origin psychologically speaking may have derived from the experience of biological birthing in which life emerges out of the amniotic fluid of the mother. Subconsciously, the individual feels a primal connection with the warmth and dampness of that in utero existence, and perhaps even desires to return to it, while consciously recognizing that life itself depends upon successful separation from the safety and comfort of that watery world. Perhaps it is out of the subconscious that images of humankind's collective emergence from the sea arise.

Whatever its origin, the belief that human existence begins with its separation from water is accompanied by fears of an involuntary return to the water. We find these fears reflected in stories of a great deluge that sometimes appear in conjunction with creation stories. Consider, most obviously, the tale of Noah's ark. References to floods, waves, and tides allude to forces beyond our control. They connote the power of the natural and supernatural and reflect an underlying recognition and fear of a power greater than our own. But we don't restrict their use to the natural and supernatural. In phrases like "the Red tide," a Cold War expression for the spread of communism, or "waves of immigrants," which reflects apprehension about the numbers of foreign-born people in the United States, these words conjure up images of being engulfed and extinguished as in a flash flood.

Postmodernists attribute the antipathy toward wetness and liquidity in modern society to capitalism's need to control and dominate natural resources and human labor. In modern bourgeois culture, the vocabulary of water—words like "floods," "fluids," and "dampness"—is the means for expressing anxiety over loss of control. In *Discipline and Punish,* Michel Foucault (1977) connected the rise of prisons and other institutions of confinement in the seventeenth century to capitalism's need to control a then nomadic workforce. Physical confinement of the indigent was intended to produce a culture of self-discipline wherein workers, held in by fear of physical punishment, would be incapable of resisting the boundaries set by the ruling class. While the relative stability of class relations in the United States in the late twentieth century attests to the success of capitalism's quest for hegemonic control, periodic urban rebellions and worker resistance to managerial authority are constant reminders that this hegemony is never total.

Fluids are defined by their tendency to move freely unless restrained, and allusions to fluidity are often employed to suggest that the dominance of the ruling class is problematic, not a given, and that the ability to render nature (including human nature) predictable is limited. Thus, many of our tropes for social and political dangers are constructed from this watery lexicon: business journalists write of waves of strikes and novelists create anti-war activists who spit.[1]

The idiom of wetness in myth is also gendered in ways that help us understand why the stories of spat-upon veterans frequently tell of women or girls doing the spitting. From the Age of Enlightenment, if not before, Western culture has emphasized a link between women and nature. The man (or mankind) pole of the man-nature dichotomy is *not* gender inclusive. Rationality, the sine qua non of humanity, was understood by Enlightenment philosophers to be an attribute of the male, emotionality, of the female. "The search for abstract and speculative truths, for principles and axioms in science, for all that tends to wide generalization," wrote Rousseau ([1911] 1986, 349), "is beyond a woman's grasp." Girls, he argued, require "habitual restraint" (332).

The control of women became representative of the control of nature, and with their equation to nature, women became the object of oppression. The "naturizing" of women was followed by their sexualizing. Seventeenth-century writers valued women for their erotic physiognomy, especially their breasts and vaginas. But the ambiguity inherent in humankind's postaquatic existence was paralleled by the male's ambivalence toward women: revered for her life-giving powers, the female simultaneously beckoned the male to return to its folds and threatened to reengulf the life that had emerged from it. As Barbara Ehrenreich (1987) writes:

> The dread arises in the pre-Oedipal struggle of the fledgling self, before there is even an ego to sort out the objects of desire and the odds of getting them: It is a dread, ultimately of dissolution—of being swallowed, engulfed, annihilated. Women's bodies are the holes, swamps, pits of muck that can engulf. (P. xiii)

It is this misogynous equation, of woman equals nature, sexuality, wetness, engulfment, which is etched deeply in the Euro-american culture, that is the basis for the myth of women spitting on defeated soldiers. But it is only the basis. Only when we investigate the role of spit in mythologies related to the politics of the anti-war movement does the myth of the spat-upon Vietnam veteran begin to make sense.

The "Evil Eye"

To understand the myth of the spat-upon veteran, one has to make a distinction between spitting as a mere physical act and as a symbolic act of communication. The latter assumes a relationship between the person spitting and the person (or persons) who are "reading" or interpreting the act. The message is delivered with the expectation that the observer "reads" in the act the same meaning the spitter intends.

Spitting as an act of communication appears to be rooted in superstitions associated with the "evil eye." In many cultures, there is the belief that certain persons possess the power to afflict others through a look, eye contact, an action, or a remark. Protection against the evil eye is sought in anticipation of such events as weddings, births, and other occasions of uncertain outcome, such as meetings between strangers. Protection takes the form of both tangible signs, such as the wearing of amulets, and intangible signs, such as spoken words. In actual practice, tangible and intangible signs are often combined. Sometimes the intangible is added to the tangible. A charm worn as an amulet, for example, might be inscribed with a curse. At other times, the tangible is added to the intangible. Spitting is an example of the latter. Saliva is material, tangible; yet, emitted from the mouth, it is oral and signifies communication. "Therefore," writes Knuf (1992, 478), "the tangible act of spitting universally stands in a potentially iconic relationship to the intangible one of speaking; it serves as its concrete manifestation."

Spitting to ward off the evil eye is found in almost all parts of the world including Africa, Europe, Scandinavia, India, Asia, and Native America. The following story from Greece illustrates the practice:

> It often happens that you see one of our people, on a visit to a sick person, spit three times on the doorstep; or a relative of a woman in labor stand at the window and spit three times, glancing around her with a stern look. . . . And finally, one sees mothers who catch some dubious woman kissing their babies, spit energetically in her direction as soon as they see her turn her back. (Knuf 1992, 472)

It is clear that, when used as a communicative device, spitting establishes spiritual or social distance between the spitter and the person who is casting the evil eye. Spit marks the boundary of the power of the evil eye. In cases where, for instance, a child is spat upon by a parent to protect the child from the glance of stranger, it is clear that the spit is not aimed at the child but at evil. Likewise, in instances where spit is used in healing, the object of the spit is not the sick person but the sickness.

In American culture it is men, not women, who spit. Women spitters are thus all the more interesting. In the first place, the displacement of women by men as healers in modern society and the scientizing of healing have eliminated the traditional contexts in which women practiced spitting. This being the case, the accusation that a woman in late twentieth century society spits asks the listener to view the accused woman as unwomanly, perhaps even as an alien outsider akin to the traditional, premodern healer, i.e., a witch.

More or less coterminus with the displacement of women from their traditional roles as healers, patriarchy and the private property system merged to increase the territorial imperative of male dominance. Because control of territory was an essential element of capitalism's colonial development, the marriage of the sword and the dollar, military might with economic logic, was inevitable (Storper 1989; Parenti 1989). In the paramilitary culture spawned by Western expansionism, the society defended by the male warrior is defined by the area he can secure against his enemies. The paramilitary warrior lives inside what Gibson (1994, 87, 89) calls, " 'concentric rings of power,' each ring measuring how big he can become and how close his enemies are. . . . The warrior is deeply afraid that no matter how many weapons he has, the enemy will penetrate each and every ring. No matter how many enemies he kills with his sniper rifle, carbine, and pistol, he will still be left alone to face just one more with his knife."

It is no surprise, then, that, in defeat, the warrior imagines his demise as a penetration of his perimeter defenses and a reduction of his own capacity to project. And it is no surprise that he feminizes the image of his enemy. In *Male Fantasies* (1987), Theweleit examined the diaries, novels, and poems written by German veterans of World War I who were members of the ultranationalist Freikorps. The Freikorps was a paramilitary movement that sought to avenge what it alleged had been the betrayal of German troops on the home front. Freikorps literature often portrayed "the enemy" as not only female but female with the power to project. Freikorps fiction writers frequently represented the traitor as a proletarian woman with a pistol hidden beneath her skirt. The imagined pistol, Theweleit says, was an expression of the male's fear of a female with male power, that is, a female with a penis. In Freikorps fiction, the bodily fluid projected by these women was spit. In *Die Geachteten*, Ernst Salomon describes an antimilitary demonstration against the Berthold Freikorps in Hamburg:

> Shaking their fists, the women shriek at us. Stones, pots, fragments begin to fly. . . . They hammer into us, hefty women dressed in blue, their aprons soaked and skirts muddied, red and wrinkled faces hissing beneath wind-whipped hair, with sticks and stones, pipes and dishes. They spit, swear, shriek. . . . Women are the worst. Men fight with fists, but women also spit and swear—you can't just plant your fist into their ugly pusses. (Quoted by Theweleit 1987, 65)

The threatening element is so great, concludes Theweleit (1987), that it must be annihilated. When Manfred von Killinger, leader of the Freikorps Ehrhardt Brigade, enters Munich on a mopping-up assignment he reports:

> I am presented with a slut. . . . "What's the story with her?"
>
> She slobbers out, "I'm a Bolshevik, you bunch of cowards! Lackeys of princes! Split-lickers! We should spit on you! Long live Moscow!" Whereupon, she spits into the face of a corporal.
>
> "The riding crop, then let her go," was all I said.
>
> Two men grab hold of her. She tries to bite them. A slap brings her back to her senses. In the courtyard she is bent over the wagon shaft and worked over with riding crops until there isn't a white spot left on her back.
>
> "She won't be spitting at any more brigade men. Now she'll have to lie on her stomach for three weeks," said Sergeant Hermann. (183)

Betrayal: The Alibi for a Lost War

The literature on the role played by myth in human groups is vast. What is clear from this body of work is that myth operates on a number of levels ranging from the micro level of the individual psyche to the transnational level of ethnic and cultural identities. The preponderance of the literature on myth, however, seems to focus on the role it plays as a cohesive element in group formation and maintenance.

Myths are usually considered characteristic of primitive cultures. Making only a vague distinction between past and present, primitive cultures do not have histories, at least not histories in the way in which we understand the term. Instead, they use stories—myths—to account for their existence and to deal with contradictions within the society. Usually, myths are stories about gods, demigods, and heros, men with god-like qualities.

At first glance, stories of abused veterans do not conform to this classical standard of what constitutes myth. Most such stories arise out of modern, highly literate societies with strong historical traditions. Nor are they stories about a mystical distant past; rather, they describe a specific recent history, and the characters in them are mortals. Upon closer inspection, however, it becomes clear that stories about spat-upon Vietnam veterans did arise in the context of a kind of historical vacuum. Following the liberation of Saigon in 1975, the United States was faced with the fact that it had lost its first war. How was a country steeped in its own mythologies of national and cultural supremacy to come to terms with losing to an undeveloped nation of what some Americans thought of stereotypically as little yellow people? What kind of stories could it tell about the war? What kind of movies could it make about it? How should it treat the men who had fought and lost the war? There was no prior experience to draw upon for guidance, no rituals appropriate for the occasion of a lost American war.

Moreover, the country as a whole wished to distance itself from its painful recent past. The war had brought death, injury, interrupted personal lives, and bitter political division. Many Americans needed a break. Americans across the political spectrum heaved a sigh of relief when the South Vietnamese government fell and the war was finally over. It was time to forget the war and get on with life.

On one level, forgetting the war was purely cognitive; on another level it was emotional and psychological. It meant cutting ourselves off from the past and starting over with a new sense of self and new sense of the body politic. It meant reconfiguring where and who we were as a people. Like a chain with its closest link broken, our separation from our most recent history also severed us from our more distant past. Like primitive people without history we had a gap to fill, and we turned to myth.

The element of spit in the stories of defiled veterans also suggests that the stories functioned to reestablish a sense of order in a society that had been rife with instability and uncertainty, even chaotic, for over a decade. Writing about the post-Vietnam rise of the environmental movement, the anthropologist Mary Douglas (1984) argued that the sudden concern about pollution in the early 1970s reflected the collective desire of a people needing to reestablish social order. Pollution, she says, is defined as such when something is where it is not supposed to be; therefore, talk about the pollution of the natural environment was partially a way of talking about a sociopolitical environment out of order.

Analogously, talk about spit and spat-upon veterans reflected a collective need to reestablish a sense of order in the social space. The Vietnam War had left people confused about right and wrong, good and bad. People needed a historical and moral reorienting, an epilogue, to explain what it had all been about. Spit does not belong on the lapels of a soldier's uniform. Stories about how it got there helped us place those alleged to have done the spitting and those supposedly spat upon within a hierarchy of "good" and "bad," "us" and "them." The stories helped us resolve our leftover ambivalence about the war years. Was the anti-war movement a good thing or not? Were our soldiers good or bad? The stories confirmed for us that anti-war activists were bad because only bad people spit on others and that the spat-upon soldiers were good—why else would the bad anti-war people have spat on them?

Myth, however, does more than fill in the missing pages of history. "Modern societies," note Studlar and Desser (1991, 277) "are cognizant of a past but frequently find it filled with unpleasant truths and half-known facts, so they set about rewriting it." In this sense, myth functions to displace existing but uncomfortable memories. In *American Myth and the Legacy of Vietnam* (1986), John Hellmann writes that Vietnam is the disruption of our story, our explanation of the past and vision of the future. "Our story," as he calls it, grew out of the early American Protestant theological conceptions of America as a new world with a special purpose in God's redemptive plan. It was a story in which the Puritan's were chosen people and America was the redeemer nation, the leader of the forces of light against the forces of darkness, the agents of Satan. Americans' destiny was to bring the light, first to the natives of North America and later, to Asia. The world consisted of Christians and heathens, whites and people of color, the civilized and savages. Thus Americans had a sense of who they were derived in part from what the story told them about who they were not. The outcome of the Vietnam War, however, was not understandable within the contours of this story. The historical evidence was that U.S. policy in Vietnam had hardly been civilized and our soldiers had not always comported themselves in a Christian manner. Most seriously, God's Chosen People had been defeated by the Asian "others." The historical record was discomforting and would have to be displaced.

Examined in this light, the role of spit in the coming-home stories suggests a more complicated function for the myth, one more consistent with a view of a society riven by conflict that ran along political, class, and gender lines. As seen in chapter 2, the story of Vietnam veterans being spat upon by anti-war activists worked to reconfirm for many Americans that their country had acted with honor in Vietnam. By providing an alibi for why the war was lost, namely that we were defeated by a disloyal internal enemy in the form of the anti-war movement, the story allowed those of us who wished to continue to believe that our military presence in Vietnam really was desired by the Vietnamese people and that our mission was righteous. We had not been defeated by a no-account third world nation; we had been defeated by the only adversary capable of such a feat: ourselves. The image of the spitting anti-war activist functioned as an icon of betrayal that shored up the boundary between who "we" were—loyal patriotic Americans—and the un-American seditious "others." On the level of the individual soldier, the stories functioned to rehabilitate the warrior identity of the Vietnam generation of American males: were it not for the soft, female side of American culture (manifested in the women's movement, longhaired males, the gay rights movement, etc.) we would have won.

But the alibi was inconveniently contradicted by the historical record. In truth, GIs and veterans were an integral part of the anti-war movement. Indeed, by the end of the war, veterans were playing a leading and militant role in opposition to it. In order for the alibi to take root in the culture, the truth had to go. The image of the militant anti-war veteran, empowered by his wartime experiences, was thus displaced by the image of the besieged and bedraggled victim-veteran.

The construction of the veteran-as-victim image was multifaceted, with the Nixon administration and Hollywood playing roles alongside the well-meaning psychiatrists and social workers who worked tirelessly to establish the legitimacy of PTSD during the 1970s. As the war itself receded in memory, the coming-home experiences of veterans took center stage. In the narrative that took shape over the ensuing years, the rejection and hostility reportedly directed at veterans by their anti-war peers assumed larger proportions in the public's memory.

From Times Square to San Francisco: Memories of Homecomings

How we remember important historical events is a complex process. While there is much we do not know about how memory works, material representations such as photographs and films are particularly important. They help us to recall events, and in so doing, to remember emotions associated with those events. The photograph of the Stars and Stripes being raised on Iwo Jima, for example, helps Americans remember their victory in World War II. That photo, reproduced in large statues adorning public spaces and small ones for living room mantels, evokes feelings of pride in the victory.

The nation's elation at the end of World War II and its appreciation for the service of the men who fought is embodied in yet another photograph. On V-J Day, August 15, 1945, photographer Alfred Eisenstaedt noticed a particularly exuberant sailor kissing every woman within reach. Eisenstaedt ran ahead of the kissing sailor and snapped him embracing a nurse in a white uniform. The photo appeared in *Life* magazine and has since become the most widely recognized representation of how World War II–era GIs came home from the war.[2]

The contrast between Eisenstaedt's photograph and the image of soldiers being spat upon when they came home from Vietnam is instructive. The use of women in both images suggests that the structure of our memory about wars is closely related to the structure of our gender relations. The memory of America's victory in World War II is encoded in Eisenstaedt's photograph. The soldier is in a decidedly dominant position with one arm around the nurse's waist, his hand pressing into the small of her back. His other arm is around her shoulders, bending her backward. The nurse appears to have gone limp, with her left arm dangling loosely and her right foot extended behind her for balance. This image of the aggressively affectionate World War II soldier, very much in control of his own homecoming experience, stands in sharp contrast to the image of GIs returning from the lost war in Vietnam. Encoded in the image of the spat-upon veteran are the country's collective "memories" of Vietnam returnees being assaulted by aggressive anti-war females and effeminate males. The loss of war is represented in the image as emasculation, the loss of manhood. The Vietnam veteran is victim, not victor.

More revealing still is the fact that the homecoming of World War

II victors is remembered through a photograph, while that of the Vietnam victim-veterans is remembered through a conjured up image. A photograph is a form of documentary evidence. It shows that an event really did happen. But there is no photographic or other documentation of soldiers returning from Vietnam and being spat upon. The icon of homefront betrayal, the spat-upon veteran, is a figment of the imagination that has been popularized through storytelling. Recall the similarity in the stories. The spitting occurs at an airport, usually in San Francisco, and the spitter is a girl or male "longhair" who calls the soldier a murderer or baby killer. The stories have been repeated so often that, if asked to do so, thousands of Americans could probably draw pictures of Vietnam veterans coming home to such scenes. Although it is a picture that thousands of people have in their minds, it simply does not exist outside of their minds. In my research for this book, involving the search of newspaper reports about anti-war rallies and peace marches, the viewing of almost 150 films, and conversations and correspondence with dozens of individuals, I found only one material representation of the spat-upon veteran image—in a "GI Joe" comic book panel from the mid-1980s.

......

The fictive nature of Vietnam-era homecoming iconography confirms that America has never come to grips with the war itself. Rather than dealing with the events of that war and the flesh-and-blood veterans who opposed it, the country escaped into its own collective imagination. Today, opponents of the war in Vietnam are remembered as a marginal, pathetic, and ineffective rabble who resorted to extreme measures in order to overcome their isolation. That memory, false though it may be, has the effect of discrediting social activism in the present. In the mid-1990s college-aged students report feeling "weird" about political involvement. Activism, many say, reminds them too much of the 1960s and they don't want the stigma that is attached to it.

America's pro-military right wing, meanwhile, feeds on the same misrepresentations of history. As late as 1996, elements central to the myth of the spat-upon Vietnam veteran, such as the betrayal of the public good by big government, cultural decadence, and the softness of the baby-boomer generation, coursed through the campaign rhetoric of right-wing Republican Party candidates. One could hear the election rhetoric of the mid-1990s and easily mistake it for the rantings of Richard Nixon and Spiro Agnew against the anti-war movement thirty years earlier. If only we were all hard-edged warriors of World War II vintage, like Republican presidential candidate Bob Dole, whatever was wrong with the country would be righted.

Electoral rhetoric was only the tip of the iceberg, however. Across the nation's heartland, a large number of Americans were feeling the hurt of thirty years of political and economic disruption. The lost war, the oil crisis and inflation of the 1970s, factory closings, the influx of immigrants, and the farm crisis of the early 1980s left many people searching for answers and a new sense of national identity. Separated from the union cultures they were once a part of and sometimes separated from family and community by their search for work, Americans made vulnerable by despair and social isolation were lured to the easy solutions posed by the ultraright. In the 1980s, traditional right-wing groups like the Ku Klux Klan experienced renewal, while in the 1990s a new generation of neo-Nazi groups sprung up. In rural areas, armed militias spouting antigovernment rhetoric and sporting high-tech weaponry symbolized, for many, the return of something lost in Vietnam.

The rise of the paramilitary right is inextricably linked to the Vietnam War. The right's "new war," as James William Gibson calls it, is largely an imaginary one, fought against the forces held responsible for the loss of the last war. Those forces are largely internal to America. They are the enemy within: immigrants, feminists, homosexuals, liberals, and the soft, effeminate, immoral, and treasonous side of the culture.

The image of warriors betrayed and then forgotten has been the centerpiece of paramilitary cultures throughout the twentieth century.

Just as the protofascist Freikorps movement of interwar Germany stoked the engine of Nazism with visions of warriors stabbed in the back on the home front, America's paramilitary movement of the 1990s propagates the myth of the spat-upon Vietnam veteran. The wrong done the men we abandoned, whether POWs, soldiers in the field, or veterans who returned home without parades, must be avenged.

It is the imaginary nature of the right's war that makes it dangerous. The wrongs it seeks to avenge are figments of fear and loathing generated in the minds and culture of the paramilitary movement. The enemies in this war are imagined ones. In the absence of any material manifestation that Vietnam veterans were spat on, the anger and resentment generated by the stories to the contrary is transferred onto surrogate targets. Individuals and groups alleged to have something in common with those who supposedly abused veterans become the objects of scorn and violence. Unless it is laid to rest, the myth of the spat-upon Vietnam veteran will continue to feed the politics of division and violence.

NINE

Myth, Spit, and the Flicks

Coming Home to Hollywood

EXT   MARINE AIR BASE   DAY

Sally stands watching injured Marines unloaded. Bob waves to Sally as he comes from the plane with only a slight limp. Sally waves back.

BOB

What the hell did ya do to your hair?

SALLY

I stopped straightening it.

BOB

Where's all the demonstrators? The asshole on the plane told us there would be a bunch of flowerheads out here.

SALLY

Well, there are some kids out there . . . but they can't come in the gate. Does your leg hurt?

BOB

No.

SALLY

Motions to the car behind her.

What do you think?

BOB

About what?

SALLY

About our new car?

BOB

A Speedster? Outstanding!

SALLY

I'm glad you're back.

EXT MARINE AIR BASE GATE DAY

A small group of anti-war demonstrators is circling in front of the gate. They chant: "One, Two, Three, Four, we don't want your rotten war!" The Porsche comes to a stop. A female demonstrator, chanting, leans into the Porsche on Sally's side. A male demonstrator on Bob's side flashes a peace sign and says, "Peace, brother."

Bob returns the peace sign, letting his index finger drop . . .

BOB

Peace on you too, brother.

The preceding scene is from the 1978 movie *Coming Home.* The film won four Academy Awards and contributed mightily to American interpretations of the Vietnam War. But there are a number of things wrong with this scene.

First, it inverts the historical reality: anti-war activists protested the dispatching of GIs *to* Vietnam, not the return of veterans *from* Vietnam. At the entrance to the Oakland, California, army terminal, for example, protestors would sit down in front of the buses carrying soldiers into the base from which they were to be transferred to Vietnam. Their protests were couched in rhetoric that conveyed sympathy for the men being sent overseas. By moving the staging for the encounter from the entrance to the base (and metaphorically from the entrance to the war) to the exit from the base and the war, the film reframes the story as a movement against Vietnam veterans.

Second, the rhetoric and symbolism in this homecoming scene convey feelings of apprehension and hostility between the Vietnam veteran and the anti-war movement. The reality, as shown in chapter 2, was that by 1969, the year in which *Coming Home* was set, soldiers were returning from Vietnam having already embraced the purposes and rhetoric of the anti-war movement. Bob's sneering, "Where's all the demonstrators?" and his derisive putdown of war opponents as "flowerheads" distances him from the movement and betrays his dislike of its purposes.

Third, the activists outside the gate are identified as "demonstrators" for us by Bob, and they are clearly portrayed in a demonstration mode. In the context of the scene, the "your" in the chant "We don't want your rotten war" can only refer to veterans. The touch of ambiguity given the scene by the male protestor's "Peace, brother" is erased by Bob's middle-finger salute. Ambiguity, however, even if that is what the film had given us in that scene, would hardly be satisfying. By 1969, relations between the anti-war movement and Vietnam veterans was not ambiguous. In reality, anti-war activists approached Vietnam returnees, if at all, with informational leaflets offering services and inviting them to join the movement.

Finally, this scene misleads the viewer by suggesting that the animosity displayed by anti-war demonstrators toward returning veterans leads to Bob's downfall. Bob is portrayed in the rest of the film as a troubled veteran, prone to violence, spousal abuse, paranoia, and suicide. The role played by the anti-war movement in his downfall is unmistakable: he steps off the plane looking for "the demonstrators," encounters them, and begins his slide toward suicide.

But if *Coming Home* helped consolidate the memory of animus between the Vietnam veteran and the anti-war movement, it also served to alienate mainstream America from veterans. Of the two lasting impressions created by *Coming Home,* one is of the mentally unstable, prone-to-violence veteran. When Bob falls into a drunken stupor on the night of his return, Sally, his wife, tries to awaken him and sees that he sleeps with a revolver in his hand. A few days later, he retrieves an automatic weapon from his garage where he has stored his luggage since returning home. Bob threatens Sally with the weapon because of an affair she had while he was in Vietnam. However, it was nearly impossible for soldiers to return from Vietnam with guns in their possession. Yet the filmmakers went out of their way to create an association between veterans, mental instability, guns and violence, which became a staple of American perceptions about Vietnam veterans.

The other powerful image created by *Coming Home* was that of the disabled veteran. Sally's boyfriend, Luke (Jon Voight), with whom she has an extramarital affair, is a paraplegic Vietnam veteran she meets in the VA hospital where she has volunteered since Bob went to Vietnam. When the film opens, Luke is portrayed as an angry, self-pitying vet. Unable to cope with his war injuries, he self-destructively lashes out at the world around him. His world consists of the VA hospital and the people who work there. Luke's problem is clearly his attitude, the fact that he regards everyone except himself as obligated to promote his recovery. It is Luke and other paraplegic veterans (not Bob) who dominate the film. By setting much of the story in the VA hospital, the film suggests that we can meaningfully view the coming-home experience of Vietnam veterans through the window of that institution. When we look, though, we see spilled urine bags, legless young men, and psychotic behavior, images that turn our stomachs more than our hearts. Interpreted anthropologically, this film reflects the deep-seated cultural boundary between wellness and sickness, making veterans the "other" by placing them across the boundary from those of us who are well. The film puts distance between the viewer and veterans, setting up, rather than removing, emotional and experiential barriers to the connectedness that Americans had (or could have had) with Vietnam veterans.

As the first statement made in a major motion picture about the anti-war movement and Vietnam veterans, a statement that had the power to affect American perceptions of veterans and the relationship between veterans and the anti-war movement for years to come, *Com-*

ing Home was a major mythmaker. But *Coming Home* did not create myths from scratch. By 1978, Vietnam veterans had already been maligned by filmmakers, and relations between the anti-war movement and Vietnam veterans were badly distorted. *Coming Home* was a key film in that it consolidated the images of the troubled veteran and veteran/activist animus that had been emerging in minor films for over a decade. Moreover, it pushed that trajectory forward into another period of filmmaking that lasted well into the 1990s.

Vietnam War Movies before 1978

Unlike films about World War II, which often recreated the heroic battles of the European and Pacific theaters, very few films are set in Vietnam or tell stories about the war itself. With a few exceptions—notably *Apocalypse Now, Platoon,* and *Full Metal Jacket*—almost all Vietnam War films are about veterans and their coming-home experiences. Film, in other words, has been a major player in the process by which the memory of the near-genocidal destruction of the Vietnam War has been displaced by the story of American soldiers coming home from that war.

Early Images of Vietnam Veterans in Film

The image of the troubled Vietnam veteran was constructed against a backdrop of veteran innocence largely borrowed from previous wars. The first veteran film of the Vietnam War era was *The Lively Set.* This 1964 film was a slice of 1950s culture. Casey, the Vietnam veteran, is a Ken Doll clone who goes from the parking lot at Los Angeles State College to road racing fame with a Gidget girl in the seat next to him and Bobby Darin music on the radio. Portrayed in kitchen scenes fit for a Ronald Reagan G.E. commercial, this is a vet with *no* adjustment problems.

Only slightly more sophisticated is the image given us by *Bus Riley's Back in Town* in 1965. Bus (Michael Parks) has some problems—an unscrupulous employer takes advantage of him and his girlfriend Laurel (Ann-Margret) has a new boyfriend. While Bus's problems are relatively minor ones, both of these themes—employment problems and female betrayal—reappear numerous times in the coming-home narratives of the Vietnam War era. However, the image of the innocent veteran is short-lived, appearing only once more, in the 1969 film *Norwood*.

Nineteen sixty-nine was the end of the trail for the happy-go-lucky veteran and the beginning of a more structural good vet/bad vet narrative in which the "bad" identity of Vietnam veterans was developed through story lines that show them in conflict with "good" veterans of previous wars, often their fathers. In the 1972 films *Deathdream* and *Parades*, for example, fathers invoked their own military experiences as a way to bridge the gulf between themselves and their just-returned sons. This man-to-man approach only widened the gap, and in both films mothers intervened to buffer their sons from the frustration expressed by the fathers. This maternal intervention provided viewers with a device with which to measure the difference between the two generations of veterans: gender. By drawing the line of conflict with mothers and sons on one side, and veteran fathers on the other, filmmakers avoided the simplicity of the generation-gap theme. The gap, in these films, was a gap in maleness.

We find an on-screen juxtaposition of good and bad veteran images throughout the war period. But far more prominent is the simple disparagement of the Vietnam veteran. It begins early and never lets up. Born alongside Casey and Bus in 1965 were the Frankensteinian "Joe Corey" and the psychopathic "Brahmin." In *Blood of Ghastly Horror*, Joe Corey is a brain-damaged Vietnam veteran who is given an electronic implant that makes him prone to homicidal fits. While Joe Corey's brain damage was due to physical injury, Brahmin's damage in *Motor Psycho* was due to the psychological trauma of war. Brahmin and his biker pals terrorize two couples before Brahmin is killed by the husband of one of the women they have raped. In the scenes before he is killed, Brahmin lapses into delirious recollections about fighting the Viet Cong. What is interesting about Brahmin's on-screen delirium is that it anticipates by several years the actual diagnosis of post-Vietnam syndrome (later post-traumatic stress disorder), of which "flashbacks" were a major symptom.

By the end of 1965, then, several motifs of the Vietnam veteran genre have been presented. *Blood of Ghastly Horror* bundled physical disability, mental damage, and criminal behavior, themes that will reappear singly and in various combinations in films throughout the late 1960s and 1970s. The freaked-out Brahmin in *Motor Psycho* will have many descendants, including Bob in *Coming Home.* These images of the "bad" veteran put distance between the filmgoing public and the Vietnam veterans whose credibility needed to be neutralized if the myth of anti-war movement hostility toward veterans was ever to take root.

The Political Years, 1968–1970

Politics and Vietnam veterans do not appear together in film until the 1968 film *Greetings.* Directed by Brian DePalma, this film borrowed its title from the popular expression for the letters notifying men that they had been drafted—the "greetings" having come from Uncle Sam. Toward the end of the film, we see a Vietnam veteran at a party of what seems to be an upper middle-class, Eastside New York City twenty-something crowd. We hear him talking about the war and how the Vietnamese people are stoned all the time. The veteran makes no statement about the anti-war movement or his own activity regarding the politics of the war. What is important, though, is that he seems to feel comfortable in this setting, where people his own age are opposed to the draft (if not the war), and they appear to feel comfortable with him. Nobody spits.

During 1969, the portrayals of veterans and the anti-war movement become more political. In the widely seen *Alice's Restaurant,* Jacob is a black Vietnam veteran who has lost a hand in the war. He is staying at Alice's and is befriended by members of the counterculture who are trying to make a commune out of an old church in Stockbridge, Massachusetts. In the film, the well-known folk musician and political activist, Arlo Guthrie, plays himself, a draft resister, so there is no mistaking the anti-war politics of the film; and when in the end Jacob bids a moving farewell to a member of the group who has died, there is no mistaking his affinity for the group.

Still more political was *The Activist.* This film may have been the best of several films about campus activism set in the late 1960s. It is the first in which we see a veteran of the Vietnam generation as a political activist and the first in which there is reference to spit. The rough stuff that occurs in this film is all aimed at opponents of the war, and it is one of the activists who tells a fellow radical that she had been spat upon at a previous demonstration. The film is also important because it is a marker by which we can tell that, as late as 1969, Hollywood was able to portray relations between the anti-war movement and Vietnam veterans accurately.

But Hollywood wasn't getting everything right, even in 1969. In *Hail Hero!* Carl, played by Michael Douglas, is the son of a wealthy ranchowning family who comes home and announces that he is dropping out of college. The story develops around the intergenerational conflict between Carl and his father, a veteran of World War II. His is a socially prominent family that hobnobs with the state's political elite, and in a conversation between Carl and a congressman, we get the first on-screen invocation of the soldiers-as-the-reason-for-the-war: responding to Carl's question about the need to send men to die in war, the congressman asks, "What about the voices of those who have lost their sons? They don't want to hear that their sons have died in vain."

The congressman's response was probably Hollywood's first major attempt to cast aspersions on the anti-war movement. In the same year, the B-grade *Satan's Sadists* used a clean-cut marine veteran named Johnny to make a clearer statement against the movement. Johnny engages in desert battle against a rampaging motorcycle gang. Filled as it is with rape, snake bites, and gunfights, this film's political moment is easy to miss. But it is there, and it is an important one. The bikers have just raped a cop's wife, and they are about to kill her and her husband. Johnny had earlier come to the defense of the couple. The scene has the motorcycle gang smoking pot, dropping acid, and saying "groovy," as the head of the gang, a character named Anchor, tells the cop that his friends are peace-loving long-hairs who get their doors knocked down by the cops. This drawing of the ideological lines puts Johnny, the "good" Vietnam veteran, and the cop, a veteran of a previous war, on one side and the villainous motorcycle gang and the anti-war movement on the other. As a technique that (mis)associates the anti-war movement and the violence of the motorcycle gang and (mis)associates the Vietnam veteran with the opposition to the anti-war movement, this scene creates subtle but powerful inversions of historical reality. No matter how improbable these twists seemed in the contemporary context (1969), the technique employed—the discrediting of the anti-war movement through its association with repugnant behavior and the misrepresentation of the Vietnam veteran either through his mythologization as the "good" veteran or his "otherization" as a person who was criminal, crippled, or crazy[1]—came to characterize Vietnam films by the end of the 1980s.

Nineteen seventy was a big year for films on politics and social movements. In *Getting Straight,* Elliot Gould plays Harry, a Vietnam veteran and veteran of several social movements of the 1960s. But now he is trying to "go straight," finish his degree, and get on with his career. Although the film contains an effective critique of suburban, middle-class life, which Harry rejects, the film is ultimately a backlash film that attempts to make passé progressive social movements and political Vietnam veterans. If writing the political veteran out of history is worse than writing him into history, then *The Strawberry Statement* is considerably worse. This film about a campus-based anti-war movement's struggle against the construction of a new ROTC (Reserve Officer Training Corps) building was a major effort on the part of Metro Goldwyn Mayer (MGM) to exploit the college-aged market. There is no criticism of soldiers or veterans in it, but neither are there any Vietnam veterans, as there surely would have been by 1969, the year in which the film is set. Worse still, was *R.P.M.*, in which the only Vietnam veteran is a member of the police swat team that breaks up a campus rally. This was especially misleading in view of the fact that during 1969 and 1970 large numbers of Vietnam veterans were participating in campus protest movements.

The most overtly political film of 1970 was *The Revolutionary,* in which Jon Voight plays a campus activist who joins a Leninist-type organization called "The League" and is expelled from college after distributing leaflets calling for a general strike. He is drafted, but when he finds out that army troops are going to be used to break a local strike, he deserts and joins the workers. Helen (played by Jennifer Salt) harbors him at the home of her wealthy parents. This film is almost unique in its attempt to bring in the organized political left and connect it to the anti-war movement and the working-class struggle. Although he is not portrayed as a veteran of Vietnam, Voight's character is the only instance in a film that we see a veteran playing a leading and revolutionary role.

Ultimate Otherizations, 1971–1972

Whatever his inadequacies, the Vietnam veteran as anti-war activist had a short screen life. By 1971 he was gone. On one level this is ironic because the most visible public persona of the Vietnam veteran by 1971 was the activist veteran who was often associated with campus-based chapters of Vietnam Veterans Against the War. On another level, however, the absence of political veterans from the big screen was symptomatic of filmdom's complicity in the Nixon-Agnew effort to distort the record of events almost as they happened.

Politicized Vietnam veterans could appear in film after 1970 but only if they were pathologized through cultural, disability, or behavioral typing. Doing so allowed film viewers to attribute a character's on-screen politics to essentially nonpolitical factors, or at least to factors unrelated to the politics of the war.[2] The best example of this was in *Billy Jack.* Billy Jack is a half-Indian who defends a countercultural school from attack by local bigots. The kids at Freedom School are stand-ins for the anti-war movement, but the film relegates politics to a clash of cultures and renders Billy as an "angry Indian." In a phrase, Billy's fight is particularized—it is his fight, not white middle America's.[3]

The racial/ethnic flavor of Vietnam veteran films dominates in 1972, but in that year the genre turns bizarre. In *Blackenstein*, Eddie is a quadriplegic under the care of a Dr. Stein. Experimenting with DNA, Dr. Stein is able to rehabilitate Eddie physically, but a lab assistant switches some serum and Eddie awakens as an ape-like monster. Eddie-the-ape goes on a killing spree, dismembering a male nurse and disemboweling other victims.

If the story line of *Blackenstein* allows the attribution of Eddie's pathologies to factors having nothing to do with the war, the storyline of *Stanley* (1972) does not. Tim Ochopee, a Seminole Indian and Vietnam veteran, befriends, and is apparently befriended by, *snakes*. The degradation of war, and his treatment at the hands of an especially brutal sergeant, has led Tim to identify with snakes and, eventually, as the film develops, to serial killing with snakes as weapons. Of the vet-as-psychopathic-killer films, this is one of the purest.

Nineteen seventy-two gave us other ethnic variations on a theme. In *Slaughter*, football hall-of-famer Jim Brown plays a black James Bond out to avenge the killing of his parents by Mafia hitmen. Mostly notable for its gratuitous violence, this blaxploitation shoot'em up and its sequel, *Slaughter's Big Rip-Off*, fed the public perception that Vietnam veterans brought the war home with them. In *Journey through Rosebud*, Danny, a conscientious objector, goes to the Rosebud Sioux Reservation in South Dakota. There he meets Frank, who leads the community's fights with the Bureau of Indian Affairs despite the fact that he drinks too much. In the end, Frank is killed while driving drunk. Like Billy Jack, Frank's struggle seems to be only partially related to the war.

If Eddie-the-Ape, Tim, and Frank were hardly the vets from down the block, the white guys are just as likely to lower the property values. In *Welcome Home, Soldier Boys,* four returning soldiers buy a cheap car and head for California across country. They pick up a girl, have sex with her, and throw her out of the car while it's going fifty-five miles an hour. At film's end, the four vets, armed with weapons they have brought home from Vietnam (including a bazooka) launch a raid on the small town of Hope, New Mexico. Reenacting the My Lai massacre, they "burn the 'Ville" before being taken down by an army unit sent to the scene from Fort Bliss, Texas.

But the ultimate otherization occurs in *Deathdream* (1972). Andy, who died in Vietnam, has now come home as a vampire. He kills the family puppy, the family doctor, his girlfriend, and his sister's boyfriend. Perhaps the most bizarre of all the coming-home stories, *Deathdream* is also the strongest metaphor for the way America was dealing with the reality of a war that had politicized a generation of veterans. Andy, the son that Charles and Christine had sent off to Vietnam did not come home. The Andy who came home was some*thing* else. Real-life families had also sent their Andys to Vietnam, and what returned home was unintelligible, unreal, alien. The horror that *Deathdream* mirrored was America's realization that the boundary between life and death was not the ultimate boundary. Andy was the very incarnation of death. Just as the politically active Vietnam veteran represented the incarnation of the political and cultural values of "the other" that America had gone to war to kill, Andy was "living" proof that the reality of this war was going to stalk America long after its end. Worse than the horror of death, Andy represented the living Vietnam veterans who embodied the death of America.

The Mike and Tony who come home in *The Visitors* are not the same either. They have just gotten out of a military prison to which they were sentenced for raping and killing a Vietnamese civilian during a My Lai–type raid. They went to prison because their friend Bill had testified against them. Mike and Tony have contempt for Bill, not only because he ratted on them but because he didn't have the same stomach for war that they did, and now they have come to visit him. Bill's father-in-law, a macho veteran of World War II, is also contemptuous of Bill and tells them that he thinks Bill is "half queer." Completing the picture, Bill has married Martha, who actively opposed the war they had fought.

After drinking and watching football on television Tony and Mike rape Martha and beat Bill. Just before the rape, Tony asks Martha if she was one of those who marched in the demonstrations. He says, "I used to wonder over there, what kind of people went to those things. I always thought they were long-haired freaks, almost like Indians."

Produced and written by Chris Kazan and directed by his father, Elia Kazan, *The Visitors* was not a simpleminded denigration of Vietnam veterans, but even so the film manages to mislead. It gives us a choice between Tony and Mike—bad vets, by any measure—and the "half-queer" Bill who doesn't like war and has married the enemy. Either way, we get vets who are better forgotten about than listened to. Beyond the bad Vietnam veteran image, this film also gave us the first movie (mis)characterization of the relationship between the anti-war movement and GIs. While there may have been soldiers in Vietnam who imagined demonstrators as "long-haired freaks, almost like Indians," they would have been the exception. Why popularize the exception when by 1970, the time when the script was being written, it was clear that the Nixon-Agnew administration was trying to falsify history by portraying relations between soldiers and the anti-war movement as hostile?

The large number of Vietnam veteran films made in 1972—eleven, the largest number made in any year until 1985—should not surprise us. Such events as the VVAW's Dewey Canyon III and the government's trial of the Gainesville Eight made Vietnam veterans highly visible. But their real-life anti-war political image never made it onto the screen. The films that opened in 1972 were most likely produced in 1970, at the time when Vietnam veterans were coming out politically and the bonds between veterans and the anti-war movement were being forged. Yet, in the proliferation of veteran films in 1972, not one portrayed what was surely the modal experience of the Vietnam generation veteran. The image of the *organized* expression of veteran opposition to the war, VVAW, never made it to the screen—period. However circumstantial, the evidence that Hollywood's momentary flirtation with the political veteran was dropped after 1970 supports the conclusion that the Nixon-Agnew line—that political veterans were not the real thing—was being heard as clearly by film producers as by Legionaires.

Fast-Forward to the First Spit

The number of Vietnam veteran films declined during each of the next three years to an all-time low of one in 1975 (*The Eiger Sanction*), while the maligning of veterans continued within motifs that were becoming well-established. The avenging black gunslinger appears in *Slaughter's Big Rip-Off* (1973) and *Gordon's War* (1973). *The Black Six* (1974) and *Brotherhood of Death* (1976) cast black professional football players in all-vets gangs of motorcycle avengers and anti-Klan crusaders. There are vets with adjustment problems in *Electra Glide in Blue* (1973), vets as paramilitary vigilantes in *The Crazies* (1973) and *Mr. Majestyk* (1974), and psychopathic vets in *Captive* (1974), *Mean Streets* (1973), *Vigilante Force* (1976), and *A Field of Honor* (1973).

The Stone Killer (1973), the emblematic piece of the period, wrote off the whole generation of Vietnam vets as wackos. Lipper, a black vet, is a PTSD case, prone to violence, with no detectable neurological problems. The doctor tells Lou (Charles Bronson) that Lipper "was one of the victims, no noticeable scars; aggression and violence are part of the learning process. . . . Vietnam doesn't make heros, it makes a generation of Lippers. . . . After we've carried out the burning of children, we have nothing left but the psychopaths." Later in the film, twenty veterans hired for a Mafia hit are said to be "trained killers."

Taxi Driver (1976), directed by Martin Scorsese and with Robert De Niro cast as the depressed and sexually obsessive Vietnam veteran cab driver, Travis Bickle, was probably the most widely viewed Vietnam veteran film prior to *Coming Home*. Bickle's fixation on an attractive political campaign worker leads him to attempt to assassinate her candidate. Later, he attempts to avenge a twelve-year-old prostitute who has been mistreated and with whom he has also become emotionally entangled. (This was the film that real life imitated when John Hinckley's obsession with Jody Foster led him to attempt the assassination of President Ronald Reagan in 1981.) The connection between Bickle's war experience and his twisted personality is only implicit in the film, but by 1976 film fans hardly needed to be drawn a picture—Bickle was the cliché that cinematic cobblers had been assembling for more than decade. *Taxi Driver* is sometimes credited with providing the prototype for the crazed veteran that would be endlessly emulated for years to come. More accurately, *Taxi Driver* must be seen as the end of an eleven-year period of filmmaking. It was Brahmin, Russ Meyer's crude creation for *Motor Psycho* in 1965, who paved the way for the more nuanced and compelling Bickle.

Nineteen seventy-six also marked the end of the wartime period of Vietnam War films. Formally, the U.S. role in the war had ended with the signing of the peace accords in January of 1973. By spring of that year the draft had ended, and the last U.S. troops left Vietnam. The war had been turned over to America's junior partner, the South Vietnamese government of Nguyen Van Thieu, which resumed the fighting a year later. One possible explanation for the small number of Vietnam War films in 1974 and 1975 is that the industry, like the rest of the country, was in limbo about the war. Was it over? Who won? Was this another Korea? Nobody made films about Korea. By 1975, the dust was settling. Richard Nixon and Spiro Agnew had both resigned, and on April 30 South Vietnamese general Duong Van Minh surrendered Saigon to Vietnamese liberation forces. The war was over. And the war was lost, which meant that films going into production after May 1975 would have to deal with an American war story for which there was no precedent.

By 1976, we began to get our first glimpse of how Hollywood was going to treat America's first lost war. *Tracks* (1977) opens with Sgt. Jack Falen on a train. He is accompanying a casket containing the body of his buddy. From a radio comes the voice of President Nixon announcing, "Today, January 23 1973 . . . a peace agreement has been signed. . . ." There is something World War II–ish about Jack—his uniform, age, body carriage—that is reinforced by the vintage 1940s music that he plays on his tape player. But if Jack is the "good vet," he is also damaged goods. Merely nervous at the beginning of the film, Jack is soon hallucinating and brandishing a handgun. These two stock images of the crazed vet, carried over from the previous decade's films, set up the first on-screen hostilities between an anti-war activist and a Vietnam veteran. The activist, Mark, identifies himself to Jack as an "underground radical" and asks Jack to help him elude capture by the authorities. When Jack expresses reluctance to help, Mark pleads, "I wanted to bring you back [from Vietnam] alive, man. I've been working my ass off." But Jack screams back: "My buddy died because of guys like you. You're the guys that killed them! You're the guys that killed them!"

What is remarkable about this first on-screen attempt at an explanation of why the United States lost the war is that after more than a decade of film in which Vietnam veterans and the anti-war movement were almost never juxtaposed, they are now, a mere one year after the war's loss, portrayed as being at each other's throat. Once the filmmakers have established the conflict between Mark, the anti-war activist, and Jack, the good but damaged Vietnam veteran, the authority figures pursuing Mark become a stand-in for Jack: when Mark spits, repeatedly, in the faces of his captors, Hollywood's role in creating the myth of the spat-upon veteran has begun.[4]

Tracks pointed the finger at the anti-war movement for having lost the war and, only a little less directly, for the defilement of Vietnam veterans. *Twilight's Last Gleaming* (1977) gives those twists on history yet another twist. In this film, which stars Burt Lancaster as renegade air force general Lawrence Dell, Vietnam veterans are portrayed as the scapegoats for a society coming to terms with a lost genocidal war. Dell commandeers a missile silo in Montana and demands that the president of the United States tell the truth about the war in Vietnam. In a flashback conversation, another veteran and former POW tells

Dell: "I wasn't home five minutes before they had me believing it was all my fault—VC, the war, the orphans, the massacres. Damn it man, I took so much shit I wished I was back in the jungle." The "they" who are blaming the veteran are unspecified but the list of symbolic indictments—orphans, massacres, etc.—sound very similar to the acts of wrongdoing that Spiro Agnew and others of his persuasion had said the anti-war movement unfairly accused Vietnam veterans of committing.

However, the antipathy of the anti-war movement toward veterans is a mere subplot in *Twilight's Last Gleaming.* The more fateful twist given history by the film may have been General Dell's indictment of the country's political leadership for not telling the truth about the war in Vietnam. The truth that Dell wants told is that the war had been unnecessarily prolonged in order to preserve the image that the United States had not lost the will to fight. Dell aims his attack at "the president" and, as the plot unfolds, the president is forced to negotiate with Dell, who has his finger on the missile triggers. As Dell has drawn the line of conflict, "the president" represents "the government." On the other side of the line are "the people." The aggrieved party in this picture is America. This populist twist was to be amplified in 1979 in a made-for-television film, *Friendly Fire.* This theme, which was taken over by the political right, built to a crescendo during the 1980s and 1990s.[5]

The years 1976 and 1977 were transitional in the sense that the Vietnam War films from this period both continued to explore themes that had been over a decade in the making and added new themes that would be built upon later. The anti-war movement, having been written out of history by filmmakers until the war was lost, was brought back as an enemy of the Vietnam veteran, the reason why the war had been lost (as in *Tracks*), and even, in *Hamburger Hill* (1987), the reason why the war had been fought. Anti-war Vietnam veterans will remain marginal in Hollywood's renditions of the war and organized veteran opposition to the war will stay offscreen. The disparagement of Vietnam veterans, which had become standard fare by 1978, continued throughout the 1980s. The image of the armed and violent vet continued to be prominent. What is new from 1978 on is the conflation of cause and effect in the presentation of the psychopathic veteran. Up to 1978, most on-screen representations of gun-toting veterans implied that the veteran's wartime experiences accounted for his postwar violent behavior. Beginning in 1978, cause and effect are not always so clear. As treatments of the war and the postwar experiences of veterans are depoliticized, narratives about them become increasingly psychologized. In effect, the disparagement of the veteran image was given still another twist: did the brutality of the Vietnam War produce a generation of damaged veterans or did the damaged psyche of American males produce the brutality of the war? Two blockbuster films of 1978 put the question on the screen and struck the fatal blow to veteran credibility.

1978

The popular wisdom with respect to Vietnam War films is that Hollywood ignored the war until 1978. Film buffs are likely to say that there was only one film on the Vietnam War before *Coming Home* and *The Deer Hunter* opened that year and that was *The Green Berets* in 1968. Scholars might add that there was also the documentary, *Hearts and Minds,* from 1974. But even with these qualifications, the perception remains that 1978 was the signal year for the genre.

The reality, however, is somewhat more complex. Hollywood had been making films about Vietnam for almost fifteen years by 1978. True, all of these films, with the exception of *The Green Berets,* were coming-home narratives about Vietnam veterans rather than films about the war per se. But *Coming Home* and *The Deer Hunter* continued, rather than departed from, the trend toward displacing the story of the war itself with stories about soldiers home from the war. These two award-winning films consolidated well-worn approaches to the Vietnam War in film and reflected the historical revisionism already underway.[6]

As coming-home narratives, for instance, they perfected the presentation of the war as something that had happened *to* American Vietnam veterans rather than as a historical and political event. Probably more effectively than any other film, *Coming Home* revised history so that the American people, and even many Vietnam veterans, remember the war as a veteran home-coming story. *Coming Home* also added to the marginalization of Vietnam veterans, giving us the paralyzed, if political, Luke and the frightening, wigged-out Bob, while *The Deer Hunter* used racist caricatures of the Vietnamese to establish an image of veterans with unbelievable appetites for violence. *Coming Home* revised the history of the relationship between the anti-war movement and veterans from one of solidarity to one of hostility; *The Deer Hunter* simply left politics out.

The Making of "Coming Home"

Coming Home was a keystone in the building of an interpretation in which "the war" became, in popular consciousness, a story about the men who fought in Vietnam and how they were treated upon return home. The film was Jane Fonda's project from its inception. Fonda had begun to speak out politically while living in France in 1968. When she returned to the United States, she helped set up a GI lobby service in Washington, D.C. She also formed the Free Theater Association (FTA), which presented antimilitary skits that were very popular at off-base GI coffeehouses in this country and in Southeast Asia. (FTA was also the acronym for a military recruitment slogan, "Fun, Travel, and Adventure," which anti-war GIs had appropriated to stand for "Fuck the Army.") By 1971, Fonda had declared herself a revolutionary, and in July 1972 she traveled to Hanoi to talk to American prisoners of war and to broadcast a plea to American pilots to stop the bombing of North Vietnam. Eighteen months later, Fonda married Tom Hayden, a founder of Students for Democratic Society and a defendant in the Chicago Eight conspiracy trial.

Fonda's professional identity as a filmic sex kitten was out of sync with her political identity as a radical activist. So in 1973 she began searching for scripts that, as she stated in an interview published the following year, would "reduce that contradiction as much as possible." But how much was possible? The country was already beginning to turn conservative. Nixon had been reelected the year before and the OPEC oil boycott was signaling what life in a declining world empire was going to be like. The returning POWS were tugging at the country's patriotic heartstrings. Fonda herself was feeling the effects of a political backlash, as boycotts by the Young Americans for Freedom and the Veterans of Foreign Wars threatened the market strength of her films. Wishing to avoid being typecast as a young revolutionary woman, Fonda said she wanted to "play the antithesis of what I feel—a prowar or apolitical kind of woman existing in a situation most average people live in." Fonda turned to her friend Nancy Dowd to write a script for her.[7]

In March 1973, Fonda contracted with Dowd to write the first draft of a screenplay. Dowd's draft, apparently completed in late 1975, was titled *Buffalo Ghost,* and its story was essentially unchanged in *Coming Home.* Between the time *Buffalo Ghost* was completed and *Coming Home* was made, were months during which the principals involved in the making of the film reflected on the war and postwar years and discussed among themselves what they wanted to put on the screen. They proceeded with a level of self-consciousness seldom seen in the industry. The archival record of the making of the film, found in the Margaret Herrick Library of the Motion Picture Academy of Arts and Sciences in Beverly Hills and the UCLA Research Library contain hundreds of pages of transcribed recordings, including a hard copy of recorded "story conferences" in which Fonda, screenwriter Waldo Salt, writer Bruce Gilbert, and director Hal Ashby, sometimes accompanied by others, discussed everything from the story line of the script, to casting, character development and production. There are also transcriptions of taped interviews done with Vietnam veterans, veterans' spouses, and others whose stories Waldo Salt drew upon for the script.[8]

From the records it is not clear when Waldo Salt entered the picture as the credited screenwriter and what his initial relationship was to the script begun by Nancy Dowd.[9] What is clear is that by October 1974 he had begun interviewing veterans and their spouses and that he developed the film's lead characters out of those interviews. The availability of those interviews enables us to compare what Salt was told with what he actually wrote. We can also compare what veterans said with what we know to have been historically possible. Both comparisons reveal discrepancies and point to *Coming Home* as a major piece of historical revisionism.

One of Salt's first interviews was with Bill Hager, a marine veteran of Vietnam. In the interview, Hager describes himself as gung ho, a John Wayne type. He was proud of having survived combat. But the hard-core combat veteran is only one side of the man revealed in the interview. Hager's fight was as much with the Marine Corps as with the Vietnamese. He talks a lot about the pettiness of military discipline and the incompetence of Marine Corps leadership. Most of the interview sounds more like *Catch 22* than *Battle Cry*. Hager tells Salt how the officers used to harass troops for smoking dope and how he was supposed to report on the men in his platoon if they were smoking. He remembers with pride that he refused to turn anyone in.

Hager's "war stories" are more about survival within an authoritarian military structure than they are about surviving jungle warfare, and the bulk of his interview is taken up with his account of his involvement with Vietnam Veteran's Against the War, his reflections on American society, and the difficulty that Vietnam vets have encountered in trying to communicate with, as he put it, a "society that don't fuckin' listen." Speaking of what was then being called post-Vietnam syndrome, Hager said the problem was that vets were "having to put up with little bullshit jobs that don't really count," jobs that were reminders of military duty. Their Vietnam experience had taught veterans that American society was a lie and now that society did not want to deal with them.

Bill Hager's interview was very political, very analytical, and resonant of the historical experiences of GIs and veterans as seen in chapter 2. But this is not the Bill Hager who makes it to the screen via Waldo Salt's construction of the character Bob, for which Hager was the ostensible prototype. Bob is never shown, even implicitly, as resistant to military authority and certainly has no affinity for the anti-war movement. Unlike Hager, who joined the anti-war movement as a member of VVAW and who comes across in his interview as a strong, committed, and politically astute if angry man, Bob, as played by Bruce Dern in the movie, gives us the image of a veteran who is confused and self-pityingly weak. His unfocused anger is soon turned on himself.

He Shot Himself in the Foot

Just as important as what Salt did not use from Hager's interview is what he did use. Salt picked up on a small piece of Hager's story and made it a major part of his portrayal of Bob. Toward the end of his interview Hager told Salt about fragging incidents in which GIs tried to kill or injure their own officers with hand grenades and how, in return, the Marine Corps command had employed divide-and-conquer tactics against the troops by pitting black, white, and Latino GIs against one another. In that context, Hager reveals how he happened to shoot himself in the foot. Drunk and fearful of the fragging and racial attacks that had been occurring in the showers, he ran to the shower one night carrying his M-16. It went off accidentally, hitting him in the foot.

Hager's account of shooting himself in the foot is very short, and he tells the story solely to make the point that "It was a real deterioration process that was taking place over there." But Salt used the foot-shooting incident to establish Bob's character as a hapless military failure who comes home with a giant Napoleon complex. Bob, in the movie, gets off the plane limping. He waves off Sally's interest in his injury, thus establishing for the moment a kind of masculine mystique about the wound. Much later, after Sally and her friend Vi persist in wanting to know how he was wounded, he sheepishly tells them that he shot himself while on the way to the shower. Unlike the story of Hager's wounded foot, which serves to make a larger political point, Bob's wound was dramatized as simply a dumb accident, and his embarrassment about how he got it is a major element of his character at this point in the film. Not having lived up to his own self-styled macho image, Bob begins "acting out" as a studly tough guy around his buddies and his wife, eventually threatening to kill Sally.

At first glance, it would appear that the discrepancies between what Salt got from Hager and what he actually wrote for the screenplay were simply due his picking and choosing what he wanted out of the interview. But he constructed "Bob" less from what Bill Hager had said about himself than from what Hager's wife said about him. Salt learned about Terry Hager in his October interview with Bill. About a week later, he began interviewing Terry and, from the available records, it appears he spent more time with Terry Hager than any other single interviewee. Terry and Bill had gotten married when she was sixteen and Bill was in Vietnam. The marriage took place by proxy in Las Vegas, and it is the basis for the scene in *Coming Home* where Sally and her friend Vi go bar hopping after Vi receives a letter from Dink, her boyfriend in Vietnam, saying he wants to get married. By 1974, when Salt interviewed Terry, she had left Bill and was ending an involvement with another Vietnam veteran, Richard. Richard was a paraplegic.[10]

At the beginning of Salt's interview with Terry Hager, they ramble a bit about paraplegics, the loss of manhood, and the adjustment that paraplegics have to make with respect to sexual dysfunction. It soon becomes clear that, for Salt, speaking about the physical paralysis of paraplegics is a way of speaking metaphorically about the psychological and emotional paralysis of all Vietnam veterans. It is almost as if Salt has already decided that the returning veteran in his script has to be a dysfunctional character and that, in order to write the character, he has to be able to imagine his prototype, Bill Hager, as being disabled. The conversation between Salt and Terry slides so imperceptively from talking about physical impairment to talking about what they see as Bill's psychic impairment that one has to read and reread the transcript to confirm that Bill is not physically disabled.

The image of the physically whole but mentally crippled Vietnam veteran in which Terry Hager was casting her former husband was well-established in popular culture by 1974. Leaving aside the pathological extremes such as Tim Ochopee in *Stanley,* Vietnam veterans were almost uniformly depicted as socially isolated loners who find it difficult to connect with others. Mr. Majestyk (*Mr. Majestyk*), Steven (*Captive*), and Lawrence Dell (*Twilight's Last Gleaming*) to name but a few, either inhabit a world without women or have troubled relations with them. The Bill Hager we meet in his interview with Waldo Salt could not have been the basis for any such characters, but the Bill Hager described by his ex-wife could be the moody and broody Travis Bickle having stepped off the screen of *Taxi Driver* and into Terry Hager's life.

What Waldo Salt got from Bill Hager was neither macho war stories nor veteran rejection stories. Hager gave Salt an indictment of America but Salt, assisted by his interview with Terry Hager, reversed the verdict. It is hard to watch *Coming Home* and not conclude that Bob is the problem: he is immature in the beginning of the film and armed and dangerous at the end. The war remains offscreen, leaving viewers to wonder whether the war produced Bob's character defects or characters like Bob produce wars. The victim blaming that is otherwise implicit in *Coming Home* is foregrounded by the shot-in-the-foot incident. "He shot himself in the foot" is the perfect expression of self-defeat. It works metaphorically in this instance as an explanation for the problems of Vietnam veterans—they have no one to blame but themselves—and it worked politically to further stigmatize Vietnam veterans as losers.

The Hippies Would Try to Kill You

The other piece that Salt used from his interview with Bill Hager became a major contribution to historical revisionism. The scene with which this chapter begins shows Bob encountering anti-war demonstrators as he arrives home from Vietnam. The staging of the scene conveys hostility between the demonstrators and the returning veteran. In the annals of film study, the importance of this scene can hardly be exaggerated because it is the first on-screen juxtaposition of the anti-war movement (as opposed to a single activist such as Mark in *Tracks*) and a Vietnam veteran.

When I first saw the film shortly after its release, I came away asking where in the world the filmmakers found the basis for the scene. The short answer is that Waldo Salt got it from Bill Hager. In his interview Hager told Salt the following:

> In fact they told us in Nam, man, when you got off the plane that the hippies would try to kill you. Man, we all believed it, we all had hand guns. We all came back with hand guns. Some dude up in Chicago wound up with a whole handful of grenades. He almost wiped out a whole group of people up in Chicago. He saw all of these long-hairs and pulled a pin. He was going to—he didn't want to come back from Vietnam and let a bunch of freaks kill me [*sic*].

Any doubt that Hager's words inspired Salt's construction of the scene is erased when we look at the stages of development that the script went through on its way to the screen. In Salt's first draft he has Bob telling Sally as they approach the demonstrators at the gate, "Would you believe I'm carrying a revolver. Some cats have grenades." Later in that draft, Bob retrieves "an arsenal" from his footlocker, takes hostages, and flees to the hills before engaging a special police combat team in an armed standoff. In a later draft, Salt had Bob telling Sally, "That asshole briefed us . . . [to] be prepared for demonstrators throwing stones and all that shit."[11] While the details change, the image of the armed and paranoid veteran touched off by hostile anti-war protestors is present from Hager's story, through the early drafts, and onto the screen.

In this case, Salt's rendition is reasonably faithful to what he was told, but there is little in Hager's story that could be true. In the first place, returning soldiers were never, to my knowledge, told to expect hostile greetings from protesters. Second, the idea that GIs could have returned from Vietnam carrying handguns or grenades, much less an entire arsenal, is pure fantasy. No soldiers, with a few exceptions, such as those in the military police, were issued a handgun. Moreover, weapons were the property of the unit, not the soldier. When the soldier left his unit to return home, he checked his weapon in and then departed for a transportation center such as the one at Cam Rahn Bay where he was then processed for his return to the states. Processing out involved turning everything in, right down to one's socks, oand then being issued a single set of new fatigues for the flight home. All luggage and personal belongings were thoroughly searched for such contraband as drugs and weapons. A soldier could not have gotten anywhere near a boarding area with a weapon in his possession.[12]

So where did Hager get his story and why did Salt use it? The part of the story about GIs returning with weapons probably reflects the influence of popular culture. By 1974, the on-screen portrayal of Vietnam veterans with heavy weapons in hand was fairly common. Since, at the time, automatic and semi-automatic weapons were not yet easily obtainable on the street—as they would be fifteen years later—the viewer would reasonably conclude that the weapons came home with the veterans. In *Welcome Home, Soldier Boys* (1972) and *Tracks* (1977), little was left to the imagination. We don't know if Hager watched these films, but he does refer in his interview to *The Stone Killer* (1973) which, like the others, was not a widely viewed film.[13]

By the time Salt was conducting his interviews in the mid-1970s, the image of hostility between veterans and anti-war activists, planted by the Nixon-Agnew administration during 1969, had been part of the culture for a half-dozen years, and the image of the gun-toting Vietnam vet was standard film fare. The fact that Bill Hager not only reproduced both images in his interview but linked them together to actually create a new image—that of the Vietnam veteran armed for defense against hostile anti-war forces—suggests the power of political and popular culture not only to rewrite history but to reconfigure memory.

The study of culture being the empirically elusive pursuit that it is makes it difficult to say where Hager and thousands of other Americans, veterans and nonveterans alike, got ideas like these. What is interesting, though, is that Waldo Salt and the other makers of *Coming Home* did not correct for the inaccuracies they were fed through their interviews with veterans. They used them. It is as if Salt's "research" was a kind of foraging for impressions of veteran coming-home experiences that had already become popularized through film and other entertainment media. He gathered these impressions, reworked them, and fed them back into the culture. The making of *Coming Home* was an exercise in popular culture feeding on popular culture.

The Prototype for "Luke"

To the film's credit, Luke is Hollywood's first attempt to portray a Vietnam veteran with some political orientation. After his transformation, Luke is shown fighting for improved conditions at the VA hospital and protesting at a local Marine Corps recruitment center. Near the end of the film, he speaks to a group of high school students and delivers what is surely one of the strongest anti-war messages ever filmed.

The basic story line of *Coming Home,* however, neutralizes its political content. Luke's conversion is more psychological and personal than it is political. His political identity strikes us as more of a coping device than a commitment. Like the "displaced" worker who turns to volunteer work in search of "meaning," Luke will seek self-esteem through outreach to kids. He acquires his new identity, moreover, through therapy and intense personal involvement with Sally rather than through political activism. Through conversations with Sally, Luke rethinks his life, from his days as a high school star athlete and a war hero to his present condition. The process is psychotherapeutic. His change for the better comes through introspection and self-healing, not social interaction; political activism is the outcome of his change, not the means through which he achieves change. Vietnam Veterans Against the War is not part of the story.

In constructing Luke, the writers made some clear choices. In November 1974, Salt interviewed Ron Kovic. Kovic's name was almost synonymous with the activism of anti-war Vietnam veterans. He had been interviewed by Roger Mudd for CBS News on the floor of the Republican Party's national convention in Miami Beach in 1972 while VVAW was attempting to disrupt the proceedings. His book, *Born of the Fourth of July*, was soon to be released.

In his interview with Salt, Kovic talks about conditions for paraplegics in the Veteran's Administration hospitals, his involvement in VVAW, and his relations with women. Kovic comes across as very angry but articulate. Everyone, it seems, had problems with Kovic's personality and his politics. The problem with the former was his preoccupation with his sex life; the problem with the latter was that he had political views at all. By September, the filmmakers had started working with another veteran, Bobby Muller, and Muller would be the inspiration for a softer and less political Luke. The Luke underwritten by Muller would be a segue to the reassertion of classical warrior imagery in Hollywood's portrayal of Vietnam veterans.

Muller had been active in VVAW, but in 1976 he was trying to establish another organization, Vietnam Veterans of America. He was one of the Vietnam veterans featured in *Hearts and Minds*, the Oscar-winning 1974 documentary, and had already parted company with Kovic. With Muller to work with, Kovic became more of a negative referent—what the filmmakers didn't want Luke to be—than a positive model. Unattributed "Continuity Notes," dated September 16, 1976, reveal where the filmmakers were headed:

> The quality of daredevil self-destructiveness which seems to be so attractive to most of us—in fact and fiction, Lindbergh, John Wayne, Evil Knievel—is probably part of the very basic need to test death as a way of heightening life. Primitive ritual, bull dancing, initiation rites, etc. The life force is attractive in whatever guise it appears. I think that the dif-

> ference between Bobby and Ron . . . is the level of consciousness of a life force. At the highest level, there's a recognition of the total interdependency of life forms. The most charismatic figures in history of course are those who have been willing to test death and die in the larger interest of life itself—Buddha, Christ, Galileo.

In "Notes on Continuity and Procedure," dated December 3, 1976, the writer said, "It is agreed that Muller rather than Kovic is the prototype for Luke. Kovic's monolithic self-concern tends to become boring without the more complex needs and commitment of a man like Muller." Muller is characterized as "mature," having outgrown his impulsive anger at his situation. He accepts the "human frailty" that his condition symbolizes. "All of us are handicapped," said the note writer, "socially, mentally, physically, emotionally, spiritually." Muller is the basis for a Luke who is

> a thinking man, an intellectual in the sense that he has curiosity and social concern, even before joining the Marines. It does not matter whether he is poor, working class, or urban intellectual middle class. He was able to understand and justify his participation in the war while still being able to see and respond to the nature of the war.

In short, the Luke that Muller gives life to is an Everyman, one who transcends social and historic specifics, whose limitations are universal, and whose capabilities in the face of adversity are extraordinary, yet human. Luke is a mythic character. Luke is a Hero. The fates could have put anyone of us in Luke's wheelchair. Had they done so, we would have responded as Luke did.

The appeal to myth in *Coming Home* marked yet another transition in Vietnam War films. The mid-1970s was a period for forgetting about the war. The dearth of cinematic and other representations of the war during those years created a hiatus, a blank space during which mental recall relaxed. Stories were not told so often. Names, dates, and interpretations lay unused for months. Remembering went unpracticed. Those who had fought the war and had fought against the war turned to other matters. Some tried to restart lives interrupted by the war, others started their careers and families. The reality of the war faded.

But prewar rumblings stirred in the postwar quietude of the declining empire. In the wake of the American defeat in Vietnam a wave of Third World revolutionary movements swept into power in Africa, Asia, and South America. The Soviet incursion into Afghanistan signaled a heating up of the Cold War and the success of the Sandinista revolution in Nicaragua in 1979 made visions of communism lapping at the north shore of the Rio Grande seem real. That same year, Iranian militants stormed the U.S. embassy in Tehran, taking fifty-two American hostages. In this climate, the Carter administration floated a proposal to reinstate draft registration. Jimmy Carter lost his bid for a second term, and Ronald Reagan, who promised to bring the U.S. hostages home from Iran, was elected president.

Vietnam loomed large in the calculations of policymakers heading into the 1980s. The American people, having answered anticommunism's clarion call to the jungles of Southeast Asia, would likely strangle the next bugler playing that tune. America's will to fight, if there was any left, would not be summoned through images of the last war. The last war, if it could not be entirely forgotten, and it couldn't, would have to be re-remembered. The memories of it would have to be revised. The grey space of the mid-1970s would have to be colored in with images of a Vietnam War that never happened. The Vietnam War would have to be mythologized if America was going to war again.

But myths are created in historical contexts that no mythology can completely transcend. The mythologizing of the Vietnam War would be done with representations of the war that were already a decade and more in the making. Chief among those was the representation of the war as a coming-home experience of American soldiers. The image of the veteran as a character disabled by physical, emotional, or mental damage loomed large in those representations. The figure of the unstable and violent veteran, already universal by the late 1970s, marches hegemonically into the 1980s. And finally, the idea of Vietnam veterans having to fight on two fronts, at home and abroad, an idea to which *Coming Home* had given credence, gains prominence during the first years of the Reagan administration.

The Road to Rambo

Coming Home consolidated the representations of the Vietnam War that Hollywood had been inventing since the mid-1960s, and its turning toward myth set a trajectory that would lead to the Rambo films a few years later. *The Deer Hunter* (1978) boosted the Vietnam War film along that path. In this film, Mike, Steve, and Nick leave their tightly knit working-class community of Clairton, Pennsylvania, for Vietnam. When Mike comes back a Green Beret and a war hero, he learns that Steve has lost his legs and is in a VA hospital, and that Nick was last reported to be AWOL in Vietnam. Mike returns to Vietnam in 1975 to find Nick and bring him home. Nick is found in the Saigon underground, apparently acculturated to a dehumanized world where betting on human lives in games of Russian roulette is routine. When Mike tries to talk him into coming home, Nick spits in his face.

Viewed one way, this film is merely a racist defamation of Vietnamese culture and a simple treatise on the power of evil to corrupt even good American boys. Viewed as a coming-home story, on the other hand, it is about cultural and political divisions in American society. At the point at which Nick spits on Mike, Nick represents the rejection of everything Mike stands for: the manly deer hunter who always gets his prey with one shot, the war hero, and the America that Mike wants to bring him home to.

That *The Deer Hunter,* with all its flaws, among which were an interminably long wedding scene at the beginning and the clumsy use of the stag image to invoke mythic maleness, could win the Academy Award for Best Picture in the same year that *Coming Home* was panned by critics and still won three Oscars, suggests that the filmmaking establishment was conferring legitimation on a genre more than it was recognizing quality filmmaking. Nineteen seventy-eight was not so much a seminal year for the Vietnam War film as it was the year in which those with power in the film industry identified a package of themes and images that they thought investors would back, political leaders would not object to, and the filmgoing public would pay to watch.

The films produced between 1978 and 1982, when *Rambo* opened, were eclectic in content. There were attempts to recycle the 1960s with *Hair* (1979), *More American Graffiti* (1979), and *The Line* (1980), a remake of *Parades* (1972) about a rebellion by GIs in a military prison.[14] *Hair* was probably the best of all the Hollywood-produced films about the impact of the war on the home front. A musical based on the late 1960s play by the same name, it was not about veterans, but it was the one film that put the true story of the solidarity between anti-war activists and GIs on the screen. Although the film's story of anti-war activists willing to put their bodies between draftees and the war righted the history that *Coming Home* had inverted a year earlier, it had an air of nostalgia about it that diminished its effectiveness.[15] In 1979, *Hair* was a displaced remnant of the previous decade, more useful as the exception with which to gauge the increasing conservatism of the times.[16]

Veterans-as-drifters films were big during those years. *Ruckus* (1980) and *Americana* (1981) were classic stories of the stranger arriving in a small town and causing a stir. *The Stunt Man* (1980) and *The Pursuit of D. B. Cooper* (1981) were variations on the theme of the disaffected veteran at odds with the traditionalism of rural Middle America. The drifter films captured an element of the reality of the Vietnam veteran experience, which is that it was the veteran who often rejected America. For many veterans, life on the road, at the margins of society, on the edge was preferable to the mindless humdrum of the middle. But rather than presenting this in political terms as a critique of a society that had put business as usual above the decade-long slaughter in Vietnam, these films give reality a Nietzschean twist. With the illumination gained from their experience at life's edge, the veterans in these films are able to see the mundane and repressive side of American culture. The normal becomes problematic. But their proffered alternative is more violence, more war even. What's more, the target of their frustration has been redefined: it is not an America that waged a war of aggression against a small and poor nation struggling to be free, but an America that lacked the will to win the war in Vietnam. "The government," reflecting the mediocrity of the masses, tied the hands of our warriors in Vietnam. What these films conjure up is the existence of a warrior class composed of Vietnam veterans at odds with virtually all other segments of American society. Measured against the actual history of Vietnam veterans, it's the stuff of fantasy, certainly, but it's also nourishment for an ideological and political trend that gains momentum during the 1980s and emerges as the militia movement in the 1990s.[17]

Reminiscent of the opening scenes of *Ruckus* and *Americana*, the first scene of *First Blood* begins with a drifter, a Vietnam veteran, arriving in a small, rural, conservative town. The drifter, John Rambo, played by Sylvester Stallone, is harassed by the town cop. Given a one-way ride to the city limits by the cop, Rambo turns around and walks back toward town. From this point, the conflict escalates and Rambo is arrested and abused by the town authorities. He escapes from jail and resorts to guerrilla warfare tactics against his pursuers. Colonel Trautman, who was Rambo's Green Beret commander in Vietnam, arrives on the scene and tries to defuse the situation, telling Rambo that if he does not surrender peacefully, friendly civilians will be hurt. "There are no friendly civilians," replies Rambo. With that, he begins a rampage that ends with the destruction of the town. In the final scene, surrounded by local police and the national guard, Rambo is once more confronted by his mentor, Colonel Trautman.

Trautman: This mission is over, Rambo. You understand me? This mission is over. . . . It's over Johnny. It's over.

Rambo: Nothing is over. Nothing. You just don't turn it off. It wasn't my war. You asked me, I didn't ask you. And I did what I had to do to win. But somebody wouldn't let us win. Then I come back to the world and I see all those maggots at the airport. Protesting me. Spit-

> ting. Calling me baby killer, and all kinds of vile crap. Who are they to protest me? Huh?

The Rambo films consolidate vigilante and avenger themes with the populist theme of big but incompetent government and the right's themes of betrayal. In *Rambo: First Blood Part II* (1985) Trautman gets Rambo out of prison to help him find POWs left behind in Southeast Asia. Rambo's question, "Do we get to win this time?" keeps the issue of home-front betrayal alive. Upon arriving in Vietnam, Rambo explains to his Vietnamese scout why he has returned: "When I came back to the States, I found another war going on. . . . A war against the soldiers returning."

Hollywood-made vets who return to Vietnam to continue the mission are common in films from the mid-1980s on. Many of these films, such as *Missing in Action* (1984), are "Rambo" knockoffs about searching for MIAs or rescuing POWs, while others depict searches for other things lost in the war or left behind. Joe, in *Heated Vengeance* (1982), goes back to find a woman and the child he fathered.

For the most part, the films of the mid-to-late 1980s are the reworked stock of the previous twenty years. Vets with PTSD can be found in *Cease Fire* (1984), *Exterminator II* (1984), *The Park Is Mine* (1985), *Birdy* (1985), *Kill Zone* (1985), *Alamo Bay* (1985), and *House* (1985). Vets are treated "like shit" in *Operation Nam* (1987), women betray vets in *Alamo Bay* (1985), *Cease Fire* (1984), and *Betrayed* (1988), while Mickey in *Choose Me* (1984) is a dangerous predator. The idea that soldiers brought their weapons home with them was never more explicit than in *Armed Response* (1987), when Jim retrieves an automatic weapon and a hand grenade from a box and says, "I had a feeling I'd need this stuff again someday. Brought it back from 'Nam."

The Return of the "Political" Veteran

There was one new important story line that emerged during the 1980s. Almost as if Hollywood was anticipating a revival of interest in the politics of Vietnam veterans during the Gulf War of 1990–91, veterans with some political identity began to reappear around 1982. Viewers hoping that filmmakers would finally get the story right, however, were disappointed. Most of the films in this category were good vet/bad vet films that drew the line between the two types of Vietnam veteran rather than between Vietnam and World War II vets, as earlier films had. Unlike such earlier films as *Electra Glide in Blue* (1973), which was a postwar story juxtaposing "troubled" vets alongside veterans who had made the adjustment to civilian life, the 1980s versions of this genre usually returned to Vietnam to locate the origins of the disagreements between veterans. The "bad" vets are introduced to us as having been discipline problems or as having taken a political stand during the war. Then they are shown in the postwar years as deranged, often criminal, characters at odds with "good" vets.

The strongest entry on this list is *Final Mission* (1984). Through a flashback we see Vince Deacon and Will Slater in Laos in 1972. Slater has defected to the enemy and is captured by Deacon. After the war, Slater goes looking for Deacon, who is now a Los Angeles cop. Slater employs his military demolition skills to kill Deacon's wife and son. This pushes Deacon over the edge. He finds Slater in the small town of Pineville and kills him before going on a rampage. The final scenes of the film show Deacon in a one-man war against a posse of Pineville residents and the National Guard. Its ending, plagiarized from *First Blood,* has Deacon's former commanding officer, Colonel Cain, talking Deacon down from his mountaintop retreat. Unlike Rambo, though, Deacon is ultimately brought down in a hail of gunfire.

Made by Cirio H. Santiago, said to be "the most prolific of Vietnam B-movie directors" (Malo, 1994, 149), *Final Mission* is interesting because of its willingness to even suggest that GIs were less than loyal to the cause. But Santiago overplays his hand and gives us a caricature. GI desertions were not uncommon in Vietnam, but defections were rare. Moreover, disloyalty to the cause does not mean disloyalty to the country. The flashback scene of Slater's capture doesn't put his defection in context for us. When Deacon captures Slater, he asks, "Why?"

Slater simply answers, "You wouldn't understand." With this unqualified portrayal of Slater as a traitor, Santiago cast aspersions on the loyalty of all dissenting GIs. Santiago's effort to clarify Slater's motivation for us only makes matters worse. In the first present-time scene, we see him as a bandanna-wearing member of a terrorist group holding a hostage—a collection of symbols commonly used to mischaracterize 1970s-era leftist radicalism. It is now clear: GI opposition to the war, treason, crime, and terrorism all fit in the same package. And if Slater the dissident vet is "bad," Deacon the "good" vet is so badly damaged that he too must be destroyed.

Eye of the Eagle and *Night Wars*, both released in 1987, also featured defectors. The video jacket for the first tells the story: "The enemy is murdering U.S. soldiers. The enemy must be destroyed. The enemy . . . is American." The enemy is the "Lost Command," a unit of disgruntled AWOLs and deserters who are shown as anti-officer roughnecks who smoke pot and shoot up dope. The unit has taken up arms against the regular army that has not been allowed to win the war it was sent to fight. At best, the film is a gross exaggeration of the actual incidents of fragging and unit refusals to fight that actually took place during the war.

In *Night Wars*, Trent and Jimmy suffer from what their counselor calls "survivor guilt." Through their flashbacks and nightmares, we learn that they left Johnny behind when they escaped from a POW camp nine years earlier. While prisoners, they had all been tortured by McGregor, a dissident GI who had gone over the Vietcong. Again, the film gives us no clue as to McGregor's motives but in the context of the conservatism of the late 1980s, that was not necessary. Disloyalty to the mission was treasonous, and the simple reminder that dissent within the military was a factor in America's first lost war was enough to stir the emotional juices of filmgoing patriots. And, as in the earlier films *Deathdream* and *House*, zombies haunt postwar America. In one nightmare scene, McGregor's zombie speaks to Jimmy from Vietnam: "There is no death here. Just pain. And we're all going to be here a long long time." When Trent and Jimmy return to Vietnam in their dreams, their mission is as much to rescue America by "killing" the dissident GI and zombie McGregor as it is to rescue Johnny.

. . . . . .

In the fall of 1990, Rep. John Murtha of Pennsylvania visited U.S. troops stationed in the Persian Gulf region. Murtha told the *New York Times* that he found soldiers there preoccupied with the level of support they were receiving from the folks back home. Murtha said it was "the aura of Vietnam. . . . They've seen all these movies. They worry. They wonder." Murtha, of course, had no way of knowing whether the troops he had talked to had seen *any* Vietnam movies, so his comment is mostly interesting for what it tells us about him. What it tells us is that, as a policymaker, he was less interested in the actual historical record than in what the public believed to be true, regardless of how people had come by their beliefs. Murtha was aware that film had created a widespread climate of anger and anxiety about how Vietnam War veterans had been treated, and he was willing to tap that well of emotion to evoke the political response he wanted—support for the administration's war in the Gulf.

Film was the most important medium through which the history of the Vietnam War was rewritten as a story of veterans coming home. Mediated by film, American memories of the war in Vietnam changed during the 1970s and 1980s to the point that the details of the war itself were forgotten and memories of the abuse of veterans were constructed. Anti-war GIs and veterans made it to the screen in very small numbers and then almost always as characters whose mental and physical disabilities overshadowed their political identity. The image of the violent and emotionally dysfunctional veteran dominated the films made about Vietnam during these decades.

The full extent to which cinema led the way in the re-imaging of the Vietnam veteran is debatable. The proliferation of wigged-out movie vets in the wake of PTSD's legitimation by DSM-III in 1980 suggests that Hollywood was just reflecting what mainstream America had already accepted as a truthful legacy of the war. But PTSD appeared in film long before the mental health professionals had identified and named it, suggesting that filmmakers were leading, rather than following, mental health practice. Brahmin's behavior in Russ Meyer's *Motor Psycho* (1965) fits the description of PTSD years before it was named as such in a clinical context. *Jud* (1971) and *Stanley* (1972) also predated the public recognition of post-Vietnam syndrome, while *Twilight's Last Gleaming* (1977), *Heroes* (1977), and *The Choirboys* (1977), with their PTSD-related flashbacks, and *Black Sunday* (1977), called the "archetypal 'crazy vet' movie" by one critic, all appeared before PTSD became an authorized diagnostic category.

Moreover, "flashbacks," said to be a symptom of PTSD, is itself a term borrowed from film. Flashbacks were widely used in Vietnam War films to tell about the war from some later point in time. But the flashbacks in Vietnam War films weren't of the usual sort; they were not descriptions of earlier events spliced into a narrative. The flashbacks in Vietnam War films were in the minds of the veterans portrayed, vivid memories of traumatic events. Filmmakers thus virtually created the definition of a flashback as a trauma-induced, mental phenomenon. The use of flashbacks allowed filmmakers to filter the history of the war through the memories of filmic veterans. It was a technique that lent credibility to the story being told, which thus seemed to be an eyewitness account. But flashbacks added an interpretative layer between the audience and historical reality. Filmmakers took enormous license with this film-about-a-memory-about-a-war device and largely invented a war of their own imagining.[18]

If flashbacks migrated from screenplays to psychiatry journals it is probably because they functioned similarly in both settings. Cinematic flashbacks created a blank space between the historical record of the war and the viewer that could be sketched in by the artist, whereas mental flashbacks filled a space between wartime experience and actual memory. It was the term assigned by psychiatrists to some, but not all, memories about the war. Those memories that mental health professionals wanted to treat as symptoms of trauma and associated with behavioral pathologies were labeled flashbacks. Flashbacks were not blank slates for psychiatrists to write on in quite the same way that they were for filmmakers, but the *meaning* of mental flashbacks *was* something created out of the interaction between psychiatrist and patient. The flashback put mental distance between memory and experience, allowing the veteran to reinterpret and even reimagine what had actually happened to him. In conjunction with psychiatric intervention, popular culture, and the additional difficulties of life in post-Vietnam America, flashbacks functioned to reconfigure memory for individual veterans, just as they had functioned through film to rewrite history for America.[19]

TEN

We Are What We Remember

> A crucial question to examine is the role of intellectuals as interpreters and perhaps even fabricators of the national imagination.
> —David Schalle, *War and the Ivory Tower*

This or any other attempt to rethink our history produces additional challenges.[1] The new perspective on post-Vietnam America presented in this book reopens questions that for many people have been closed and filed away. One of those questions concerns the well-being of the men and women who fought the war. There is no gainsaying the fact that wars exact an enormous price from those who fight them. Fifty-eight thousand Americans were killed and three hundred thousand wounded in the Vietnam War. The families and communities who lost their loved ones and friends in the war continue to bear that burden. Yet, broken bodies are only part of the cost of war. Short-term military service, such as that demanded of draftees and those who entered service under the threat of the draft, disrupts lives. It interrupts educational plans, derails employment and career opportunities, and wreaks havoc on family and love lives. Attempts to measure the impact of the war on the lives of veterans have proved inconclusive, but the high rates of divorce, suicide, and drug and alcohol addiction among Vietnam veterans suggest that those who fought the war have been accorded anything but privileged treatment.

The hurt and confusion that many Americans felt with the loss of the war was exacerbated by the inadequacy of the attention given veterans. Assessing blame for those wrongs was part of the process by which the country put the war behind it and moved on. But the laying of blame for the loss of the war and the mistreatment of veterans at the feet of the anti-war movement was misdirected. It was a form of scapegoating, and as such it left the real sources of peoples' troubles unaddressed. The war itself went unexamined, and the leaders who got us into it were never held accountable. America's war in Vietnam remains a festering sore covered over by such mythic bandages as the spat-upon veteran.

Myths help people come to terms with difficult periods of their past. They provide explanations for why things happened. Often, the explanations offered by myths help reconcile disparities between a group's self-image and the historical record of the group's behavior. The myth of the spat-upon veteran functions in this way by providing an alibi for why the most powerful and righteous nation on earth (as America perceives itself to be) lost the war to an underdeveloped Asian nation. The myth says, in effect, that we were not beaten by the Vietnamese but were defeated on the home front by fifth columnists.

The myth also functions to reverse the verdict of history, to find the innocent guilty and the guilty innocent. The indicters were themselves indicted as the responsibility for the loss of the war was shifted from those whose policies had failed to those who were critical of the policies all along. In the process, the resolve and resourcefulness of the Vietnamese people was denied, and the credibility and character of Vietnam veterans, who were the most convincing witnesses for the case against the government, was attacked. Initially dismissed as impostors and then discredited as deviant malcontents, this generation of "bad" war veterans were eventually recast as "mad" war veterans.

The myth sullies the reputation of those individuals and organizations who dared to dissent, and strips Vietnam veterans of their true place in history as gallant fighters against the war. The identity crisis supposedly suffered by Vietnam veterans because they were denied the military victory of their youth might better be laid at the feet of a culture that confers manhood on warriors, but not on peacemakers.

In *The New Winter Soldiers*, Richard Moser writes about what he calls the "soldier ideal." The soldier ideal is constituted of the images we have of soldiers and the values we attach to those images. There is a duality in the American soldier ideal, he says, between the dominant vision of the frontier fighter and the defender of empire, and the alternative figure of citizen-soldier. Soldiers of the first sort live in a world separated from civilian concerns, fighting wars with neatly drawn lines between good guys and bad guys. The citizen-soldier, on the other hand, as represented by the Revolutionary War's minuteman and by the armed fugitive slave of the Civil War era, is someone who fights to create or defend freedom. He is a character capable of crossing boundaries, of fighting as a soldier but also as a citizen against wars he deems unjust. It is this spirit of the citizen-soldier that anti-war Vietnam veterans connected with, and thus began to transform what it meant to be an American soldier. The loss of the war in Vietnam made their identification with the citizen-soldier ideal all the more imperative for Vietnam veterans. But their place as citizen-soldiers who stood up against military authority, racism, and genocidal warfare was stolen from them. By the late 1970s, the culture of empire and its dominant image of the soldier ideal was reasserting itself, and the fabricators of the national imagination lent themselves to the pathologizing of the Vietnam veteran's image.

On a societal level, we have largely forgotten that much of the energy and inspiration for the anti-war movement came from veterans themselves. Such political amnesia can be dangerous. For militarists, the failure to remember the GI and veteran opposition to the war could lead to overly optimistic assessments of what to expect from soldiers in a future conflict. The Bush administration, indeed, may have made just such a miscalculation in leading the country into the Gulf War. Writing in the *Catholic Radical* (1998, 5), Australian peace activist Ciaron O'Reilly reported that more serious resistance to the Gulf War "came from within the military than from the peace movement." According to him, more than one thousand U.S. soldiers filed for conscientious objector status during the war. On the other end of the spectrum, some peace activists fed pro-military propaganda during the Gulf War by giving credence to erroneous claims of the antiwar movement's hostility toward Vietnam veterans. They had forgotten their own history.

The Gulf War of 1990–91 is a marker by which we can assess the impact of the myth of the spat-upon Vietnam veteran on American political culture. The myth's awesome power to sow confusion, stir political passions, and lead large numbers of citizens into war was exhibited at the time. But that was by no means the end of the story. Just as the Vietnam War was used to frame our rationalizations for invading the Persian Gulf, so too, it appears, has the return of soldiers from the Gulf been made to conform to the now-dominant coming-home narrative of the Vietnam veteran.

The Gulf War, like the Vietnam War, was a strange event. Although nominally it was a victory for the United States, it was fought entirely from the air by a small number of elite pilots who inflicted a kill ratio on the Iraqis even more obscene than that visited upon the Vietnamese. Notwithstanding the yellow ribbon hoopla that surrounded their mission, there was little that Gulf veterans could take pride in. As veterans qua veterans just what were they supposed to feel? What could they ask their countrymen to feel for them? What identity could they derive from a war that was not really a war?

Most Gulf War veterans grew up in the 1970s and 1980s when the images of the dysfunctional Vietnam veteran were being constructed. The only veterans they had to model their own coming-home experiences after were the veterans of the Vietnam era. Likewise, their ideas of what to expect from the society were shaped by the stories of veterans spat upon by activists and forgotten by their own government. One of the most singularly powerful films about a Vietnam veteran appeared in 1990, just as the Bush administration was committing another 150,000 troops to the Gulf. *Jacob's Ladder* was about the government's conspiracy to cover up its use of GIs in Vietnam for a drug experiment. The veteran, Jacob Singer, (or his zombie—we're never sure) is tormented by demons. Through his deranged flashbacks and flashforwards, the story of America defeated by the only power on earth capable of such a feat—America itself—is told yet again. Starring Tim Robbins, Danny Aiello, and Macaulay Caulkin, *Jacob's Ladder* hit the cultural mainstream on November 2, 1990, just as the country's emotions were being revved up for war.

The outcome was predictable. Within months after the bombing stopped, men home from the Persian Gulf complained of mysterious ailments and reported erratic behavior. One vet complained of fluorescent vomit, others of semen that burned or blistered their wives. Stories of birth defects in veterans' children proliferated. Newspapers reported high levels of cancer among Gulf War veterans.[2]

The failure of epidemiological studies and other medical research to confirm the reality of the sicknesses didn't stop the rumor mill from churning out causes. Nerve gas, secret drug experiments, and deadly toxins spread by the Iraqis were alleged to be the culprits. Many of the stories contained more than a hint of conspiracy. Either our own government was covering up its use of GIs as guinea pigs or hiding information it had about Iraqi chemical agents. Years later, news stories about Gulf War syndrome appear on a weekly basis, while the war itself recedes from memory.

We are what we remember, but how do we remember? Writing about the legacy of Vietnam in *Tangled Memories* (1997), Marita Sturken reminds us that memory is a narrative rather than a replica of an experience that can be retrieved and relived. We remember through the representations of our experiences, through the symbols that stand for the events. While the events themselves are frozen in time, their representations are not. Our memories of what happened can be changed by altering the images of the events. The power to control memory is thus bound up with the power to control the representations of history.

e Are What We Remember

e a society with a strong oral tradition, America today remem- history through visual imagery. Film, print, and electronic media are very capital intensive, which means that most Americans are consumers, not producers, of the images through which they remember. Our sense of who we are, derived as it is from the icons through which we collectively represent our historical selves, is heavily mediated by the institutions of popular culture and mass communication. As we approach the twenty-first century, the twisted imagery of Vietnam continues to infect our culture and cloud our political discourse. Today, mention of Vietnam veterans is likely to elicit a nodding recognition of the retarded Forrest Gump in the film of the same name, or the derelict, Russell, who self-destructs for Old Glory in *Independence Day,* both Hollywood products of the 1990s. To look into these films, observes film scholar William Adams (1989, 166), "is to watch an historical image in the making, a public memory in the course of construction."

Reclaiming our memory of the Vietnam era entails a struggle against very powerful institutional forces that toy with our imaginings of the war for reasons of monetary, political, or professional gain. It is a struggle for our individual and collective identities that calls us to reappropriate the making of our own memories. It is a struggle of epic importance. Studies of the twentieth century will shape America's national identity for decades to come. How Vietnam is to be remembered looms large on the agenda of turn-of-the-century legacy studies. Remembered as a war that was lost because of betrayal at home, Vietnam becomes a modern-day Alamo that must be avenged, a pretext for more war and generations of more veterans. Remembered as a war in which soldiers and pacifists joined hands to fight for peace, Vietnam symbolizes popular resistance to political authority and the dominant images of what it means to be a good American. By challenging myths like that of the spat-upon Vietnam veteran, we reclaim our role in the writing of our own history, the construction of our own memory, and the making of our own identity.

NOTES

Notes to Chapter Two

A longer version of this chapter can be found in Lembcke 1995.

1. "Operation Yellow Ribbon" was founded in the fall of 1990 by Gaye Jacobson, a manager for a Silicon Valley, California, defense contractor. Later incorporated in the state of California, Operation Yellow Ribbon eventually grew to twenty-seven chapters with five thousand members in six states. Jacobson, who had a son in the Gulf, initially volunteered her time to the organization but her board of directors eventually voted her $4,000 a month in salary. In April 1991, she founded another organization, the American Awareness Foundation ("Gaye Jacobson" 1991).

2. See the statement of Archbishop Daniel Pilarczyk, the president of the National Conference of Catholic Bishops, in Goldman 1990.

While the question of "proportionality" was a hypothetical one in the fall of 1990, it was clear within a few weeks after the bombing of Iraq began in January 1991 that the United States was inflicting massive civilian casualties on the country and generally engaging in gross overkill.

3. The first reports were about Sgt. Michael R. Ange's lawsuit over the constitutionality of the orders that he be transferred with his unit to the Gulf. The same story told of marine corporal Jefferey A. Patterson's court-martial for refusing to be shipped to the Gulf. By November 26, the War Resisters League, a pacifist group, was reporting "several hundred" applications for conscientious objector status by in-service soldiers while the Pentagon gave a lower number (Gonzalez 1990; LeMoyne 1990a).

4. On December 9, Bush claimed in a speech that his "alliance" was firm on the need for war against Iraq even though there were no longer hostages and even if Iraq pulled out of Kuwait (Dowd 1990a).

5. See the *New York Times*, December 17, 1990, p. B14, for an example of the advertisement.

6. Operation Eagle was founded during the fall of 1990 by two retired marines, Paul F. Roughan and Ray M. Kelley although it was not incorporated in Massachusetts until February 25, 1991. Articles of incorporation for Operation Eagle were obtained from the Commonwealth of Massachusetts.

7. Most of the information on Operation Eagle comes from copies of its own literature and a collection of newspaper stories kept on file at the Catholic Worker House in Worcester, Massachusetts.

8. Horowitz wrote, "To disarm their critics, [Gulf War protesters] volunteer their past 'mistakes,' like spitting on U.S. soldiers returning from Vietnam." Given that the press was trying to frame the opposition to the Gulf War with the narrative of anti-war movement hostility toward war veterans, it is also possible that Vietnam-era activists were misquoted or had their words taken out of context.

9. Until memoirs are written, we might not know how consciously the Bush administration pursued the tactic of switching from one reason to another in order to make nonsense out of any effort to figure out what the war was about. In a moment of rare incisiveness, however, the *New York Times* suggested on November 1, 1990, that the tactic was rehearsed. Referring to the way the administration had handled Congress during the just-completed struggle over the budget, the *Times* wrote, "In an eerie replay of the budget ordeal, the President and his advisers are talking in different voices, sending different messages and moving back and forth between opposing positions—sometimes at the same moment." The *Times'* suggestion, however, that the resulting "confusion" was functioning to "redirect the public's attention in the week before elections away from the budget battle" seems superficial. Rather than redirecting the public's attention, the shuffling of narratives was rendering attention to the Gulf War, in any cognitive sense, nearly impossible. See Dowd 1990b.

10. This is Virginia Carmichael's explication of how perfecting myths perform (1990, 1–7). She attributes the notion of perfecting myth to Kenneth Burke (1969, 240–41).

11. The best of such analyses are MacArthur 1992, and Kellner 1992.

Notes to Chapter Three

1. Useem (1973, 54) reports a "series of isolated but public draft card destructions" that took place during 1964–66. Primary sources cited in this chapter by the author indicate that veterans from previous wars participated in as least some of these burnings.

2. The Ia Drang Valley, near Pleiku in the Central Highlands of Vietnam, had been the site of a major battle in October 1965. Two thousand Vietnamese and three hundred U.S. soldiers died in the fight, the highest one-week casualty rate of the war for the United States. On November 30, 1965, CBS television aired a special report on the fight for the Ia Drang Valley.

3. Simultaneously, a group called Veterans and Reservists to End the War

in Vietnam was also formed. The two groups differed over membership, politics, and strategy, although they cooperated on many fronts.

4. The early activities of Veterans for Peace chapters in several cities are reported in "Minutes of Meeting at Hotel Sheraton-Carlton, Washington, D.C.," dated May 14, 1966. The document is located in the Veterans for Peace collection at the Wisconsin State Historical Society Library (hereafter cited as WSHSL), Madison.

5. This account is complied from various newspaper stories. See the *Chicago Tribune*, the *New York Herald Tribune*, and the *New York Times* of March 27, 1966. The incidents of spitting were reported in the *Chicago Tribune* story.

6. This account of the Fort Hood Three case is taken from Halstead 1991, pp. 174–84.

7. Bojarski's letter was reproduced as a leaflet titled "GI's in Vietnam want to come Home!" Fifth Avenue Peace Parade Committee files, WSHSL.

8. Many of the details in the following paragraphs come from the files of the GI Press Service in the Student Mobilization Committee Collection, WSHSL.

9. Halstead (1991, 479) provides a good summary of the refusal of GIs to fight. In April 1970, Colman McCarthy wrote a lengthy *Washington Post* column about the "warriors who oppose war." In it he noted, "Their numbers are still small but more and more are falling out of line. Which is a new kind of domino theory."

10. The September 29 memo and the November 22 letter are in the Vietnam Moratorium Committee Collection (hereafter cited as VMC), box 1, folder 4, WSHSL.

11. VMC, box 1, folder 7, WSHSL.

Notes to Chapter Four

1. Wells (1994, 326) recalls Nixon's "fixation" on the role of Jews in the protests.

2. The Johnson administration's counterattacks against the anti-war movement were halfhearted and ineffective. Some officials, concluded Wells (1994, 150), "feared the political fallout of stifling dissent too much and of appearing frightened of even small clusters of protesters.

3. Press release from Rep. Bob Wilson's office, October 30, 1969, VMC, box 1, folder 4, WSHSL; Associated Press wire service copy, November 11, 1969, VMC, box 1, folder 7, WSHSL.

4. The reports of atrocities that follow are all from the same source.

5. There was no *New York Times* coverage of Winter Soldier. Thorne and Butler noted that television news "barely covered the event."

6. Turner (1996, 42) cites a poll showing widespread public disbelief that "our boys" were responsible for My Lai: "the assigning of 'madness' to and the blaming of veterans for crimes committed" functioned as an alibi for America's political culture. It enabled Americans to feel it was a few "crazies" who were responsible, rather than their government's policy or themselves.

7. My own experience illustrates the point. Most men I was with in the Headquarters Battery of the Forty-first Artillery Group during 1969 laughed at the idea that they would ever consider themselves "veterans." The image of the veteran was a conservative, pro-military one that these anti-military soldiers had contempt for. Upon returning home from Vietnam, many of us accommodated the veteran identification in the qualified sense that it meant *anti-war* veteran.

8. There are reports (see Loeb 1994, 78) that Vietnam veterans were spat on by convention delegates, but these reports have proved impossible to document. One source referred me to a September 4, 1972, *Time* magazine story, "A New Majority for Four More Years?" but that story (p. 17) only reported protesters spitting at delegates.

9. The historian Christian Appy has argued that homecoming experiences varied by socioeconomic status and that working-class veterans perceived more hostility from activists than did middle-class returnees. He may have a point, but there is no evidence to warrant his conclusion (1993, 314) that GIs turned to mainstream veterans organizations for support because they returned from Vietnam convinced that anti-war people would be "against them."

Figley and Leventman (1990) make even more sweeping claims, writing that veterans were "hated by the war's opponents" (xviii) and that veterans in college "found themselves rejected by their age peers" (xxviii). Research reported in U.S. Senate 1972, and in Hassemer and McCary (1974) refutes these claims.

Notes to Chapter Five

1. I obtained copies of the reports from the library of the Association of the Bar on January 29, 1996. Edwin J. Wesley, who was chairman of the Special Committee on Demonstration Observation, wrote an op-ed piece describing the project in the May 6, 1972 *New York Times*.

2. The other sources were chosen for their proximity to general anti-war activity or to specific events, such as large local demonstrations against the war.

3. The on-line Roper collection is DIALOG Information Services Inc. *Public Opinion ONLINE (POLL)*. My research of polls was assisted by John E. Lane.

This is not to say that acts of hostility against Vietnam veterans by persons not associated with the anti-war movement were not reported. One reported instance, recounted in chapter 2, was that of VFW members harassing VVAW members at Valley Forge. The psychiatrist Robert Jay Lifton noted (1973, 99) that a veteran told him about having been spat upon, but the act was not attributed to an anti-war activist.

4. The fact that the conservative political culture remembers anti-war people spitting on veterans, when virtually all the evidence points to the opposite being true, suggests that what psychologists call "projection" is at work. By "projecting" their own bad behavior onto others, the guilty parties are able to save face and deny what they actually did. A later chapter explores other psychological dimensions of the spitting stories.

5. For more on the treatment of Vietnam veterans in VA hospitals, see Scott 1993. The harassment of VVAW members at Valley Forge is recorded in the video, *Different Sons* (author's possession). Stories of rejection in American Legion and VFW halls were so common in the early 1970s that they achieved the status of folklore, according to Egendorf (1985).

6. Those linkages are explored in a later chapter.

7. Lembcke to O'Connor, February 6, 1995; Mustaciuolo to Lembcke, February 22, 1995, in the possession of the author.

8. The report of a professor calling a veteran a killer is highly believable, especially given the politically charged climate of college classrooms at that time. On the other hand, it is sometimes the case that students take personally what a professor means as a general or analytical point. Following lectures about inequality in America, for example, I have had students, sons or daughters of corporate executives, ask if I mean to say that their parents are mean and greedy people. Sometimes they will say they feel personally attacked. In similar fashion, it would be very understandable if a veteran, listening to a lecture on, say, My Lai, interpreted the professor's remarks as a personal attack on himself.

Notes to Chapter Six

1. Usually Penelope is held up as the symbol of the virtuous wife but Bell (1991, 348–51) notes versions of the story in which she had sex with all one hundred-plus suitors, thus producing Pan. What might be important is that, even in antiquity, stories about men at war cast their women in roles that raised eyebrows.

2. Katzman (1993) writes that civilian society has also been leery of its war veterans. Alfred Schuetz wrote about veterans as outsiders in the context of World War II. His 1945 article, "The Homecomer," is reprinted in Figley and Leventman (1990).

3. My research on the German and French cases was assisted by Walter Landberg and Christina Davilas.

4. There are some reports of German soldiers actually returning home to a hero's welcome.

5. A seminar I taught in the fall of 1995 provides a case in point. Most of the twelve students came into the seminar familiar with PTSD and its association with Vietnam veterans. Few, if any, knew what "fragging" was or had any knowledge of the GI anti-war movement.

6. These characterizations of the political left and right derive from sociological theory. See, for example, Zeitlin (1995).

7. Westmoreland made several speeches while in the States. See Halstead 1991, 228–29, for a summary of them.

8. Halberstam attributes the description of the *Times* to *Time* magazine.

9. Schell is quoted by H. Bruce Franklin in *M.I.A., or, Myth Making in America* (1992, 60). Franklin's book is an excellent debunking of the POW/MIA myth.

10. Spiro Agnew's speeches are collected in Coyne 1972.

Notes to Chapter Seven

1. See Kifner 1972c.

2. Calley was convicted on March 29, 1971, of the premeditated murder of South Vietnamese civilians at My Lai. The *New York Times* began publishing the Pentagon Papers on June 13, 1971.

3. Peter Bourne (1970, 40–43, 76), who was an army psychiatrist in Vietnam identified the reasons for the low psychiatric casualty rate. Among them were the predictable length of the duty tour in Vietnam (one year), excellent mail service, the availability of hot meals, quick medical evacuations, and the belief of GIs in their military superiority. Bourne also reported that "antiwar sentiment in the United States appears to have had little effect upon the motivational level of the troops in the field."

4. That June, of course, the *Times* itself took a giant step against the war when it began publishing the Pentagon Papers.

5. Wilson (1977, 54) found that fully half of Vietnam veterans he studied believed that the purpose of the war was either "U.S. Imperialism/capitalism" (27.3 percent) or for the United States to gain a "Political/Military foothold in the World" (22.2 percent).

6. In her book, *Worlds of Hurt* (1996, 13–14), Kali Tal makes a similar observation. She argues that the rehabilitation of the veteran image, which was a component of rewriting the history of the war, made stories of GI atrocities in Vietnam seem "surreal" by 1990. While I agree that the real history of the war seems unreal twenty-five years later, I don't think it is because the veteran image has been rehabilitated. Rather, the unrelenting disparagement of veterans in popular culture has destroyed their credibility. What seems unreal is

that the PTSD-stricken basket case that constitutes the popular perception of the Vietnam veteran could be the same person who terrorized Vietnamese civilians.

7. On reading Nordheimer's account (1971) of Johnson's death, one finds very little in it that would sustain a diagnosis of what we now think of as post-traumatic stress syndrome. What is clear from the story is that Johnson suffered from poverty and the feeling that the army and others were exploiting his status as a Medal of Honor winner.

8. Young (1995) attributes the legitimation of PTSD to the ascendancy of a diagnostic tradition associated with psychiatrist Emil Kraepelin, a contemporary of Sigmund Freud.

9. In their book *Deviance and Medicalization: From Badness to Sickness* (1992), Peter Conrad and Joseph W. Schneider argue that the distinction between what is considered "criminal" and what is considered "sick" or "mad" is the outcome of social and political processes. Much of the literature on the social construction of mental health categories was influenced by Michel Foucault's *Madness and Civilization* (1965).

10. Bey and Zecchinelli (1974) reported similar findings. Many of their patients were men who had been ridiculed, harassed, and scapegoated by other GIs and officers. See also *Psychiatric News,* October 3, 1986, pp. 22–23.

11. The centrality of grief to the notion of PTSD is evident from the title of Chaim Shatan's 1973 article in the *American Journal of Orthopsychiatry*: "The Grief of Soldiers: Vietnam Combat Veterans' Self-Help Movement."

12. Critiques of the PVS/PTSD formulation can also be found in Fleming 1985; Frankel 1994; and Young 1995.

13. Herman (1992) writes about the problem of sexual abuse and memory using the case of Vietnam veterans as an analogy. Loftus and Ketcham (1995) treat the link between trauma and repressed memory critically, referring to the "myth of repressed memory."

14. Solotaroff is referring to what psychiatrists call "factitious PTSD." See Sparr and Pankratz 1983; and Lynn and Belza 1984.

15. Studies of suicide are similarly difficult to interpret. The Centers for Disease Control (1987) reported that fifty-seven thousand Vietnam veterans had committed suicide by 1983. The popular interpretation of that figure attributed those suicides to combat-related PTSD. However, a similar number of non-Vietnam veterans of the same era had also committed suicide, a fact also reported in the study. This raises questions about the popular interpretation. Moreover, just because a suicide victim is a veteran does not mean there is a causal relationship between the two facts. The downturn in the economy following the OPEC oil crisis of the early 1970s and the wave of plant closings that swept the country later in the decade hit working-class veterans very hard.

Robert Huffman (1972), an army psychiatrist who served in Vietnam, reported to the Veterans Administration that only 8 percent of the 610 patients he had seen in Vietnam had combat-related problems. "Most of the patients," he said, "were support troops who had never seen combat."

16. Thompson's book, *Hell's Angels*, was very popular. The widespread association of veterans with bikers, particularly in southern California where the Hells Angels rode, probably explains why the early movies about Vietnam veterans, such as the 1965 film *Motor Psycho*, were biker stories.

17. See Fentress and Wickham 1994 for a discussion of what the authors call "social memory."

18. The best available source on the GI/veteran anti-war movement is a special issue of the journal *Vietnam Generation*, "GI Resistance: Soldiers and Veterans Against the War," vol. 2, no. 1, 1990. Richard Moser's *The New Winter Soldiers: GI and Veteran Dissent during the Vietnam Era*, which is based on oral histories, was published in 1996.

19. Maurice Halbwachs' work ([1925] 1980) undergirds much of what we know about collective memory.

20. Richard Moser develops this point more fully in *The New Winter Soldiers* (1996).

Notes to Chapter Eight

1. Theweleit (1987, 256) says, "In the bourgeois German vernacular . . . awareness of flowing . . . lives on only in a negative, defensive form: in words such as 'ejaculation' (*Erguss*) or 'copulate' (*verkuppeln*). The first is uncontrolled; the second immoral." This could explain why there are numerous references in German literature to spat-upon veterans of World War I, while spitting does not appear in the descriptions of acts of hostility against soldiers returning from Indochina in the French literature.

2. See Eisenstaedt 1990, and *Time* magazine, September 4, 1995. My research on the contrasts between the kissing sailor and spat-upon vets was assisted by Kate Christou.

Notes to Chapter Nine

1. Sometimes veterans from previous wars functioned as stand-ins for the good veteran. This was the case in *Homer* and *Joe*, both made in 1970. *Homer* is a generation-gap story that pits an anti-war high school senior against his small-town VFW chapter. *Joe* is a bit more complicated. Working-class Joe and middle-class Bill, both veterans of previous wars, share a disdain for the hippie drug culture and general permissiveness they see around them.

2. Christopher (1994, 472) points out that movies like these "displac[ed] guilt about the war from mainstream America onto the 'trash' soldiers who

fought it and lost it." My point is that the "trash" soldier image also functioned as an alibi for the politicized veteran: these veterans were political for reasons having to do with their cultural background, not the war.

3. *The Bus Is Coming* (1971), featuring a black veteran, developed similar themes in an urban setting.

4. *Tracks* ends at the cemetery. No one had come to the internment of Jack's buddy—no family, no friends. Jack chases off the cemetery's grounds crew and jumps into the grave on top of the coffin. We then see an open coffin, but in it instead of a body we see a collection of military hardware. Jack ascends from the grave in combat attire. He has bands of ammunition wrapped around him and an automatic weapon in his hand. Like Andy in *Deathdream,* Jack is a vet that America will not be allowed to forget.

5. The rest of the 1977 film fare is pretty stock stuff. *The Choirboys* is a veterans-as-cops story. The cops are corrupt. The portrayal of one cop's flashbacks inverts reality by showing him trapped in a tunnel, with the Vietcong trying to flush him out with a flamethrower. *Good Guys Wear Black* finishes the unfinished business of the Vietnam War through martial arts, assassinations, and conspiracies.

6. *Go Tell the Spartans* was set in Vietnam and was about the war, but very few people saw this low-budget film.

7. Martin Kasindorf, "Fonda: A Person of Many Parts." *New York Times Sunday Magazine,* February 3, 1974, p. 16. The biographical details in the preceding paragraphs are from this article.

8. Gilbert subsequently assigned his rights to Dowd. Correspondence and documents related to the legal settlement between Dowd and the Jayne Production Corporation can be found in box 19, folder 1 of the Waldo Salt Papers at the University of California, Los Angeles.

9. Bruce Gilbert, who worked with Nancy Dowd on *Buffalo Ghost* and with Salt on *Coming Home* provided continuity between the two stages of writing. Gilbert was present at most of the interviews that Salt conducted with Vietnam veterans.

10. There are transcripts of four different interviews that Salt conducted with Terry Hager, dated November 6 and November 11, 1974, and July 25 and August 7, 1975, Waldo Salt Papers at the University of California, Los Angeles.

11. This is from a draft dated April 23, 1976.

12. My attempts to document army policy were unsuccessful. Most veterans with whom I have spoken remember processing out of Vietnam the way I have described it here. One recalled an application procedure for permission to bring home war trophies, such as captured AK-47s. But he also recalled that weapons brought home that way had to be rendered inoperable before shipment and that except for officers very few GIs even knew there was such a procedure.

13. Hager was trying to make a point that there were a lot of frustrated veterans who have also had a lot of military skill and experience. Whereas in *The Stone Killer* the veterans become Mafia mercenaries, Hager is talking about their potential for revolutionary armed struggle.

14. *More American Graffiti,* a collage of nostalgia for the 1960s that was antiwar in content, portrayed the resistance of a soldier in Vietnam but contained no direct references to veterans or their coming-home experiences.

15. *More American Graffiti* was, like *Hair,* misplaced in time. Set in 1965–67, the absence of veterans in its story was not necessarily unrealistic, but then neither was it particularly relevant to the politics of the late 1970s, a time when the accuracy of the coming-home experience was an issue.

16. Better harbingers of what was coming were the avenger narratives of *The Exterminator* (1980) and *Nighthawks* (1981).

17. A timely film, in this regard, was *Friendly Fire* (1979), a made-for-television movie based on the true story of Michael Mullen's family when it learns of his death in Vietnam. Peg and Gene Mullen of Waterloo, Iowa, are skeptical of the explanation that Michael was killed by "friendly fire." When they request further information, they run up against a bureaucratic stone wall and begin to suspect a cover up. Like *Twilight's Last Gleaming* (1977) before it and *First Blood* (1982) after it, *Friendly Fire* blurred the real lines of home-front conflict during the war by positing a populist tale of the "the government" against "the people." *Betrayed* (1988) took this theme to another level entirely, and was the art that real life imitated when the Oklahoma City Federal Center was bombed in 1995.

18. The 1964 college edition of *Webster's New World Dictionary* defined flashback as "an interruption in the continuity of a story, play, etc. by the narration or portrayal of some earlier episode." Frankel (1994), noting the origins of the term in literature and film, says it was adapted to the drug culture in the 1960s and did not appear in the PTSD literature until the 1980s. DSM-III-R, published in 1987, included the term flashback.

19. McGee (1984, 277) objects to flashbacks being treated as pathologies. It is better, he says, "to view them as instances of normal memory processes." Frankel (1994, 321) writes, "The content of a flashbacks appears to be at least as likely to be the product of imagination as it is of memory.

Notes to Chapter Ten

1. The title of this chapter is a phrase taken from Fentress and Wickham 1994.

2. The best critique of Gulf War syndrome is in Fumento 1997. Showalter (1997) discusses Gulf War syndrome as a form of hysteria.

REFERENCES

Adams, William. 1989. "War Stories: Movies, Memory, and the Vietnam War." *Comparative Social Research* 11:165–83. New York: JAI Press.

Adler, Jerry. 1991. "Prayers and Protest." *Newsweek*, January 28, p. 37.

Ambler, John Steward. 1966. *The French Army in Politics, 1945–1962*. Columbus: Ohio State University Press.

American Psychiatric Association. 1980. *Diagnostic and Statistic Manual of Mental Disorders*, 3d ed. Washington, D.C.: American Psychiatric Association.

Apple, R. W. 1990. "Views on the Gulf: Lawmakers Versed in Vietnam." *New York Times*, September 16, p. I18.

Appy, Christian G. 1993. *Working-Class War: American Combat Soldiers and Vietnam*. Chapel Hill: University of North Carolina Press.

Beamish, Thomas D., Harvey Molotch, and Richard Flacks. 1995. "Who Supports the Troops? Vietnam, the Gulf War, and the Making of Collective Memory." *Social Problems* 42 (3):344–60.

Bell, Robert. 1991. *Women of Classical Mythology*. New York: Oxford.

Best, Joel, and Gerald T. Horiuchi. 1985. "The Razor Blade in the Apple: The Social Construction of Urban Legends." *Social Problems* 32 (5):488–99.

Bey, Douglas R., and Vincent A. Zecchinelli. 1974. "G.I.'s Against Themselves—Factors Resulting in Explosive Violence in Vietnam." *Psychiatry* 37: 221–28.

Bigart, Homer. 1969. "Dissension in City." *New York Times*, October 16, p. 1.

Bourne, Peter G. 1970. *Men, Stress, and Vietnam*. Boston: Little, Brown.

Brinkley, Joel. 1990. "Israelis' Fear of a Poison Gas Attack Is Growing." *New York Times*, October 24, p. A8.

Burke, Kenneth. 1969. *A Rhetoric of Motives*. Los Angeles: University of California Press.

"Bush Talks of Atrocities." 1990. *New York Times*, October 16, p. A19.

Butterfield, Fox. 1996. "A Portrait of the Detective in the 'O.J. Whirlpool.'" *New York Times*, March 2, p. A1.

Carmichael, Virginia. 1990. *Framing History: The Rosenberg Story and the Cold War*. Minneapolis: University of Minnesota Press.

Centers for Disease Control. 1987. "Postservice Mortality among Vietnam Veterans." *Journal of the American Medical Association* 257:790–95.

Christopher, Renny. 1994. "Welcome Home, Soldier Boys." In *Vietnam War Films,* edited by Jean-Jacques Malo and Tony Williams. Jefferson, N.C.: McFarland.

Clements, Charles. 1984. *Witness to War: An American Doctor in El Salvador.* New York: Bantam Books.

Cloud, Stanley W. 1991. "Exorcising an Old Demon: A Stunning Military Triumph Gives Americans Something to Cheer About—and Shatters Vietnam's Legacy of Self-Doubt and Divisiveness." *Time,* March 11, pp. 52–53.

Conrad, Peter, and Joseph W. Schneider. 1992. *Deviance and Medicalization: From Badness to Sickness.* Philadelphia: Temple University Press.

Cook, Fred J. 1973. "The Real Conspiracy Exposed: Justice in Gainesville." *Nation,* pp. 295–302.

Cortwright, David. 1975. *Soldiers in Revolt.* New York: Anchor.

Coyne, John R. 1972. *The Impudent Snobs: Agnew vs. the Intellectual Establishment.* New Rochelle, N.Y.: Arlington House.

Crowder, Reg. 1972. Untitled. *St. Petersberg Times,* August 25.

de Jong, Alex. 1978. *The Weimer Chronicle.* London: Paddington Press.

Douglas, Mary. 1984. *Purity and Danger: An Analysis of the Concepts of Pollution and Taboo.* London: Ark Paperbacks.

Dowd, Maureen. 1990a. "Bush Denies 'Payback' on Embassy." *New York Times,* December 9, p. I14.

———. 1990b. "Bush Intensifies a War of Words against the Iraqis." *New York Times,* November 1, p. A1.

du Berrier, Hilaire. 1965. *Background to Betrayal.* Boston: Western Islands.

Duncan, Donald. 1966. "I Quit." *Ramparts,* February.

Egendorf, Arthur. 1985. *Healing from the War: Trauma and Transformation after Vietnam.* Boston: Houghton Mifflin.

Ehrenreich, Barbara. 1987. Introduction to *Women, Floods, Bodies, History.* Vol. 1 of *Male Fantasies,* by Klaus Theweleit. Minneapolis: University of Minnesota Press.

———. 1989. *Fear of Falling: The Inner Life of the Middle Class.* New York: Pantheon Books.

Eisenstaedt, Alfred. 1990. *Eisenstaedt Remembrances.* Boston: Little, Brown.

"An Extraordinary Military." 1969. *Life Magazine,* May 23, pp. 28D–36.

Fentress, James, and C. Wickham. 1994. *Social Memory: New Perspectives on the Past.* Oxford: Blackwell.

Figley, Charles R., and Seymour Leventman. 1990. *Strangers at Home: Vietnam Veterans since the War.* New York: Brunner/Mazel.

Finney, John W. 1971. "Senators Open Hearing on Ending War." *New York Times,* April 21, p. 12.

Fleming, Robert H. 1985. "Post Vietnam Syndrome: Neurosis or Sociosis?" *Psychiatry* 48 (May): 122–39.

Foucault, Michel. 1977. *Discipline and Punish: The Birth of the Prison*. London: Allen Lane.

———. 1965. *Madness and Civilization*. New York: Random House.

Frank, Andre Gunder. 1992. "A Third-World War: A Political Economy of the Persian Gulf War and the New World Order." In *Triumph and the Image: The Media's War in the Persian Gulf—A Global Perspective*, edited by Hamid Mowlana, George Gerbner, and Herbert Schiller. Boulder, Col.: Westview.

Frankel, Fred H. 1994. "The Concept of Flashbacks in Historical Perspective." *International Journal of Clinical and Experimental Hypnosis* 42 (4):321–36.

Franklin, H. Bruce. 1992. *M.I.A., or, Mythmaking in America: How and Why Belief in Live POWs Has Possessed a Nation*. New York: Lawrence Hill Books.

Friedman, Thomas L. 1990. "U.S. Gulf Policy: Vague 'Vital Interests.'" *New York Times*, August 12, p. A24.

Fumento, Michael. 1997. "Gulf Lore Syndrome." *Reason*, March, 22–33.

"Gaye Jacobson." 1991. Spring/Summer. *People*, p. 44.

Gibson, James William. 1994. *Warrior Dreams: Violence and Manhood in Post-Vietnam America*. New York: Hill and Wang.

Gillingham, Peter N. 1972. "Wasted Men: The Reality of the Vietnam Veteran: The Report of the Veterans World Project." Edwardsville, Ill.: Southern Illinois University.

Gimbel, Cynthia, and Alan Booth. 1994. "Why Does Military Combat Experience Adversely Affect Marital Relations?" *Journal of Marriage and the Family* 56:691–703.

Gioglio, Gerald R. 1989. *Days of Decision: An Oral History of Conscientious Objectors in the Military During the Vietnam War*. Trenton, N.Y.: Broken Rifle Press.

Gitlin, Todd. 1980. *The Whole World Is Watching: Mass Media in the Making and Unmaking of the New Left*. Berkeley: University of California Press.

Goldman, Aril L. 1990. "Council of Churches Condemns U.S. Policy in Gulf." *New York Times*, November 16, p. A13.

Gonzalez, David. 1990. "Some in the Military Are Now Resisting Combat." *New York Times*, November 26, p. A13.

Greene, Bob. 1989. *Homecoming*. New York: G. P. Putnam.

Halberstam, David. 1979. *The Powers That Be*. New York: Knopf.

Halbwachs, Maurice. [1925] 1980. *On Collective Memory*. Translated by Lewis Coser. Chicago: University of Chicago Press.

Halstead, Fred. 1991. *Out Now! A Participant's Account of the Movement in the U.S. against the Vietnam War*. New York: Pathfinder Press.

Hamilton, Richard. 1982. *Who Voted for Hitler?* Princeton: Princeton University Press.

Hassemer, Peter, and Patrick W. McCary. 1974. "A Comparative Study of the

Attitudes of Veterans and Non-veterans at the University of Northern Colorado." *Colorado Journal of Educational Research* 14:11–18.

Hehir, Bryan. 1991. "The Moral Calculus of War." *Commonweal,* February, 125–26.

Hellmann, John. 1986. *American Myth and the Legacy of Vietnam*. New York: Columbia University Press.

Herman, Judith. 1992. *Trauma and Recovery: The Aftermath of Violence — From Domestic Abuse to Political Terror*. New York: Basic Books.

Herring, George C. 1979. *America's Longest War: The United States and Vietnam, 1950–1975*. New York: Wiley.

Holder, Dennis. 1973. "Witness Says Barker, Sturgis Asked Him to Discredit VVAW." *Miami Herald,* June 8, p. 1.

Horowitz, David. 1991. "Coalition against the U.S." *National Review,* February 25, 36–38.

Huffman, Robert E. 1972. "Which Soldiers Break Down: A Survey of 610 Psychiatric Patients in Vietnam." In *The Vietnam Veteran in Contemporary Society*. Washington, D.C.: Veterans Administration.

Hunter, Marjorie. 1969. "Agnew Says 'Effete Snobs' Incited War Moratorium." *New York Times,* October 20, p. 1.

Karnow, Stanley. 1983. *Vietnam: A History*. New York: Viking Press.

Katzman, Jason. 1993. "From Outcast to Cliché: How Film Shaped, Warped and Developed the Image of the Vietnam Veteran, 1969–1990. *Journal of American Culture* 16 (spring): 7–24.

Kellner, Douglas K. 1992. *The Persian Gulf TV War*. Boulder, Col.: Westview.

Kerry, John. 1971. *The New Soldier: Vietnam Veterans Against the War,* edited by David Thorne and George Butler. New York: Macmillan.

Kifner, John. 1972a. "Informer Appears Key to U.S. Case against 6 Antiwar Veterans." *New York Times,* August 14.

———. 1972b. "Veterans Face Guardsmen in Protest at Miami Beach." *New York Times,* August 22, p. 36.

———. 1972c. "War Foes Harass G.O.P. Delegates." *New York Times,* August 22, p. 1.

———. 1990. "Iraq Proclaims Kuwait's Annexation." *New York Times,* August 9, p. A1.

Knuf, Joachim. 1992. " 'Spit First and Then Say What You Want!': Concerning the Use of Language and Ancillary Codes in Ritualized Communication." *Quarterly Journal of Speech* 78:466–82.

Kovic, Ron. 1976. *Born on the Fourth of July*. New York: Simon and Schuster.

Larteguy, Jean. 1962. *The Centurions*. New York: E. P. Dutton.

Lembcke, Jerry. 1995. "The Myth of the Spat-upon Vietnam Veteran and the Rhetorical Construction of Soldiers as Means *and* Ends in the Persian Gulf

War." *Vietnam Generation: A Journal of Recent History and Contemporary Culture* 6 (3–4):24–36.

LeMoyne, James. 1990a. "President and the G.I.s: He Will Get Respect." *New York Times*, November 22, p. A23.

———. 1990b. "Troops in Gulf Talk of War, and of Vietnam and Respect." *New York Times*, September 30, p. I1.

Lester, J. C., and D. L. Wilson. [1905] 1971. *Ku Klux Klan: Its Origin, Growth and Disbandment*. New York: AMS Press.

Lewis, Anthony. 1990. "Democracy in the Way?" *New York Times*, November 26, p. A19.

Lifton, Robert Jay. 1973. *Home from the War: Vietnam Veterans, Neither Victims nor Executioners*. New York: Simon and Schuster.

Loeb, Paul. 1994. *Generation at the Crossroads*. New Brunswick, N.J.: Rutgers University Press.

Loftus, Elizabeth, and Katherine Ketcham. 1995. *The Myth of Repressed Memory: False Memories and Allegations of Sexual Abuse*. New York: St. Martin's.

Lynn, Edward J., and Mark Belza. 1984. "Factitious Posttraumatic Stress Disorder: The Veteran Who Never Got to Vietnam." *Hospital and Community Psychiatry* 35:697–701.

MacArthur, John R. 1992. *Second Front: Censorship and Propaganda in the Gulf War*. New York: Hill and Wang.

MacPherson, Myra. 1984. *Long Time Passing: Vietnam and the Haunted Generation*. New York: Doubleday.

Malo, Jean-Jacques. 1994. "Final Mission." In *Vietnam War Films*, edited by Jean-Jacques Malo and Tony Williams. Jefferson, N.C.: McFarland.

Malo, Jean-Jacques, and Tony Williams. 1994. *Vietnam War Films*. Jefferson, N.C.: McFarland.

McGee, Rob. 1984. "Flashbacks and Memory Phenomena: A Comment on 'Flashback Phenomena—Clinical and Diagnostic Dilemmas.'" *Journal of Nervous and Mental Disease* 172 (5):273–78.

Memorandum. c. 1966. "Peace Movement Now Concerned with Legalities in Order to Gain Maximum Effectiveness." Fifth Avenue Peace Parade Committee. Wisconsin State Historical Society Archives, Madison.

Mills, M. 1991. "School's Ribbon Policy Draws Bush Response." *Chicago Tribune*, February 26, p. C2.

"Minutes of Meeting at Hotel Sheraton-Carlton, Washington, D.C. 5/14/66." 1966. Veterans for Peace Collection, Wisconsin State Historical Society, Madison.

Moser, Richard. 1996. *The New Winter Soldiers: GI and Veteran Dissent during the Vietnam Era*. New Brunswick, N.J.: Rutgers University Press.

Mowlana, Hamid, George Gerbner, and Herbert Schiller. 1992. *Triumph of the*

Image: The Media's War in the Persian Gulf—A Global Perspective. Boulder, Col.: Westview.

Mueller, John. 1973. *War, Presidents, and Public Opinion.* New York: Wiley.

News Release. 1966. "Vietnam Peace Parade Committee Schedules Massive Protest Aug. 6." Fifth Avenue Peace Parade Committee. Wisconsin State Historical Society Library, Madison.

Nielsen, J. 1971. "Survey of American Veterans." *Congressional Record-Extension of Remarks,* May 17, E4471:73.

"Nixon Supporters Planning War Rallies." 1969. *New York Times,* November 9, p. 57.

Nordheimer, Jon. 1971. "From Dak To to Detroit: Death of a Troubled Vietnam Hero." *New York Times,* May 26, p. A1.

———. 1972. "Postwar Shock Besets Ex-G.I.'s." *New York Times,* August 21, p. A1.

O'Connor, John J. 1968. *A Chaplain Looks at Vietnam.* New York: World Publishing.

O'Neill, John. 1972. "The Ones Who Came Back." *New York Times,* September.

O'Reilly, Ciaron. 1998. "A Seamless Garment Pilgrimage." *Catholic Radical,* January.

Parenti, Michael. 1989. *The Sword and the Dollar.* New York: St. Martin's.

Polner, Murray. 1971. *No Victory Parades.* New York: Holt, Rinehart and Winston.

Porter, Janice. 1991. February. Interview with Carolyn Howe, Audio recording, author's possession.

Powers, Gene. 1971. "An Open Letter to Spiro Agnew." Spring Mobilization Committee. Wisconsin State Historical Society Library, Madison.

Reston, James. 1969. "A Whiff of Mutiny in Vietnam." *New York Times,* August 27.

Rhodes, Richard. 1990. "Bush's Atomic Red Herring." *New York Times,* November 27, p. A23.

Rosenbaum, David E. 1969. "Agnew Scores War Foes; Rally to Hear 2 Senators." *New York Times,* November 11, p. 1.

Rousseau, Jean-Jacques. [1911] 1986. *Emile.* London: Dent, Everyman's Library.

Safire, William J. 1990. "The Hitler Analogy." *New York Times,* August 24, p. A29.

Schalk, David. 1991. *War and the Ivory Tower: Algeria and Vietnam.* New York: Oxford University Press.

Schomp, Gerald. 1970. *Birchism Was My Business.* New York: Macmillan.

Scott, Wilbur J. 1990. "PTSD in DSM-III: A Case in the Politics of Diagnosis and Disease." *Social Problems* 37:294–310.

———. 1993. *The Politics of Readjustment: Vietnam Veterans since the War.* New York: Aldine de Gruyter.

Scriven, Michael, and Peter Wagstaff, ed. 1991. *War and Society in Twentieth-Century France*. New York: St. Martin's.

Severo, Richard, and Lewis Milford. 1989. *The Wages of War: When America's Soldiers Came Home from Valley Forge to Vietnam*. New York: Simon and Schuster.

Shatan, Chaim. 1972. "Post Vietnam Syndrome." *New York Times*, May 6, L35.

———. 1973. "The Grief of Soldiers: Vietnam Combat Veterans' Self-Help Movement." *American Journal of Orthopsychiatry* 43 (4):640–53.

Shirer, William. 1960. *The Rise and Fall of the Third Reich*. New York: Simon and Schuster.

Showalter, Elaine. 1997. *Hystories: Hysterical Epidemics and Modern Culture*. New York: Columbia University Press.

Snow, David A., and Robert Benford. 1988. "Ideology, Frame Resonance, and Participant Mobilization." *International Social Movement Research* 1:197–217. New York: JAI Press.

Solotaroff, Paul. 1995. *The House of Purple Hearts: Stories of Vietnam Vets Who Find Their Way Back*. New York: HarperCollins.

Sparr, Landy, and Loren D. Pankratz. 1983. "Factitious Posttraumatic Stress Disorder." *American Journal of Psychiatry* 140:1016–19.

Starr, Paul. 1973a. *The Discarded Army: Veterans after Vietnam*. New York: Charterhouse.

———. 1973b. "Home from the War—Vietnam Veterans: Neither Victims nor Executioners." *Worldview*, October, 53–55.

Steinberg, Stephen. 1974. *The Ethnic Myth: Catholics and Jews in American Higher Education*. New York: McGraw Hill.

Steinfels, Peter. 1990. "Church Leaders Voice Doubts on U.S. Gulf Policy." *New York Times*, October 12, p. A1.

Storper, Michael. 1989. *The Capitalist Imperative: Territory, Technology, and Industrial Growth*. London: Blackwell.

Strayer, R., and L. Ellenhorn. 1975. "Vietnam Veterans: A Study Exploring Adjustment Patterns and Attitudes." *Journal of Social Issues* 3:81–94.

Studlar, Gaylyn, and David Desser. 1991. "Rambo's Rewriting of the Vietnam War." In *Coming to Terms: Indochina, the United States and the War*, edited by Douglas Allen and Ng Vinh Long. Boulder, Col.: Westview.

Sturken, Marita. 1997. *Tangled Memories: The Vietnam War, the Aids Epidemic, and the Politics of Remembering*. Berkeley: University of California Press.

Sullivan, Ronald. 1969. "Cahill Gets an Enthusiastic Reception from Hudson Democrats." *New York Times*, October 23, p. 53.

Tal, Kali. 1996. *Worlds of Hurt: Reading the Literatures of Trauma*. New York: Cambridge University Press.

Theweleit, Klaus. 1987. *Women, Floods, Bodies, History*. Vol. 1 of *Male Fantasies*. Minneapolis: University of Minnesota Press.

Thompson, John. 1995. "Bay of the Wolf: The Feral Howl." Worcester, Mass.: Self-published Newsletter at Holy Cross College.

Tolchin, Martin. 1990. "TV Ads Seek U.S. Support on Gulf Stand." *New York Times*, December 17, p. A12.

Toner, Robin. 1990. *New York Times*, September 16, p. I27.

Turner, Fred. 1996. *Echoes of Combat: The Vietnam War in American Memory*. New York: Anchor.

U.S. Senate. 1972. "A Study of the Problems Facing Vietnam Era Veterans on Their Readjustment to Civilian Life." Washington, D.C.: Government Printing Office.

Useem, Michael. 1973. *Conscription, Protest, and Social Conflict: The Life and Death of a Draft Resistance Movement*. New York: John Wiley.

Veterans Administration. 1980. *Myths and Realities: A Study of Attitudes toward Vietnam Era Veterans*. Washington, D.C.: Government Printing Office.

"Veterans Discard Medals in War Protest at Capital." 1971. *New York Times*, April 24, p. 1.

Vietnam Veterans Against the War. 1972. *The Winter Soldier Investigation: An Inquiry into American War Crimes*. Boston: Beacon Press.

"War Veterans Plan Antiprotest Drive." 1969. *New York Times*, November 2, p. xx.

Waterhouse, Larry, and Mariann Wizard. 1971. *Turning the Guns Around: Notes on the G.I. Movement*. New York: Praeger.

Weiner, Tim. 1996. "Military Combat Insignia Signify Esteem of Officers." *New York Times*, May 18, p. A11.

"Welcome Home." 1991. *The Economist*, March 2, p. 29.

Wells, Tom. 1994. *The War Within: America's Battle over Vietnam*. Berkeley: University of California Press.

Werth, Alexander. 1958. *Lost Statesman: The Strange Story of Pierre Mendes-France*. New York: Abelard-Schuman.

Wesley, Edwin J. 1972. "Eye on Demonstrations." *New York Times*, May 6, L35.

Whitley, Glenna. 1994. "The Good Soldier." *Texas Monthly*, August, pp. 30–37.

Wilson, John P. 1977. "Identity, Ideology and Crisis: The Vietnam Veteran in Transition," part I. Research Report. Cleveland: Cleveland State University.

Wingo, Hal. 1969. "From GIs in Vietnam, Unexpected Cheers." *Life*, October 24, p. 36.

Wright, Will. 1975. *Sixguns and Society: A Structural Study of the Western*. Berkeley: University of California Press.

Young, Allan. 1995. *The Harmony of Illusion: Inventing Post-Traumatic Stress Disorder*. Princeton: Princeton University Press.

Zeitlin, Irving. 1995. *Ideology and the Development of Sociological Theory*. New York: Prentice Hall.

FILMOGRAPHY

The Activist. 1969. Regional Films. Color, 85 mins.

Alamo Bay. 1985. U.S.A. Tri-Star. Color, 99 mins.

Alice's Restaurant. 1969. U.S.A. United Artists. Color, 111 mins.

Americana. 1981. U.S.A. David Carradine Studio. Color, 93 mins.

Apocalypse Now. 1979. U.S.A. United Artists-Zoetrope. Color, 153 mins.

Armed Response. 1987. U.S.A. Cinetel Films. Color, 86 mins.

Betrayed. 1988. United Artists. Color, 127 mins.

Billy Jack. 1971. U.S.A. Warner Bros. Color, 115 mins.

Birdy. 1985. U.S.A. Tri-Star. Color, 120 mins.

Blackenstein. 1972. U.S.A. Exclusive International. Color, 87 mins.

The Black Six. 1974. U.S.A. Cinemation. Color, 84 mins.

Black Sunday. 1977. Paramount. Color, 143 mins.

Blood of Ghastly Horror. 1965–72. U.S.A. Independence International Pictures Corporation. Color, 86 mins.

Brotherhood of Death. 1976. U.S.A. Omni Capital Films. Color, 85 mins.

The Bus Is Coming. 1971. U.S.A. William Thompson International. Color, 109 mins.

Bus Riley's Back in Town. 1965. U.S.A. Universal. Color, 93 mins.

Captive. 1974. U.S.A. Colmar. Color, 82 mins.

Cease Fire. 1984. U.S.A. Cineworld Enterprises. Color, 97 mins.

The Choirboys. 1977. U.S.A. Universal. Color, 119 mins.

Choose Me. 1984. U.S.A. Island Alive Productions. Color, 106 mins.

Coming Home. 1978. U.S.A. United Artists. Color, 128 mins.

The Crazies. 1973. U.S.A. Cambist. Color, 103 mins.

Deathdream. 1972. Canada. Alpha. Color, 89 mins.

The Deer Hunter. 1978. U.S.A. Universal. Color, 183 mins.

The Eiger Sanction. 1975. U.S.A. Universal. Color, 128 mins.

Electra Glide in Blue. 1973. U.S.A. United Artists. Color, 114 mins.

The Exterminator. 1980. U.S.A. Warner Bros. Color, 101 mins.

Exterminator II. 1984. U.S.A. Cannon. Color, 88 mins.

Eye of the Eagle. 1987. Concorde. Color, 82 mins.

A Field of Honor. 1973. U.S.A. University of Southern California. Color, 15 mins.

Final Mission. 1984. U.S.A. Motion Pictures Distributors. Color, 101 mins.

First Blood. 1982. U.S.A. Orion. Color, 96 mins.

Friendly Fire. 1979. U.S.A. ABC Television. Color, 145 mins.

Full Metal Jacket. 1987. U.S.A. Warner Bros. Color, 118 mins.

Getting Straight. 1970. U.S.A. Columbia. Color, 125 mins.

Go Tell the Spartans. 1978. U.S.A. Mar Vista Films. Color, 114 mins.

Good Guys Wear Black. 1977. U.S.A. Action One Film Partners. Color, 95 mins.

Good Morning, Vietnam. 1987. Touchstone Pictures. Color, 125 mins.

Gordon's War. 1973. U.S.A. Palomar Pictures. Color, 90 mins.

The Green Berets. 1968. U.S.A. Warner Brothers-Seven Arts. Color, 141 mins.

Greetings. 1968. U.S.A. West End Films. Color, 88 mins.

Hail Hero! 1969. U.S.A. Cinema Center Films. Color, 97 mins.

Hair. 1979. U.S.A. United Artists. Color, 122 mins.

Hamburger Hill. 1987. U.S.A. RKO Pictures. Color, 110 mins.

Hearts and Minds. 1974. Touchstone/Warner Bros. Color, 90 mins.

Heated Vengeance. 1982. U.S.A. Fries Distribution Company. Color, 91 mins.

Heroes. 1977. U.S.A. Universal. Color, 97 mins.

Homer. 1970. U.S.A. Palomar Pictures. Color, 91 mins.

House. 1985. U.S.A. New World. Color, 92 mins.

Jacob's Ladder. 1990. U.S.A. Tri-Star/Carolco. Color, 120 mins.

Joe. 1970. U.S.A. Cannon. Color, 107 mins.

Journey through Rosebud. 1971. U.S.A. GSF Productions. Color, 93 mins.

Jud. 1971. Duque Films/Maron Films. Color, 80 mins.

Kill Zone. 1985. U.S.A. Spartan. Color, 86 mins.

The Line. 1980. U.S.A. USA Home Video. Color, 96 mins.

The Lively Set. 1964. U.S.A. Universal. Color, 95 mins.

Mean Streets. 1973. U.S.A. Warner Bros. Color, 100 mins.

Missing in Action. 1984. U.S.A. Cannon. Color, 101 mins.

More American Graffiti. 1979. U.S.A. Lucasfilm-Universal. Color, 111 mins.

Motor Psycho. 1965. U.S.A. Eve Productions. Black and White, 73 mins.

Mr. Majestyk. 1974. U.S.A. MGM/UA. Color, 103 mins.

Nighthawks. 1981. U.S.A. Universal. Color, 99 mins.

Night Wars. 1987. Warner Bros. Color, 89 mins.

Norwood. 1969. U.S.A. Paramount Pictures. Color, 96 mins.

Operation Nam. 1987. Imperial Entertainment. Color, 85 mins.

Parades. 1972. U.S.A. Confron/Cinerama. Color, 95 mins.

The Park Is Mine. 1985. U.S.A. Ramble. Made for Television. Color, 106 mins.

Platoon. 1986. U.S.A. Hemdale. Color, 120 mins.

The Pursuit of D. B. Cooper. 1981. U.S.A. Universal/MCA. Color, 100 mins.

Rambo: First Blood Part II. 1985. U.S.A. Warner Communications. Color, 96 mins.

The Revolutionary. 1970. U.S.A. United Artists. Color, 101 mins.

R.P.M. 1970. Columbia. Color, 97 mins.

Ruckus. 1980. U.S.A. International Vision, Inc. Color, 91 mins.

Satan's Sadists. 1969. U.S.A. Kennis-Frazer Films; Independent International Pictures Corporation. Color, 86 mins.

Slaughter. 1972. U.S.A. American International Pictures. Color, 92 mins.

Slaughter's Big Rip-Off. 1973. U.S.A. American International Pictures. Color, 93 mins.

Stanley. 1972. U.S.A. Crown. Color, 108 mins.
The Stone Killer. 1973. U.S.A. Columbia. Color, 96 mins.
The Strawberry Statement. 1970. U.S.A. MGM. Color, 109 mins.
The Stunt Man. 1980. U.S.A. 20th Century-Fox. Color, 130 mins.
Taxi Driver. 1976. U.S.A. Columbia. Color, 113 mins.
Tracks. 1977. U.S.A. Rainbow Pictures. Color, 92 mins.
Twilight's Last Gleaming. 1977. U.S.A./West Germany. Allied Artists. Color, 146 mins.
Vigilante Force. 1976. U.S.A. United Artists. Color, 89 mins.
The Visitors. 1972. U.S.A. United Artists. Color, 90 mins.
Welcome Home, Soldier Boys. 1972. U.S.A. 20th Century-Fox. Color, 91 mins.

INDEX

Activist, The, 151
Agnew, Spiro, 27–29, 36, 45–46, 49–51, 63, 68, 95–100; calls protesters "effete snobs," 49–51; gay-baits antiwar veterans, 99
Aiello, Danny, 187. See also *Jacob's Ladder*
Alamo Bay, 177
Algeria: and France, 8, 88, 89; and anti-Semitism, 9; National Liberation Front, 88
Alibi for lost war. *See* Myth of the Spat-upon Vietnam veteran
Alice's Restaurant, 150
American Legion, 54, 78
American Nazi Party, 32
Americana, 175, 176
Ann-Margret, 148. See also *Bus Riley's Back in Town*
Anti-Semitism, 7–8
Anti-war movement: splits within, 52
Apocalypse Now, 148
Armed Response, 177
Army Math Center at University of Wisconsin, 32
Ashby, Hal: directs *Coming Home*, 163

"Baby Killer," 83, 20, 141
Baker, James, 16–17
Bar Association of the City of New York, 73
Battle Cry, 164
Beck, Pvt. Jim, 47
Benade, Brig. Gen. Leo, 56
Best Years of Our Lives, The, 120
Betrayed, 177
"B-52s for Peace," 67
Bias, Dallas, 54
Billy Jack, 153
Birdy, 177
Black Six, The, 157
Black Sunday, 181
Blackenstein, 154
Bloch, Edward, 31
Blood of Ghastly Horror, 149
Body fluids: female, 9; and male fear, 9. *See also* Myth of the spat-upon Vietnam veteran
Bojarski, George, 36
Boorda, Jeremy, 115
Born on the 4th of July, 66
Bosnia, 26
Boudin, Leonard 40
Bra burning: myth of, 72
Bronson, Charles, 157. See also *Stone Killer, The*
Brotherhood of Death, 157
Burkett, B. G., 115
Bus Is Coming, The, 197
Bus Riley's Back in Town, 148
Bush administration, 13, 20, 23. *See also* Gulf War
Bush, George, 11–13, 16–18, 45. *See also* Gulf War

Calley, Lt. William, 101
Camil, Sgt. Scott, 60. *See also* Winter Soldier Investigation
Captive, 157, 167
Carmichael, Stokely, 35
Carmichael, Virginia, 25
Carter, Jimmy, 173
Catch 22, 164
Caulkin, Macauley, 187. See also *Jacob's Ladder*
Cease Fire, 1984
Central Intelligence Agency (CIA), 92
Centurions, Les, 87–89. *See also* Indochina
Cheney, Dick, 12
Choirboys, The, 181
Choose Me, 177

Christ: spat on, 7
Citizen-soldier, 185
Civil War, 84
Cleland, Max, 109
Clements, Charlie, 111–114
"Coalition Against the U.S.," 18
Coalition for America at Risk, 19
Colow, Maury, 33
Coming Home, 9, 80, 144–148, 150, 157, 161–174
Committee for Independent Action, 32
Crandell, Lt. William, 58–59. *See also* Winter Soldier Investigation
Crazies, The, 157
Creation myths, 130; and great deluge stories, 131
Cronauer, Adrian, 117

De Niro, Robert, 76, 157. See also *Taxi Driver*
De Palma, Brian: directed *Greetings*, 150
Dearborn, Mich., 36
Deathdream, 149, 155, 179
Deerhunter, The, 161, 174
Dellinger, David, 35, 37, 41, 44, 52
Democratic National Committee, 15
Democratic Party: National Convention of 1968, 55
Dern, Bruce, 165. See also *Coming Home*
Diem, Ngo Dinh, 30
Dien Bien Phu, 87
"Dolchstoss Legend," 85–87
Dole, Bob, 142
Dong, Phan Van, 50
Douglas, Michael, 151. See also *Hail Hero!*
Dowd, Nancy, 163–164. See also *Coming Home*
Drolshagen, Lt. Jon, 161. *See also* Winter Soldier Investigation
du Berrier, Hilaire, 91–92
Duncan, Donald, 33

Easter GI-Civilian demonstrations, 39
Economic crisis: and paramilitary movements, 142
Eiger Sanction, The, 157
Eisenstaedt, Alfred, 140
Electra Glide in Blue, 157, 178
Evil Eye: and spit to ward off, 133–134
Exterminator, The, 198
Eye of the Eagle, 179

"False memory syndrome," 7, 81, 115, 121
Field of Honor, A, 157
Fifth Avenue Peace Parade Committee, 4, 6, 31, 34–35, 37–38
"Fifth columnists," 2
Final Mission, 178
First Blood, 176, 178
Flashbacks, 23; in film, 150, 159, 178–179, 181–182, 187
Fonda, Jane: at 1972 Republican Party convention, 65; produces *Coming Home*, 162–165
Ford, Rep. Gerald, 50
"Forgotten Warrior Project," 121
Fort Dix, 35; stockade, 44
"Fort Hood Three," 35
"Fort Jackson Eight," 40
Fragging, 79, 87, 119, 165, 179
Free Theater Association, 162
Freikorps, 135, 143
Friendly Fire, 160
Fronaugh, Pvt. Jack, 59. *See also* Winter Soldier Investigation
Fuhrman, Mark, 115
Full Metal Jacket, 148
Fuller, Craig, 15

Gainesville Eight, 99–100, 102. *See also* Gainesville Six
Gainesville Six, 65, 69. *See also* Gainesville Eight
Germany: World War I, 2, 7, 128, 135. *See also* Freikorps
Getting Straight, 152
"GI Joe," 141
GI movement against the Vietnam War, 29, 35–44, 46–48; coffeehouses, 42, 44, 98; "GI Referendum on Vietnam," 45; GIs United, 44; newspapers, 42; support for moratorium, 46–47; Thanksgiving fast in Vietnam, 47. *See also* GI Press Service (GIPS)
GI newspapers, 41–43, 48

GI Press Service (GIPS), 38, 41–42, 46, 67
Go Tell the Spartans, 197
Good Guys Wear Black, 197
Good Morning Vietnam, 117
"Good Veterans" vs. "Bad Veterans," 5, 49, 53–55, 61–62, 68, 104–105, 124, 178–179
Gordon's War, 157
Gould, Elliot, 152. See also *Getting Straight*
Green Berets, The, 161
Greenblatt, Robert, 37
Greene, Bob, 1, 79–81
Greetings, 150
Grist for the myth of spat-upon veterans, 6, 76–79, 125
Gulf War: anti-war movement, 22–24; GI resistance to, 17, 185–186; hostage issue, 13–14, 18, 23; reasons for, 12–16, 25–26; and spat-upon Vietnam veterans, 20, 25, 128–129
Gulf War syndrome, 187
Guthrie, Arlo, 151. See also *Alice's Restaurant*

Hager, Bill: prototype for "Bob" in *Coming Home*, 164–170
Hager, Terry: prototype for "Sally" in *Coming Home*, 166–167
Hail Hero!, 175
Hair, 175
Haley, Sarah, 105
Halstead, Fred, 41
Hamburger Hill, 90, 160
Hanoi Radio, 49, 51
Harris poll, 75–76. *See also* Polls
Hayden, Tom, 162
Hearts and Minds, 161, 171
Heated Vengeance, 177
Hell's Angels, 120
Heroes, 181
Hersch, Seymour, 58
Hill and Knowlton, 15
Hinckley, John, 158
"Hippies," 73, 78, 82; "will try to kill you," 167
Hitler, Adolf, 85
Hitler-Hussein analogy, 16
Homer, 196
House, 177, 179
Hubbard, Orville, 36
Hussein, Saddam, 14–15, 18

Ia Drang Valley, 31
Indochina: France and, 7–8, 83, 87–89, 91–92, 128. *See also* Algeria; *Centurions, Les*
Iraq. *See* Gulf War

Jacob's Ladder, 187
Jews, 7, 51; and "Dolchstoss Legend," 85–86; and John Birch Society, 91
"Jody" legend, 118–119
Joe, 196
John Birch Society, 91–94; and Richard Nixon, 91–94
"John Turkey Movement," 47
Johnson, Dwight, 69, 107–108, 113
Johnson, James, 35. *See also* "Fort Hood Three"
Journey through Rosebud, 154
Jud, 181
"Just war" theory, 17

Kazan, Chris: wrote and produced *The Visitors*, 156
Kazan, Elia: directed *The Visitors*, 156
Keating, Ed, 37
Kerry, Sen. John, 21, and VVAW, 63
Keyes, SP/4 Gary. *See also* Winter Soldier Investigation
Kill Zone, 177
Kovic, Ron: at the Republican Party convention in 1972, 66, 101–102; prototype for "Luke" in *Coming Home*, 171
Ku Klux Klan: formed by Confederate veterans, 84; in the 1980s, 90–91
Kuwait. *See* Gulf War

Larteguy, Jean, 89
Lemmer, William, 64. *See also* Vietnam Veterans Against the War (VVAW)
Lifton, Robert Jay, 81, 105–106, 108–109. *See also* Post-traumatic Stress Disorder (PTSD); "Rap groups"
Lindsay, Mayor John: supports Vietnam War moratorium, 50, 93
Line, The, 175

Lively Set, The, 148
Lynd, Staughton, 35

Maddox, 30
Mallory, Capt. John, 60. *See also* Winter Soldier Investigation
"March Against Death," 48
"March on the Pentagon," 39, 81–82
Marchi, Sen. John, 50, 93
McCain, Sen. John, 21
McCarthy, Sen. Eugene, 39
McGovern, Sen. George, 52
McGovern-Hatfield Amendment, 96
Mean Streets, 157
Memory and the Vietnam War: during the Gulf War, 10, 186–188; and film, 180–182; lapse of, in 1970s and 1980s, 122–123, 173; legacy of Vietnam, 186–188; and myth, 138–143. *See also* Post-traumatic Stress Disorder (PTSD)
Meyer, Russ: produced *Motor Psycho*, 158
Miles, Pvt. Joe, 39, 44. *See also* GI movement against the Vietnam war, GIs United
Missing in Action, 177
Mollet, Prime Minister Guy, 88. *See also* Algeria
Moore, Sharon, 1
Mora, Dennis, 35. *See also* "Fort Hood Three"
Moratorium Days against the War, 44–53; GI support for, 44–48; GI Thanksgiving fast in support of, 47–48; GIs in Vietnam support, 47–48; Nixon-Agnew counteroffensive, 49–53. *See also* "Good Veterans vs. Bad Veterans
More American Graffiti, 175
Moss, David, 77. *See also* Moratorium Days against the War
Motor Psycho, 149–150, 158, 181
Mouvements des appelés et rappelés, 88
Mr. Majestyk, 157, 167
Muller, Bobby: prototype for "Luke" in *Coming Home*, 171; founds Vietnam Veterans of America, 171
Murtha, Rep. John, 21
Muste, A. J., 32, 35, 37
My Lai, 58, 95, 101, 105, 123
Myth of the Spat-upon Vietnam Veteran: 8–10, 71, 81, 87, 89, 98, 122–126, 129, 142–143; as alibi for lost war, 136–139, 184, 188; and anthropology, 137; binary structure of, 129–133; and evil eye, 133–134; in film, 159–160, 173; and male fear of body fluid, 129–133; origins of, 8, 94, 125–126; as perfecting myth of betrayal, 25, 139, 69; as urban myth, 1–2; women as spitters in, 8–9, 80, 132–143

National Council of Churches, 109
National Peace Action Coalition, 28–29
Navarre, Gen. Henri, 87
Nazism, 143
Nelson, Marjorie, 61. *See also* Winter Soldier Investigation
New Mobe, 52
Night Wars, 179
Nixon-Agnew administration: counters the moratorium against the Vietnam war, 49–70; and John Birch Society, 93–95; and neo-conservatism, 96–98; and POW issue, 94–95; veterans' day strategy, 53–56; and Vietnam veterans, 27–29, 53–56, 63–70, 94–100. *See also*, Agnew, Spiro; "Good veterans" vs. "bad veterans"

Oakland Army Terminal, 145
O'Connor, Cardinal John J., 81–82
Odysseus, 84
Operation Desert Shield, 19
Operation Dewey Canyon III, 62–64
Operation Eagle, 22–23
Operation Yellow Ribbon, 20–24

Pacific Stars and Stripes, 27
Parades, 149, 175
Paramilitary movements: culture of, 134; in film, 157; and political right wing, 142
Park is Mine, The, 177
Parks, Michael, 148. See also *Bus Riley's Back in Town*
Peck, Sidney, 37
Pentagon Papers, 101
Persian Gulf War. *See* Gulf War
Petrick, Howard, 38. *See also* GI Press Service (GIPS)
Pflimin, Prime Minister Pierre, 88. *See also* Algeria
Platoon, 148

Polls: Harris, 68, 75–76; *New York Times*, 75; Gallup, 75; Roper Center for Public Opinion, 75
Postman, Neil, 25
Post-traumatic Stress Disorder (PTSD): 7, 87; and false memory syndrome, 121; in film, 150, 157, 177, 180–181; Robert Jay Lifton and, 105–109; a mode of discourse, 110–114; and role of *New York Times* in constructing, 102–109; Chaim Shatan and, 105–109; Paul Starr's critique, 114–121; and victim-veteran image, 139–141. *See also* Gulf War syndrome; Post-Vietnam syndrome
Post-Vietnam syndrome (PVS), 103–104, 108. *See also* Post-traumatic Stress Disorder (PTSD)
Powell, Gen. Colin, 17
Powers, Ensign Gene, 27–28
POW/MIA, 20, 61, 94–95. *See also*, Nelson, Marjorie; Smith, S/Sgt. George
"Proletarian army," 41
Pully, Andrew, 44. *See also* GI movement against the Vietnam War, GIs United
Pursuit of D.B. Cooper, The, 175

Rambo: First Blood Part II, 80, 177
"Rap groups," 106. *See also* Lifton, Robert Jay; Post-traumatic Stress Disorder (PTSD); Post-Vietnam syndrome (PVS)
Reagan, Ronald: governor of California, 50; elected president, 173
Republican Party National Convention of 1972, 64–66, 69, 101–103, 109
Reston, James, 43
Revolutionary, The, 153
Ridenhour, Ronald Lee, 58. *See also* My Lai
Robbins, Tim, 187. See also *Jacob's Ladder*
Romo, Barry, 3, 66. *See also* Vietnam Veterans Against the War (VVAW)
Rosebud Indian Reservation, 38
R.P.M., 153
Ruckus, 175, 176

Salt, Jennifer, 153. See also *Revolutionary, The*
Salt, Waldo, 163–172. See also *Coming Home*
Samas, David, 35. *See also* "Fort Hood Three"
San Clemente, Calif., 44
San Francisco airport, 1, 74, 141
Satan's Sadists, 151
Saudi Arabia, 12–13
Schaumburg, Ill., 23
Schorr, SP/4 Sam, 60. *See also* Winter Soldier Investigation
Scorsese, Martin, 157. See also *Taxi Driver*
Shatan, Chaim, 69, 105–106, 108–109, 112. *See also* Post-traumatic Stress Disorder (PTSD); Post-Vietnam syndrome (PVS)
Slaughter, 154
Slaughter's Big Rip-Off, 154, 157
Smith, S/Sgt. George, 61. *See also* Winter Soldier Investigation
Socialist Workers Party, 40–41
Spat-upon veterans, 3–5, 20, 23–24, 26, 66, 71–83, 118; as "Alamo," 188; as conservative icon, 26; in film, 150, 174, 159, 176; in post-World War I Germany, 83, 85–87, 128. *See also* Myth of the spat-upon Vietnam veteran
Special Committee on Demonstration Observation, 73
Spit: as icon in myth, 128–135
Spock, Benjamin, 40
Spring Mobilization Committee to End War in Vietnam, 37
"Stab in the back," 92–93, 118; as French legend, 87–89; as German legend, 50, 85–87; as icon in myth, 128. *See also* "Dolchstoss Legend"
Stanley, 154, 167, 181
Starr, Paul, 113–114; critic of survivor guilt and PTSD, 121
Stone Killer, The, 157, 169
Strawberry Statement, The, 152
"Street-corner psychiatry," 106. *See also* Lifton, Robert Jay; Post-traumatic Stress Disorder (PTSD); Starr, Paul
Streeter, Barry, 1
Student Mobilization against the War in Vietnam, 4
Student Mobilization Committee to End the War in Vietnam (SMC), 28, 37–38, 40–41, 44, 46; and GI organizing, 38
Students for a Democratic Society (SDS), 37
Stuntman, The, 175

"Survivor guilt," 108, 121; in film, 179. *See also* Lifton, Robert Jay; Post-traumatic Stress Disorder (PTSD); Starr, Paul

Taxi Driver, 76, 157–158, 167
Tracks, 9, 158, 160, 169
Turner Joy, 30
Twilight's Last Gleaming, 159, 167, 181

Urban legend, 130; spat-upon veterans as, 1–2, 71

Veterans and Reservists to End the War in Vietnam, 31, 190
Veterans Day 1969, 53–56
Veterans for Peace, 31, 33, 35, 39, 67
Veterans of Foreign Wars (VFW), 14, 54, 62, 78, 99
Vietnam Moratorium Committee, 44–45, 48
Vietnam syndrome, 24–26
Vietnam Veterans Against the War (VVAW), 4, 39–40, 57–70, 98, 100, 106–107, 109; credibility denied by press, 62–63; in film, 9, 153, 156–157; and guerrilla theater, 78, 57–58, 62; infiltrated by Nixon's "plumbers," 64–65; members discard service medals, 62; and Operation Dewey Canyon III, 62–64; and Winter Soldier Investigation, 58–62, 69. *See also* Gainesville Eight
"Vietnam Veterans for Nixon," 67
Vietnam Veterans' Outreach Program, 109
Vigilante Force, 157
Visitors, The, 155
Voight, Jon, 147, 153. See also *Coming Home; Revolutionary, The*

Warrior dreams, 127, 115–117
Watergate: and VVAW, 64–65
Weapons brought home from Vietnam, 146–147, 155, 159; in film, 168–170, 177; myth of, 168–170, 146–147
Welch, Robert, 91
Welcome Home, Soldier Boys, 115, 169
Wilson, Maj. Gen. Winston, 54
Wilson, Rep. Bob, 56
Wingo, Hal, 47
Winter Soldier Investigation, 58–62; ignored by press, 98
Wolff, Rep. Lester, 51
Worcester, Mass., 22
World War II: films about, 9, 148; and the myth of "victory parades," 20; veterans and film, 151, 119–120, 140; veterans opposed to Vietnam war, 4, 31

Yapp, Pfc. Chris, 47. *See also* Winter Soldier Investigation
Young Socialist Alliance, 40–41

Zombies, 179–180, 187

ABOUT THE AUTHOR

Jerry Lembcke grew up in northwest Iowa. He received his B.A. degree in math from Augustana College, an M.A. in social science from the University of Northern Colorado, and the Ph.D. in sociology from the University of Oregon. He is currently an associate professor of sociology at the College of the Holy Cross in Worcester, Massachusetts. He is the author of four previous books and numerous articles on labor history and social inequality.

After service in Vietnam, Lembcke was active in Vietnam Veterans Against the War and has remained involved in peace and social justice organizations since that time. Currently, he works with the Boston-area Jobs With Justice campaign. Lembcke lives in Worcester with his wife, Carolyn Howe, and daughter, Molly Del.

CPSIA information can be obtained
at www.ICGtesting.com
Printed in the USA
JSHW021922030821
17532JS00001B/31